HOW TO STUDY LAW

HOW TO STUDY LAW

9th EDITION

by

ANTHONY BRADNEY LLB, BA, FAcSS, FRSA
Professor of Law Emeritus, Keele University
Senior Associate Research Fellow, Institute of Advanced Legal Studies

FIONA COWNIE BA, LLB, LLM, FAcSS, FRSA, PFHEA
Barrister, Professor of Law Emerita, Keele University
Senior Associate Research Fellow, Institute of Advanced Legal Studies

Previous editions also authored by:

the late VICTORIA FISHER
Lecturer in Law, University of Leicester from 1979 to 1986
Founder member of the Women and Law group

JUDITH MASSON PhD FAcSS Q.C. (hon)
Professor Emeritus, University of Bristol

ALAN C. NEAL, LL.B., LL.M., D.G.L.S.
Barrister, Employment Judge
Emeritus Professor of Law, University of Warwick

DAVID NEWELL, LL.B., M.Phil.
Solicitor
Chief Executive, News Media Association

SWEET & MAXWELL

Published in 2021 by Thomson Reuters, trading as Sweet & Maxwell.
Registered in England & Wales. Company number 1679046.
Registered office 5 Canada Square, Canary Wharf, London E14 5AQ.

For further information on our products and services, visit
www.sweetandmaxwell.co.uk

Typeset by Servis Filmsetting Ltd, Stockport, Cheshire
Printed in Great Britain by Ashford Colour Press, Gosport, Hants

A CIP catalogue record for this book is available from the British Library.

ISBN (print): 978-0-414-08807-8
ISBN (e-book): 978-0-414-08810-8
ISBN (Proview): 978-0-414-08809-2
ISBN (print and Proview): 978-0-414-08808-5

Contents

PART 2

Acknowledgments

The authors and publishers would like to thank those whose copyrighted materials are reproduced as examples throughout this book:

English Legal System in Context, 4th edition, edited by Fiona Cownie, Anthony Bradney, Mandy Burton, (2007), extracts from pp.209, 224–225, reproduced by permission of Oxford University Press.

R v Jackson [1999] 1 All E.R. 572. Reproduced by permission of RELX (UK) Limited, trading as LexisNexis.

"Are Lawyers Neurotic" by Daniel Carl Newman (2018) International Journal of the Legal Profession 25(1), Taylor and Francis (Routledge), reprinted by permission of the author and the publisher Taylor & Francis Ltd, http://www.tandfonline.com

House of Lords Act 1999, Laser Misuse (Vehicles) Act 2018, Stalking Protection Act 2019 (HMSO); *Stocker v Stocker* [2019] UKSC 17, *O'Dwyer v O'Dwyer* [2019] EWHC 1838 (Fam) (sourced from BAILII) ©CrownCopyright public sector information licensed under the terms of the Open Government Licence v.3.

Figures 1, 2, 3 in Chapter 8 taken from "Knife Possession Sentencing Quarterly Brief, October to December 2012, England and Wales", Ministry of Justice Statistics Bulletin, Published 7 March 2013 ©CrownCopyright, public sector information licensed under the terms of the Open Government Licence v.3.

The authors would also like to acknowledge the assistance provided by Patrick Greenhalgh, of the Careers and Employability unit at Keele University, in relation to the contents of Appendix I.

While every care has been taken to establish and acknowledge copyright, and contact the copyright owners, the publishers tender their apologies for any accidental infringement. They would be pleased to come to a suitable arrangement with the rightful owners in each case.

Preface

The purpose of this book is to help the reader to take part in the arguments that there are about law, legal institutions and legal rules. It explains the basic raw material that is used in these arguments. The judgments of courts, statutory material and academic studies are all important. It is necessary to understand how to find these things, either in a library or increasingly online, how to read them and how to cite them properly. Some arguments about law involve technical legal skills and material that few people not trained in law will understand. Some arguments entail engagement with material that is found in other academic disciplines in the humanities and social sciences. Both kinds of arguments are examined and explained in this book.

The law constantly changes. The nature of arguments about law changes more slowly if, at all. Some of the facts about law will be out of date a few years after you have learnt them. How you argue and write about law will remain largely the same. For this reason, the techniques that you will learn about in this book are of especial significance. Judges not infrequently differ amongst themselves about the meaning of legal rules. Academic legal scholars are often even more vehement in their disagreements about what legal rules mean, how they work in practice and whether the policies that they are intended to implement are desirable or not. You need to be able to understand these arguments but, much more than this, make your own decision about where you stand as regards the issues that are being contested. You would also like to be able to defend your decisions in ways that are convincing to others who are thinking about law. One aim of this book is to enable you to do this.

Studying law in a university setting will be new to every student when they first enter university. University is not a continuation of school. Appreciating what the purpose of different forms of studying at university are will allow you to get the most out of what is being provided. How you engage with lectures is not the same as what is expected from you when you take part in seminars. Not all academics approach lectures or seminars in the same way. Online facilities are now increasingly available alongside face-to-face learning. Learning about these matters is as important as learning about arguments about the law because it will help you to be better and quicker in learning about arguments about law. Here again, an aim of this book is to help you to do this.

Part 1

1
Sources of the law

LAW AND LEGAL INSTITUTIONS

1.1 The first question to answer is "what is law?" Most laws are not about something dramatic like murder but are, rather, about the everyday details of ordinary life. Every time a purchase is made, a contract under state law is created. Both parties make promises about what they will do; one to hand over the goods, one to pay the price. In this and other ways, everybody is involved in law every day of their lives. In many instances people are free to make their own choices about the rules that govern their lives. If they want to join a club, a religion or a company and be bound by its rules that is a matter for them. Some people regard these rules as being law just like the law that the state creates. This idea is known as *legal pluralism*. However the kind of law that comes from the state is what we most frequently think about when we think about law. University courses involving law focus on this type of law and that is what this book is about.

There are a number of generally acknowledged sources of English law. Some are more obvious than others. Thus, "the Queen in Parliament" (the House of Commons, the House of Lords and the monarch) is a vital source of modern English law. Here proposals for legislation (*Bills*) are presented to, debated by, and voted upon by the House of Commons and the House of Lords, finally receiving the assent of the monarch and thus becoming legislation (*Statutes* or *Acts*). However judges are also significant sources of law, partly because the English legal system places great emphasis upon judgments in previous legal cases as guidance for future judicial decision-making and partly because, in some instances, judges can themselves make law. There are, however, less obvious sources of English law. For example, the customs of a particular trade may be incorporated into the law by the judges or Parliament or international law (the law between states) may be a basis for national law.

All of the above are sources of *legal rules*. What precisely it is that is meant by the term legal rules is a subject much debated by philosophers of law. Generally speaking, when the term is used it indicates that a particular course of action should, or should not, be followed. Legal rules are said to be *binding*. This means if they are not followed some action in the courts may result.

It will suffice for present purposes if we consider just two of these sources of law: Parliament and the judiciary. In so doing, we will discover the central positions occupied within the English legal system by *statute law* and *judge-made law*. There is a further explanation of international law and the law of the European Union in Chapter 2.

PARLIAMENT

1.2 Parliament creates law but not all the law that is created through Parliament is of the same kind. We need, in particular, to distinguish between various levels of legislation.

The legislation with which most people are familiar are statutes. Bills proposed in Parliament become Acts. These Acts may either be *General* or *Personal and Local*. Both of these are sometimes known as *primary legislation*. General Acts apply to everybody, everywhere within the legal system. In this context it is important to remember that there are several different legal systems within the UK; one for England and Wales, one for Scotland and one for Northern Ireland. Sometimes the law in Wales is different to that in England and some people argue that a Welsh legal system is either in the process of being created or already exists. Some Acts apply to all the legal systems; many apply only to one or two of them.

Personal and local Acts apply either to particular individuals, institutions or, more usually, to particular areas. Thus, before divorce was part of the general law, it was only possible to get a divorce by Act of Parliament. The most common example of local legislation is that which applies to individual cities. The law in Leicester is sometimes not the same as the law in London. General legislation is much more common than personal and local legislation.

A legal rule in a statute can only be changed by new legislation. Judges interpret statutes but they do not have the power to change them. Any statute, no matter how important it seems, can be changed in the same way as any other.

Most legislation consists of a direct statement about how people should behave or indicates the consequences of certain behaviour. For example, a statute may define a crime and say what the punishment will be for that crime. Sometimes Parliament cannot decide exactly what the law should be on a particular point. It may not have the necessary expertise or it may be that the area is one where frequent changes are needed. In such cases Parliament may pass an Act giving somebody else the power to make law in the appropriate area. Such power is often given to government ministers or to local authorities. This is the most common example of what is known as *delegated* or *secondary legislation*. A person or body to whom legislative power is delegated cannot, as can Parliament, make law about anything. The Act (sometimes called *the parent Act*) will determine the area in which law can be made. It may say something about the content of the law but the details of that law will be left to the person or body to whom legislative power is delegated. They may also have the power to change that law from time to time. Most delegated legislation is published as a statutory instrument. Although people are frequently unaware of this type of legislation it is very important, affecting most people's lives. For example, much of the system of state benefits is based on delegated legislation.

The final thing that we have to consider is the range of directives, circulars, and guidance notes produced by various State agencies and bodies such as HMRC. Some of these documents bind the people to whom they are addressed to behave in particular ways. Many, however, are not legally binding. They do not compel people to do things in the way that statutes or statutory instruments do. Even so, such documents are often very influential. In practice officials receiving them may always act in the way they indicate. Thus we might consider them all as almost equivalent to legislation.

In Chapter 4 you will find an explanation of how to find statutes and statutory instruments. In Chapter 5 there is an explanation of how you read them to find out where the law stands about something. The methods that the judiciary use to decide how a particular legislative provision is to be interpreted are explained in Chapter 7.

JUDGES, COURTS AND TRIBUNALS

Precedents

Not all legal rules are laid down in an Act of Parliament or some other piece of legislation. A number of legal rules are found in the statements of judges made in the course of deciding cases brought before them. Rules that ultimately come from judicial decisions, rather than from legislation, make what is called the *common law*. A common law rule has as much force as a rule derived from statute. Many important areas of English law, such as contract, tort, criminal law, land law and constitutional law have their origins in common law. An explanation of the different divisions of law is to be found in Chapter 2. Some of the earliest common law rules still survive, though many have been supplemented or supplanted by statute. Common law rules are still being made today, though, as a source of new legal rules, common law is much less important than statute. ▶ 1.3

Strictly speaking, the term common law is confined to rules that have been developed entirely by judicial decisions. It excludes new rules made by judges when they interpret statutes. Most decisions made by judges now involve, at least in part, interpreting statutes. The term *case law* covers both kinds of decisions.

The application of case law is easiest to understand when the issue presently before the court has been raised in some previous analogous case. In such a situation the court will look to see if there is a potential applicable rule in the reports of previously decided cases. Then they will decide whether they have to, or should, apply that rule. It is therefore vital that accurate and comprehensive records be kept of past court decisions and judicial pronouncements. Thus the importance of the numerous and varied series of law reports can be appreciated. Anybody entering a law library in England can hardly help being impressed at the volume of materials falling within this category of Law Reports. Row upon row of bound volumes, containing the judgments in thousands of past cases, dominate the holdings of any major English law library. In the modern era cases are not only published in printed form. They are also published electronically, either by the courts themselves or by various commercial publishers.

More information about the various kinds of Law Reports and how to use them can be found in Chapter 4.

Not every judgment in every case or every part of a judgment is of equal importance in terms of the creation of law. The weight that is to be given to a judgment as an indication of what future judicial decisions will be depends upon two things. One is the level of the court in which that case was decided. In English law there is a principle of a *hierarchy of precedents*. Judgments given by superior courts in the hierarchy are binding on inferior courts; these judgments create a precedent. The second is whether the part of the judgment that is under consideration is the ratio of the judgment or whether it is obiter dicta. An explanation of the hierarchy of precedents and the rules for determining whether something is ratio or obiter in a judgment is to be found in Chapter 6.

Courts

Cases are decided in courts or tribunals. We look at what tribunals are in the section below. Different kinds of legal disputes are decided in different kinds of courts. Sometimes it is possible to bring a legal dispute before two or more different kinds of court. In some situations, once a court has given judgment, it is possible to appeal against that judgment to another court. Some courts only hear appeals. ▶ 1.4

SUPREME COURT, formerly the HOUSE OF LORDS (deals only with appeals)

COURT OF APPEAL (deals only with appeals)

HIGH COURT different divisions deals with different kinds of legal dispute (deals with both appeals and new cases)

FAMILY DIVISION | CHANCERY DIVISION | QUEEN'S BENCH DIVISION

COUNTY COURT (deals with civil law disputes) | CROWN COURT (deals mainly with criminal law disputes) | FAMILY COURT (deals with family law matters)

MAGISTRATES' COURT (main business—criminal, matrimonial and licensing matters)

The highest court in the English legal system is the Supreme Court, formerly known as the House of Lords. Cases in the Supreme Court are normally heard by five judges (called Justices) but cases involving more than five Justices are becoming increasingly common. Because there is more than one Justice in a case before the Supreme Court the decision may be a majority one.

The Privy Council has a varied jurisdiction. It includes hearing appeals from courts in some Commonwealth countries. Its decisions are not technically binding on courts within the English legal system but, because the judges in the Privy Council are mainly the same as the Justices in the Supreme Court, its decisions are highly influential within the courts in the English legal system.

The court below the Supreme Court is the Court of Appeal. Like the Supreme Court the Court of Appeal has jurisdiction over virtually every area of law. Cases in the Court of Appeal are usually heard by three judges.

The court below the Court of Appeal is the High Court. Both the Supreme Court and the Court of Appeal are basically appellate courts. They hear appeals about the decisions of other lower courts. However the High Court has both an original jurisdiction, that is to say it is a place where a case is first heard there, and an appellate jurisdiction. The High Court is divided into three different Divisions. In practice these Divisions function as though they were separate courts. The Chancery Division mainly hears cases that are concerned with mortgages, the sale of land, the administration of estates of deceased persons or other probate business. The Family Division hears cases about matrimonial matters, including civil partnerships, and matters relating to children. The Queen's Bench Division is the largest of the three Divisions and has a much wider jurisdiction than the other two Divisions. Its jurisdiction includes, amongst other things, judicial review (broadly cases challenging the decisions of bodies with statutory powers such as government departments), criminal law, the law of tort and the law of contract.

Few of the courts and tribunals below the High Court create precedents; that is to say that few of their decisions create legal rules that are binding on other courts. This is not to say that these courts are unimportant. They hear more cases when they first come to court than the High Court does. For most people if they have a case come to court it will be to a court below the High Court. In terms of the operation of the legal system it is the courts below the High Court that matter most. However, most law courses at university are concerned, at least in part, with the analysis of legal rules. This means that courts below the High Court are rarely mentioned in these courses.

The courts immediately below the High Court are the Family Court, the County Court and the Crown Court. The Family Court's jurisdiction deals with a broad range of family matters. The County Court has a civil jurisdiction whilst the Crown Court has a mainly criminal jurisdiction, dealing with the more serious criminal offences. In the Crown Court cases are decided by a judge and a lay jury comprised of 12 people randomly selected from the population at large.

The lowest court in the English legal system is the magistrates' court. Judges who are legally qualified preside in the other courts within the English legal system. However, in the magistrates' court decisions are mostly made by magistrates who are lay people. They receive only a very minimal training in law. Legally qualified clerks advise them. Magistrates' courts are often thought of as courts with a criminal jurisdiction. However, whilst it is true that magistrates' courts do deal with a very large number of minor criminal cases, dealing with approximately 98 per cent of all criminal cases heard each year, they also have a significant civil jurisdiction, dealing with, amongst other things, some family law matters and licensing decisions.

Tribunals

▶ 1.5

Courts are not the only state institutions that hear cases and make legal decisions. Tribunals have a very similar role to that of the courts. Their hearings tend to be more informal and their decisions tend to be about less serious matters than cases that are heard in court. Tribunal cases are usually decided by a panel comprising of a legally qualified chairperson, who is now oftencalled a judge, and two other people who have knowledge of the area that the tribunal is concerned with. Thus, for example, in an Employment Tribunal the panel might consist of an Employment Judge, a trade union official and someone who is an employer. Tribunals have their own appellate system. Most decisions of tribunals will not constitute a precedent and they will not be reported in the way that decisions of the higher courts are. There are, however, exceptions to this such as the Employment Appeal Tribunal.

COMMON LAW AND EQUITY

▶ 1.6

In the section above the term *common law* is used as a synonym for rules of law derived from judicial decisions rather than statute. This is the most common way in which the phrase is used.

However, another sense of the word is as an antonym to *equity*. English law has deep historical roots. The opposition of common law and equity refers to the system of rules that originally developed in different courts within the legal system. Common law rules arose first. Later, these rules were seen as being over-formal and concerned too much with the way a case was presented rather than with the justice in the issues at stake. Thus a less strict system of equitable rules was developed. In time, the rules of equity also became formalised. Eventually, the different courts were merged and now all courts can apply both the rules of common law and equity.

2
Divisions of law

INTRODUCTION

2.1 Not all legal rules are of the same type. Legal rules can be divided up in many different ways. This chapter introduces some common ways of classifying law. They show differences in purpose, in origin and form, in the consequences when the rules are breached, and in matters of procedure, remedies and enforcement. The divisions described below are of the broadest kind. One kind of division of legal rules has already been introduced, that between statute and case or common law. This division and the others now described overlap. For example, the legal rule defining murder originates in common law, not statute. It is a rule of criminal law rather than civil law; and of national law rather than international law.

CRIMINAL AND CIVIL LAW

2.2 One of the most fundamental divisions in law is the division between criminal and civil law. Newcomers to the study of law tend to assume that criminal law occupies the bulk of a lawyer's caseload and of a law student's studies. This is an interesting by-product of the portrayal of the legal system by the media. Criminal law weighs very lightly in terms of volume when measured against civil law. There are many more rules of civil law than there are of criminal law; more court cases involve breach of the civil law than involve breach of the criminal law. Law degree students will find that criminal law is generally only one subject out of twelve or more subjects in a three-year law degree, although some criminal offences may be referred to in other courses.

Criminal law means the law relating to crime. Civil law can be taken to mean all the other legal rules within the legal system. The distinction relies not so much on the nature of the conduct that is the object of a legal rule but in the nature of the proceedings and the sanctions that may follow. Some kinds of conduct give rise to criminal liability, some to civil liability and some to both civil and criminal liability.

The seriousness of the conduct does not necessarily determine the type of liability to which it gives rise; conduct that is contrary to the criminal law is not always "worse" than conduct that is against the civil law. Few people would consider every criminal offence a moral wrong (except, perhaps, in the sense that every breach of the law will be thought by some to be a moral wrong). Equally, some actions that are purely breaches of the civil law might be considered breaches of morality. If you breach your contract you break a promise. Nor is harm, in the sense of damage done to individuals, something that is always found to a greater degree in the criminal law as compared with the civil law. The person who "speeds" at 31 miles per hour on an empty road in broad daylight breaches the criminal law. The company that fails to pay for the goods that it has bought, thereby bankrupting another company, commits only a breach of the civil law. Who has done the greater harm? Concepts of morality have had some influence on the development of English law but historical accident, political policy and pragmatic considerations have played just as important a part in developing our law.

Some conduct which might be considered "criminal" by many people gives rise in law only to civil liability or to no liability at all and some conduct which you may consider "harmless" may rise to either criminal or civil liability. It will be easier to see that "harm", "morality" and the division between criminal and civil law do not follow any clear pattern if you consider some fictitious examples. In considering them, ask yourself whether or not the conduct described should give rise to any legal liability; if it should, what form should that liability take and what should the legal consequences be which flow from the conduct described? Should any of the people be compensated for the harm done to them and, if so, by whom and for what? Should any of the characters be punished and, if so, for what reason and how? Who should decide whether or not legal proceedings of any variety should be instigated against any of the individuals? The probable legal consequences that follow from each example are found at the end of the chapter. Do not look at these until you have thought about the examples yourself.

Examples

1. *Norman drinks five pints of beer as he does each day. His car suffers a puncture and, as a consequence, he drives into a queue at the bus station injuring a young woman and her child.*
2. *Meena, who is an accountant, regularly takes recreational drugs.*
3. *Sue, who is pregnant, lives with Chris. She smokes 50 cigarettes a day. Sue is also carrying on an occasional affair with Richard.*
4. *Robert agrees to pay Usha, a professional decorator, £5000 if she paints his house. She completes the work to a very high standard. Robert, who is a millionaire, refuses to pay her.*

Even when a person's actions clearly infringe either the criminal law or civil law, it does not necessarily mean that any actual legal consequences will follow. In criminal and civil cases persons with the legal right to take any legal action have a discretion as to whether or not they initiate legal proceedings. There is a difference between *liability* and *proceedings*. Conduct gives rise to liability. It is for someone else to decide whether or not to take the matter to court by starting proceedings.

In criminal proceedings a *prosecutor* prosecutes the *defendant*. The case is heard in the magistrates' court or the Crown Court, depending on the seriousness of the offence. The prosecutor will normally have to prove to the court, *beyond all reasonable doubt*, that the defendant committed the offence charged. The court will have to determine whether or not the defendant is guilty. In the magistrates' court it will usually be for the magistrates to determine this question, in the Crown Court it will be for the jury to decide questions of fact and for the judge to decide questions of law. A finding of *not guilty* will lead to the defendant's acquittal. A finding of *guilty* will lead to a conviction and may lead to a sentence of imprisonment or some other form of punishment such as a fine or probation.

One of the major objectives of the criminal law is to punish the wrongdoer for action that is deemed to be contrary to the interests of the state and its citizens. Criminal proceedings do not have as a major objective the provision of compensation or support for the victim of crime. It is significant that the exercise of the discretion to prosecute is seldom carried out by the victim of the crime. Criminal proceedings are normally initiated by the state or its agents and brought in the name of the Queen or the prosecuting official.

In civil proceedings it is generally the *claimant* (the party harmed) (before April 1999 known as the *plaintiff*) who sues the *defendant*, although in some areas of the civil law other terms are used. For example, in the case of a divorce there is a petitioner and a respondent. The case will usually be heard in either the County Court or the High Court, depending on the nature of the case and the size of the loss involved. The plaintiff usually has to prove, on *the balance of probabilities*, that the events took place in the manner claimed. This is a lower standard of proof than in criminal cases. If the plaintiff proves their case, the court will make some kind of order. What this will be will depend upon the kind of case and what the plaintiff has asked for. The basic choice before the court is whether to order the defendant to compensate the plaintiff for their loss by awarding damages or to order the defendant to act, or refrain from acting, in some specific way in the future, or to make both kinds of orders.

Historically the civil law was primarily founded on the law of contract and tort, which are still mainly areas of common law. The law of contract determines which forms of agreement entered into between individuals are legally binding and on whom they will be binding. The law of tort covers categories of civil wrong, other than breach of contract, which may give rise to legal causes of action. It includes the law of negligence, trespass and libel and slander. Just as a set of facts can give rise to conduct that may result in both civil and criminal proceedings, so a set of facts can give rise to both actions in contract and in tort. Most claimants' primary motivation for bringing civil proceedings will be to obtain an effective remedy for the civil wrong which has been perpetrated. The fact that there is liability will not, however, necessarily mean that they will take action. For example, there may be little point in suing a person for damages if you know they have no money.

In the latter part of the twentieth century areas of civil law other than those related to contract and tort came to be of increasing importance. Some took a very different form to contract and tort. Divorce, for example, necessitates an action in court but, unlike actions in contract and tort, such cases are rarely contested, although there may be separate court cases about what happens to either any children the divorcing couples may have or the property and income that they have. One area of law that is very important in the higher courts is public law. Public law is the law that governs those that are given powers by statute. These are largely bodies or individuals which form part of either central or local government. There is a more detailed explanation of the nature of public law in the final section of this chapter.

The emphasis of the civil law has changed over the last hundred years with an increase in the role of the state and the importance of legislation as opposed to case law as the major source of law. Civil law does not just regulate relations between individuals covering such matters as their property transactions, but also deals with relations between the state and individuals. It covers unemployment and social benefit entitlement, tax and planning questions, and council tenants' relationships with their local authorities. All of these areas are covered by statute law that has created new rights and obligations. These are often enforced in tribunals as opposed to courts.

Statutory provisions have also been enacted in order to change the common law rights that have resulted from the judicial development of contract law and the notion of freedom of contract. For example, employment protection and landlord and tenant legislation give employees and tenants statutory rights that will often modify or override terms in their contracts that give their employers or landlords specific rights to dismiss or evict them.

NATIONAL, INTERNATIONAL AND EUROPEAN UNION LAW

2.3 The term *national, municipal* or *state law* is used when referring to the internal legal rules of a particular country. In contrast *international law*, usually termed *public international law*, deals with the law that applies to external relationships of a state with other states. In the UK, national law is normally unaffected by international legal obligations unless these obligations have been put into national law by an Act of Parliament. *European Union law*, however, cuts across this conventional notion that national and international law operate at different and distinct levels. It is a form of international law in that it is in part concerned with legal relations between Member States, but EU law may also directly affect the national law of Member States. It will therefore be considered separately from both national and international law.

NATIONAL LAW

2.4 The system of national law has already been considered in Chapter 1.

INTERNATIONAL LAW

2.5 Public international law regulates the external relations of states with one another. (*Private international law* is a type of national law that deals with cases where individuals find themselves in legal disputes that involve a number of different countries; for example when someone from the UK makes a contract in France). Public international law, but not private international law, is a form of law that is very different from national law. There is no world government or legislature issuing and enforcing laws to which all nations are subject. The international legal order is essentially decentralised and operates by agreement between states. This means that the creation, interpretation and enforcement of international law lies primarily in the hands of states themselves. Its scope and effectiveness depends on the capacity of states to agree and the sense of mutual benefit and obligation involved in adhering to the rules.

International law is created in two main ways: by treaty and by custom. Treaties are agreements between two or more states, and are binding, in international law, on the states involved if they have given their consent to be so bound. Customary law is established by showing that states have adopted broadly consistent practices towards a particular matter and that they have acted in this way out of a sense of legal obligation. International law is neither comprehensive nor systematic. Few treaties involve the majority of world states. Most are bilateral understandings or involve only a handful of parties to a multilateral agreement.

Disputes about the scope and interpretation of international law are rarely resolved by the use of international courts or binding arbitration procedures of an international organisation. This is because submission to an international court or similar process is entirely voluntary and few states are likely to agree to this if there is a serious risk of losing their case or where important political or national interests are at stake. Negotiation is far more common. International courts are used occasionally, for example where settlement is urgent, or protracted negotiations have failed, where the dispute is minor or is affecting other international relations; in other words, in cases where failure to settle is more damaging than an unfavourable outcome. Where international law has been breached, an injured state must rely primarily on self-help for enforcement. There is no effective international institutional machinery to ensure compliance when the law is challenged. This means that in practice powerful states are better able to protect their rights and assert new claims.

Breaching established rules is one, rather clumsy, way of changing international law. In a decentralised system, change can only be effected by common consent or by the assertion of a new claim being met by inaction or acquiescence by others. The lack of powerful enforcement machinery does not mean that international law is widely disregarded. On the contrary, legal rules are regularly followed, not least because states require security and predictability in the conduct of normal everyday inter-state relations.

International law also plays an important role in the promotion of common interests such as controlling pollution, restricting over-fishing, or establishing satellite and telecommunication link-ups.

A large number of global or regional international organisations have been established for the regulation and review of current inter-state activity. The best-known example, though perhaps not the most effective, is the United Nations, whose primary function is the maintenance of international peace and security.

In the UK, international law has no direct effect on national law and, on a given matter, national law may in fact be inconsistent with the United Kingdom's international obligations. The Government has authority to enter into treaties which may bind the UK vis-à-vis other states. However a treaty will not alter the law to be applied within the UK unless the provisions are adopted by means of an Act of Parliament. Customary international law may have been incorporated into national law but will enjoy no higher status than any other provision of national law and is, therefore, liable to be superseded by a new statute. However, it is a principle of judicial interpretation that, unless there is clear legal authority to the contrary, Parliament does not intend to act in breach of international law. In some other countries, international law is accorded a different status. In the Netherlands and Germany, for example, international law takes effect in municipal law and, where these conflict, international law prevails.

The lack of direct application should not be taken to mean that international law is of no importance in UK courts or for UK citizens. National courts regularly decide domestic cases having presumed the existence and application of international law. For example, under the Vienna Convention of 1961, diplomats enjoy immunity from criminal prosecution. If a defendant claims immunity, a court must decide whether the defendant falls within the terms of the treaty before proceeding further. Secondly, individuals may have rights under international law, enforceable not through national courts but through international institutions. The European Convention on Human Rights gives individuals the right to complain of breaches of the Convention to the European Commission on Human Rights which may then refer the case to the European Court of Human Rights (these institutions should not be confused with European Union institutions: they are quite separate). Although the UK ratified the Convention in 1951, it was only in 1966 that the UK agreed to the articles of the treaty that recognised the right of individual petition and the compulsory jurisdiction of the Court. The Human Rights Act 1998 now gives an individual the right to enforce certain rights found in the Convention against public authorities.

EUROPEAN UNION LAW

2.6

The European Union is an international organisation established and developed by treaty between Member States. The basic framework is set out in the EEC Treaty of 1957 (the Treaty of Rome), which defines the objectives of the Community, the powers and duties of Community institutions, and the rights and obligations of Member States. This treaty goes much further than just creating law that binds both Member States and Community institutions. It contains many detailed substantive provisions, some of which create rights for individuals that are enforceable directly in national courts. The EEC Treaty, and certain others which have followed it, are thus primary sources of European Union law. The European Union has a number of major institutions: the Council of the European Union, the Commission, the Assembly (or European Parliament), the Court of Justice (and the Court of First Instance) and the Court of Auditors. The terms of the various treaties give the European Union a powerful legislative, administrative and judicial machinery. The Treaty provides that further legislation may be made by the Council of Ministers and the Commission. This is called secondary legislation and takes three forms:

- *Regulations*, once made, pass into the law of a Member State automatically. Regulations are *directly applicable*, that means that Member States do not have to take any action (such as passing an Act of Parliament) to implement them or to incorporate them into national law. Regulations are intended to be applied uniformly throughout the Community, and override any conflicting provisions in national law.

- *Directives* are binding on Member States as to the result to be achieved, but leave each Member State with a choice about the method used to achieve that result. Member States are given a transitional period in which to implement the directive. This may involve passing a new law, making new administrative arrangements, or, where national law already conforms with the directive, taking no action. The Commission can initiate proceedings against a Member State if it believes the steps taken do not achieve the desired result. Although directives are addressed to Member States, in some circumstances an individual may be able to rely directly on certain parts, whether or not the Member State has taken implementing action. This is when the relevant part lays down an unconditional obligation and grants enforceable individual rights.

- *Decisions* can be addressed to Member States, individuals or companies. They are binding only on the person to whom they are addressed and take effect on notification.

EU law is applied in Member States by their individual system of national courts and tribunals. When a point of EU law is crucial to a court's decision, the court may refer the case to the Court of Justice for a preliminary ruling on the interpretation of the point in question. Courts against whose decision there is no appeal (e.g. the Supreme Court) must make a reference to the Court of Justice when the case hinges on EU law unless the Court has already ruled on that particular issue. Once the Court of Justice has given a preliminary ruling, the case is referred back to the national court from which it originated, which must then decide the case. The Court of Justice will only answer questions put to it about the interpretation of EU law; it will not rule on national law or on conflict between national and EU law or apply its interpretation to the facts of the case. These are all matters for national courts. The Commission may bring an action in the Court of Justice against a Member State for breach of an obligation, such as the non-implementation of a directive. Proceedings may be taken against the Commission or the Council for failing to act where the EEC Treaty imposes a duty to act. There are also provisions for annulling legislation adopted by the Commission or Council, for example, where the action has exceeded the powers laid down by treaty.

The United Kingdom has now withdrawn from the EU. However this does not mean that EU law is now irrelevant in the UK. First the UK's longstanding membership of the EU has had an impact on many areas of law. Whether this impact will diminish or disappear remains to be seen. Secondly, since the UK trades with countries within the EU the law of the EU will still be relevant. Finally, Northern Ireland, unlike the rest of the UK, remains within the European Union's single market for goods. This means that Northern Ireland will remain subject to, amongst other things, the rules of the EU's customs union.

PUBLIC AND PRIVATE LAW

▶ 2.7

Another distinction that may be drawn between different types of law is the division between *public law* and *private law*. Public law is largely concerned with the distribution and exercise of power by the state and the legal relations between the state and the individual. For example, the rules governing the powers and duties of local authorities, the operation of the NHS, the regulation of building standards, the issuing of passports and the compulsory purchase of land to build a motorway all fall within the ambit of public law. In contrast, private law is concerned with the legal relationships between individuals, such as the liability of employers towards their employees for injuries sustained at work, consumers' rights against shopkeepers and manufacturers over faulty goods, or owners' rights to prevent others walking across their land.

The significance of the public/private law distinction operates at two levels. First, it is a very useful general classification through which we can highlight some broad differences, such as those in the purpose of law, in sources and forms of legal rules, and in remedies and enforcement. This is the way the idea of public/private law will be discussed here. However, the distinction is also used in a second, narrower sense; as a way of defining the procedure by which claims can be raised in court.

One way of thinking about a legal rule is to consider its purpose. The primary purpose underlying most private law rules is the protection of individual interests, whereas the aim of most public law provisions is the promotion of social objectives and the protection of collective rather than individual interests. The methods used to achieve these purposes also differ. A characteristic feature of public law is the creation of a public body with special powers of investigation, decision-making and/or enforcement in relation to a particular problem, whereas private law achieves its ends by giving individuals the right to take action in defence of their interests.

Many problems are addressed by both public and private law. Sometimes a single statute may include both private rights and liabilities alongside public law provisions.

Public and private law also show differences in their origins and form. Some of the most important principles of private law are of ancient origin and were developed through the common law as individuals took their private disputes to court and demanded a remedy. The rules of private rights in contract, over land and inheritance, to compensation for physical injury or damage to property or reputation, were all first fashioned by judges in the course of deciding cases brought before them. In contrast, most public law rules are of comparatively recent origin and concern the use of statutory powers.

Example

Ann lives next door to an industrial workshop run by Brenda. The machinery is very noisy and the process discharges fumes that make Ann feel ill. This sort of problem is tackled by both public and private law in a number of different ways.

(i) *As a neighbour, Ann may bring a private law action in nuisance, which is a claim that Brenda's activities unreasonably interfere with the use of Ann's land. Ann could claim compensation for the harm she has suffered and could seek an injunction to stop the harmful process continuing.*

(ii) *There are also public law rules that may be invoked whether or not an. individual has or may be harmed, aimed at preventing the problem arising in the first place or controlling the situation for the public benefit. For example, when Brenda first started her workshop she would have needed to get planning permission from the local authority if her activities constituted a change in the use of the land. Planning legislation thus gives the local authority an opportunity to prevent industrial development in residential areas by refusing planning permission, or control it by laying down conditions. Other legislation gives the local authority powers to monitor and control various kinds of pollution and nuisances in their area, including noise and dangerous fumes. A further complex set of private rights and public regulations govern the working conditions of the workshop employees, who would also be affected by the noise and smells.*

An important function of public law has its roots in constitutional theory. The actions of public bodies are only lawful if there is a legal rule granting the body authority to act in a given situation. A private individual needs no legal authority merely to act. It is assumed that a person acts lawfully unless there is a legal rule prohibiting that behaviour. Public law therefore has a facilitative function, for which there is no equivalent in private law, permitting a public body to take action that would otherwise be unlawful.

A feature of much recent public law is a shift towards the grant of broad discretionary powers to public bodies. This means that the same legislative framework can be used more flexibly, accommodating changes in public policy as to the purposes to which the powers should be put or the criteria for the exercise of these powers. This characteristic form of modern public law contrasts quite sharply with the relatively specific rights and duties to be found in private law, and in turn affects the way public and private law can be enforced. All private law is enforced by granting individuals the right to take action in defence of a recognised personal interest. For example, a householder may make a contract with a builder over the repair of a roof, and may sue the builder if the work or materials are of a lower standard than was specified in the contract. Not all public law can be enforced by way of individual action.

The enforcement of public law can be viewed from two perspectives. First, public law can be enforced when an official ensures that individuals or companies comply with standards set in statutes or delegated legislation, e.g. Environmental Health Officers making orders in relation to or prosecuting restaurants. Secondly, the enforcement of public law can also be seen as the matter of ensuring public authorities themselves carry out their duties and do not exceed their legal powers. Here, the form of public law statutes, mentioned above, rarely ties a public body to supplying a particular standard of service, as a contract may tie a builder, but gives a wide choice of lawful behaviour.

Even where legislation lays a duty on a public authority, there may be no corresponding right of individual action. For example, under the Education Act 1996, local education authorities are under a duty to ensure that there are sufficient schools, in numbers, character and equipment, for providing educational opportunities for all pupils in their area. However, nobody can sue the authority if the schools are overcrowded or badly equipped. The only remedy is to complain to the Secretary of State, who can make orders if satisfied that the authority is in default of their duties. The mechanism for controlling standards of public bodies is generally by way of political accountability to the electorate or ministers rather than the legal process.

Some parts of public law do create individual rights and permit individual enforcement. In social security legislation, for example, qualified claimants have a right to certain benefits and may appeal against decisions on benefit to a tribunal. There is a procedure, special to public law, called *judicial review of administrative action* (usually referred to simply as *judicial review*), whereby an individual may go to the High Court alleging unlawful behaviour on the part of a public body. However, in order to go to court, the individual must show *sufficient interest* in the issue in question (this being legally defined) and the court has a discretion whether to hear the case or grant a remedy. This is quite different from proceedings in private law, where a plaintiff does not need the court's permission for the case to be heard but has a right to a hearing if a recognised cause of action is asserted and also a right to a remedy of some kind if successful.

CRIMINAL LAW AND CIVIL LAW ANSWERS

Legal consequences in questions 1–4: 2.8

1. Norman's actions may give rise to both criminal and civil proceedings. He may be prosecuted for drink driving and related road traffic offences and, if convicted, will have a criminal record. He may also be sued by the woman or child who would wish to recover damages for the personal injuries they have suffered. Such an action would be a civil action. The same set of facts may give rise to both criminal and civil liability.
2. The use of some drugs is prohibited by law. Legislative changes from time to time alter both which drugs are prohibited and the punishment that follows from conviction.
3. Sue has committed no criminal offence. Neither the unborn child nor Chris, if it is Chris' child, have any right of civil action for any harm they may consider Sue has done to them. If Sue is not married to Chris her affair with Richard does not give rise to any possible legal action.
4. Robert has not committed any criminal offence. He is in no different a position in law to the person who has no money. Usha will be able to commence civil proceedings against him. She will be able to sue him for breach of contract. Robert's wealth makes it more likely that Usha will consider it worth suing him as she is more likely to be able to recover any damages. However she will also have to remember that Robert will, if he wishes, be able to hire the best lawyers so as to delay Usha's inevitable court victory.

3
Law and its Social Context

INTRODUCTION

3.1 This chapter is about the different kinds of questions that arise when studying law and the different techniques you need when studying them.

You might think that studying law is purely a matter of learning a large number of legal rules. If this were the case only one kind of question would ever arise, what is the content of any particular legal rule? However, simply learning a large number of legal rules is not a very useful way of learning about law. Learning the rules is like memorising the answers to a set of sums. It is of no help when the sums change. If all you do is learn a set of legal rules, when the rules change, when the law is altered, you are back where you started. At the very least, to use your legal knowledge, you also need to know how to find legal rules and how to find out if they have been changed. Thus, to the question "what is the content of the legal rule?" are added questions about how to find them. More importantly all legal scholars would agree that legal rules are sometimes not clear. The content of such rules, and some scholars would argue that most legal rules are like this, is the subject of debate. If you are studying law you therefore need to know not just what the legal rules are but how you argue about what the content of legal rules might be.

Not everyone interested in law is interested in questions about the content of legal rules. For example, we might ask whether it is ever right to disobey the law. Here we are concerned not simply with what the rule is but what we ought to do because of that rule. This is a question of ethics that might, in part, relate to the content of a legal rule but is much more about the nature of moral judgment. We need to decide what we should do but we also need to learn how to construct arguments that will convince others that we are right about what we do.

Legal rules are intended to change behaviour; they should have an impact on society. However knowing what a legal rule is does not tell us whether the rule is in fact being obeyed. Equally knowing what a legal rule is does not tell us whether the impact that it is having, even if it is being obeyed, is that which was intended. Scholars have long observed that there is a difference between *the law in books*, legal rules, and *the law in action*, what happens in practice once a legal rule has been created. This is so even if we are just concerned with what happens in the courts. The hierarchical nature of the courts means that the lower courts should obey the rulings in the higher courts but research has shown that this is not always the case. Whether we are concerned with looking at what the law is for an individual client or what influence the law has on society knowing what the legal rules are is not enough. We need to know what happens in practice.

The distinction between the law in action and the law in books is both easy to see and useful to use but it also has its limitations. Some questions about law seem to fit into neither category. For example, is our earlier question about disobedience to law a question about the law in action or the law in books? Information about what actually happens in the legal system will only tell us what people do, not whether their action is morally correct. Equally, being told what the legal rule says is of little help in helping us assess whether we are correct to obey it or not. The question does not appear to fall into either category.

The distinction between the law in action and the law in books is broad but crude. More sophisticated categories provide narrower, more precise distinctions. Thus questions about the nature of law that can include whether or not one has a duty to obey it can be grouped together under the title the philosophy of law or *jurisprudence*. Such categories are not firmly fixed and may be defined by different people in different ways. Thus some people would use the term the *sociology of law* to refer to all questions about the operation of the legal system in practice. Others would distinguish between questions about the relationship between law and other social forces and questions about how effective a legal rule is. They would see the first kind of question as falling within the sociology of law and the second as coming under the heading *socio-legal studies*. It is more important to be able to identify the different kinds of questions than give them the labels.

DIFFERENT QUESTIONS MEAN DIFFERENT ANSWERS

3.2

Knowing that there are different kinds of questions asked when studying law is of intellectual interest but does it have any further significance? What happens if you fail properly to identify the kind of question that you are asking? We can answer these questions by looking at one way in which different kinds of questions are commonly confused.

For many years it was assumed that legal rules that laid down what should happen were an accurate guide to what actually happened. The law in action was thought to correspond more or less exactly with the law in books. It was accepted that there were divergences but these were thought to be on a small scale and of no importance. However, academics have now shown that there is often a very great difference between legal rules and the practice in the legal system. One example of this can be seen in the area of criminal justice, when people are arrested and taken to the police station for questioning.

The Police and Criminal Evidence Act 1984 (generally referred to as "PACE") lays down a large number of rules relating to the treatment of suspects who are detained in police stations. The purpose of these rules is to try and provide a balance between providing safeguards for the person who is being questioned and enabling the police to carry out a thorough investigation. One of the rules that PACE contains is that the suspect must be told of his/her right to seek legal advice. However, researchers have found that most people do not receive legal advice at the police station. This can happen because many suspects do not appreciate how important it is to have legal advice at an early stage in criminal investigations. However, another significant reason influencing suspects in their decision not to seek legal advice is that the police may use a number of ploys to discourage suspects from taking advice, including minimising the significance of what is happening by saying the suspect will only be there for a short time, or emphasising what a long time the detainee will have to wait until their legal adviser arrives. Merely looking at the law in the books could only tell us what is supposed to happen; that suspects are entitled to be told about their right to seek legal advice. It is only when we look at the law in action that we can understand how the law really works in practice; in this case, we come to understand that merely giving a right to people does not mean that they will understand how important it is to exercise that right, nor does giving a right ensure that it will necessarily be implemented in the way it was intended.

The difference between the law in action and the law in books in this area is important for several reasons. First, confusing the different kinds of questions resulted in an inaccurate description. People accepted the wrong kind of material as evidence for their answers, and as a result thought that the law worked in practice in much the same way as the legal rules suggested it should. Secondly, because of that mistake, those involved in advising others on the law may have given misleading advice. Finally, those involved in considering whether or not the law and legal system are effective and just looked not at the real legal system but, instead, at a shadowy reflection of it.

WHICH KIND OF QUESTION AM I ASKING?

3.3 Somebody has been divorced and you are asked how their financial affairs will be settled by the courts. Are you being asked what the relevant rules are, or what will actually happen in court, or both? Outside your course of study it may be very difficult to sort out what kind of question you are being asked. For study purposes the task will generally be simpler. The kind of question that you are being asked is likely to be indicated by the nature of your course as a whole. The title of your course may give you a clue. A course on "the sociology of law" is unlikely to be much concerned with questions about the content of legal rules. Some kinds of courses are more usually taught with one kind of question in mind than another. For example, courses on "land law" or the "law of contract" are more often concerned with the law in books than the law in action. These kinds of courses are sometimes termed *black-letter law* courses. Courses on Family Law often include a great deal of material that tells us about the law in action. This kind of course is often described as *socio-legal*.

Even when it is clear what kind of question your course is generally concerned with problems may still arise. It is not only important to know the kind of question that you are interested in. You must also be able to identify the kind of question that the author of a book or article that you are using is interested in. Are they trying only to analyse the legal rules, the cases and statutes in a particular area of law, or are they also interested in exploring how the law works in practice? If you know the type of answer they are trying to give you will be in a better position to judge the quality of their argument and, thus, the value of their work. Even when you have identified the kind of question an author is most interested in you will also have to be careful to see that other kinds of question are not introduced. For example, it is not uncommon to find a book largely devoted to discussion of the content of legal rules also including a few remarks on the value or justice of those rules. There is nothing wrong with this if the author realises that a different kind of question is being addressed and uses the appropriate material to answer it. Unfortunately this is not always so.

ARE THERE REALLY DIFFERENT QUESTIONS?

3.4 There are some people who would argue that it is misleading to distinguish between different questions in the way we have done above. Some would argue that all the distinctions drawn are wrong. Others would argue that only some of them are invalid. Are there really different questions? One argument that might be advanced is about the distinction between the law in action and the law in books. The Court of Appeal has laid down strict rules about when people accused of offences can receive a lesser sentence if they plead guilty (a practice known as *plea-bargaining*). Research in the past in this area suggested that these rules were not followed in practice. If we assume that the practice of all courts is not to follow these rules, and if this practice continued for many years, what would it mean to say that the legal rule was that which had been laid down by the Court of Appeal? People would only be affected by what happened in practice that would always be different from that which the legal rules said should happen. Could we really say that the legal rule had any significance? If the legal rule has no significance, then surely all we ought to study is what happens in practice, ignoring questions about the law in books?

Other more complicated forms of the above argument exist. Some people would argue that when a judge makes a decision that decision is sometimes influenced by the judge's social background, political views and education. The result of any case is therefore not solely determined by the neutral application of legal rules but by factors personal to the particular judge in the case. If this is so, then what kinds of questions will discussion about the content of legal rules answer? If we are to advise people how to act so as to win cases in court what we need to discuss is not, or not only, the content of legal rules but, rather, who the judges are and what their background is. If we want to find out what the law is we have to ask a whole series of questions other than those about ratios or statutes.

In a similar fashion not everyone accepts that questions about the morality of law and questions about the content of law are different. For some people, the very idea of an immoral law is a contradiction in terms. They think that all law must have an irreducible minimum positive moral content. Without that content the "law", in their view, is merely a collection of words that make a command which may be backed by the physical power of the state but do not have the authority of law. Such theories are termed *natural law* theories. Others argue that the questions about whether something is a legal rule or not and questions about the moral content of that rule are quite distinct. This is usually termed a *positivist* approach to law.

The authors of this book would accept that the distinctions drawn in the previous sections are open to question. The relationship between the different questions, if there are different questions, may be more complicated than the simple divisions above. However most books and most courses in law draw the kinds of distinction outlined. At this early stage in your study of law it will be enough if you understand what the distinctions are. Even if later you come to reject some or all of them, you will still find yourself reading material that is based upon them.

ANSWERING QUESTIONS

▶ 3.5

This chapter has drawn a distinction between three types of question; those concerned with the nature of law, those concerned with the content of legal rules and those which address the operation of law and legal system in practice. Each type of question has a technique appropriate for answering it.

Questions about the nature of law are those that are most difficult to answer. The questions are basic ones, appearing to be very simple. For example, how is law different from other types of command? What is the difference between a gunman telling me to do something and the state, through law, telling me to do something? Are both simply applications of power or is there something fundamentally different between them? Neither the content of particular legal rules nor the operation of the law in practice provides any answer. Arguments in this area are abstract and philosophical. In advancing and judging such arguments it is necessary to see that all the terms are explained and that the argument is coherent. Arguments used here must also match the world they purport to explain. In practice these simple conditions are very difficult to meet.

The ultimate source for answers to questions about the law in books are the judgments and statutes that have already been discussed in Chapter 1. Only these sources will give you a definitive answer to any question you are asked. You are told how to find these materials in Chapter 4 and how to use them in Chapter 5. In some cases you may not have either the time or the resources to consult original materials. In such instance you can look at some of the various commentaries on the law. These vary in size, depth of coverage and price. Different commentaries serve different purposes. Some are student texts. Others are written for specific professions or occupations. Most cover only a limited area of law. However there are some general guides to the law and some encyclopaedias of law. The best encyclopaedia of general English law is *Halsbury's Laws of England*. This has a section on almost every area of law. Most good reference libraries will have a copy of this, and your library may also contain some of the other commentaries that are available. All commentaries try to explain legal rules. You should select one suitable to your interests. However, always remember that a commentary is one person's opinion about the law. It may be wrong. You can only be sure what the rule is if you consult the original cases and statutes.

Finding out how the law works in practice is frequently much more difficult than deciding what a legal rule means. It is easy to find opinions about how things work. Almost everybody who has contact with the law, even if only through reading about it in the newspapers, has an opinion on such questions. However, such opinions have little value. At best they are the experience of one person. That experience may be unusual or misinterpreted by that person. What we are trying to understand is how the legal system works. Anecdotes do not give us the answers that we seek. Thus, to answer this kind of question, we need to turn to the materials and techniques of the social scientist.

SEEING THE LAW IN ACTION

3.6 One starting point for looking at the law in action is looking at statistical information about the legal system. This is one way of moving from the merely anecdotal to the general. Information about the number of cases handled by a court shows in specific terms what the court's workload is. Changes from year to year may indicate some effects of changes in the law and practice. Statistics here can be used descriptively to provide a clearer picture than general phrases such as "some", "many" or "a few". Statistical tests can also establish that there is a relationship, often called a *correlation*, between different things. For example, the length of a sentence for theft may correlate with the value of the items stolen or the experience of the judge who heard the case. This means that the sentence will be longer if, for example, more items are stolen or the judge is more experienced. Statisticians have produced tests to show whether, given the number of examples you have, there is a strong correlation or not. Where this correlation fits with a theory (sometimes termed an *hypothesis*) it provides evidence tending to confirm the theory. Such confirmation is important; without it we have little to establish the effect that the law has, being forced to rely on personal knowledge of individual instances of its application and having to assume that these have general truth. Empirical study of the operation of law may reveal areas for improvement. It can also confirm that, measured by particular standards, the courts are working well.

If we want to use statistics where will we get them from? Government departments collect and publish a large number of statistical reports relating to their operations. Many of these are now available not only in hardcopy form but online via the web. Thus, for example, the Office for National Statistics' data can be seen at: *https://www.ons.gov.uk/*. The work of all Government departments is relevant when looking at how the legal system works. Some departments are, however, particularly important in this respect. The Ministry of Justice is one of the largest Government departments and is responsible for the court system, prisons and the probation service. Its website is *https://www.gov.uk/government/organisations/ministry-of-justice*. The Home Office is responsible for things such as the police, immigration and anti-terrorism. Its website is *https://www.gov.uk/government/ organisations/home-office*. The Department for Education: *https://www.gov.uk/government/organisations/department-for-education* and the Department for Work and Pensions: *https://www.gov.uk/government/organisations/department-for-work-pensions* also provide useful information. A complete list of Government departments and agencies together with their websites is to be found at: *https://www.gov.uk/government/organisations*.

Most official statistics are collected from returns filed by local offices of the relevant departments. The content of these is determined by what the department needs to know about its activities and also by what Parliament has asked it to report on. Even minor changes in the collection of official statistics means that it is often impossible to make comparisons over a period of years. The information collected in one year is about something different from that in other years. Moreover, because of the way in which information is collected and the purpose of collecting it, these statistics can only answer a few of the questions about the way the law operates. For example, the judicial statistics list the number of cases brought each year in the County Court, broken down according to the type of claim. They provide little or no information about the applicants, the specific point of law relied on or whether the judgment was successfully enforced.

Official statistics, as a source of information, are limited. They provide information about things of importance to those who collected them. These are not necessarily the things that are important to the researcher. Government departments, the research councils and some private bodies sponsor research into specific areas of law. Small-scale research is often undertaken without sponsorship. Although this research may be based upon official statistics it may involve first collecting the necessary statistics and then deciding what they mean. The researchers must collect the data they need for each project. They have to design the study that is to select the methods they will use and choose the sample to ensure that they have all the information relevant to their chosen topic. There is a more detailed discussion of some of these issues in Chapter 8, "Reading Research Materials".

The collection of statistics is only one way of gathering information about law and the legal system. Statistics are useful for describing things like numbers of events but are poor for describing things like motivations. Collecting them is one form of *quantitative research*. If researchers want to find out more about the reasons why the law affects people in certain ways, or how it affects them, they will have to carry out different types of research. This may involve interviewing people or even directly observing what is happening in the area in which they are interested. This is known as *qualitative research*. When conducting qualitative research researchers must decide how they can carry out their research so as to ensure that the material they collect represents not just the particular people or bodies they have studied but is also an accurate reflection of the world as a whole.

Socio-legal research has enabled us to understand in a whole range of situations the way in which the law works in practice. It has revealed, for example, how the work of solicitors varies widely, depending on what kind of firm is being considered and why people frequently do not seek the legal redress that they are entitled to. Socio-legal research offers us the opportunity to extend our knowledge of the law and the legal system far beyond the boundaries of the law in the books, showing us how legal rules are affected by the political, economic and social contexts in which law operates.

Part 2

4 Finding cases and statutes

In Chapter 1 the importance of cases and statutes as sources of law was explained. This chapter explains how you find reports of cases and copies of statutes and how you make sure that they are up-to-date. As has been explained, these materials are primary sources of law. From them it is possible to derive the legal rules in which you are interested. Chapters 5, 6 and 7 will explain in more detail how this is done. 4.1

FINDING CASES

In the following, the task of discovering case reports will be considered for three different sets of circumstances: 4.2

(a) Where a well-stocked and supported library is available, using non-electronic resources.
(b) With the aid of online computerised retrieval facilities.
(c) Where some research or library facilities are available, but without access to a fully-equipped law library.

Most readers will have different facilities available at different times. For example, a reader who has access to a fully-equipped law library can only use it during opening hours. It is important that you are aware of the different ways in which to find cases so that you can decide which is the best method to use at any particular time.

USING FULL LAW LIBRARY NON-ELECTRONIC RESEARCH FACILITIES

The traditional form of research in relation to law reports is performed in law libraries containing a wide selection of materials and a variety of support systems, indexes, catalogues, etc. designed to assist the researcher in the task of locating and using particular items. Such libraries are found in academic institutions, such as universities, as well as in professional institutions such as the Inns of Court. In many cases, it is possible to use such libraries even if you are not a member of the institution. What follows in this chapter is an introduction to the major series of law reports and the basic methods of locating and checking up-to-date material and of updating earlier materials. 4.3

Law reports go back over 700 years, although most of the case reports you will find in a normal law library have been decided during the last 150 years. Reports are divided into different series. The way in which these series are compiled varies. Sometimes the series are systematic in their coverage, reporting cases in a particular area of law or from a particular court. In other instances coverage is more general and even idiosyncratic. Older cases can be found in series which bear the title of the name (or names) of the law reporter(s). Such a series is the nineteenth century series of Barnewall and Alderson (Bar & Ald) (all law reports have abbreviations that are customarily used when discussing them. Whenever a series is first mentioned here its usual abbreviation will be given, in brackets, as above. Appendix II to this book is a list of useful abbreviations, including those to the main law reports). The only necessary coherence these cases have is that the reporter thought it was worthwhile to print them. The range and variety of these older cases is enormous, although some help has now been provided to modern legal researchers with some of the old series reprinted in a new collection under the title of *The English Reports* (E.R.). In 1865 the Incorporated Council of Law Reporting introduced *The Law Reports*, a series that was divided according to the different courts of the day. The Council has continued these reports though the current divisions of the reports are different. Today one can find the following divisions:

(a) Appeal Cases (A.C.)—reports of cases in the Court of Appeal, the House of Lords, the Supreme Court and the Privy Council.
(b) Chancery Division (Ch.)—report of cases in the Chancery Division of the High Court and cases appealed from there to the Court of Appeal.
(c) Queen's Bench (Q.B.)—reports of cases in the Queen's Bench Division of the High Court and cases appealed from there to the Court of Appeal.
(d) Family Division (Fam.)—reports of cases in the Family Division of the High Court and cases appealed from there to the Court of Appeal (until 1972 the Family Division was the Probate, Divorce and Admiralty Division (P.)).

This series is the closest to an "official" series of law reports. If a case is reported in several different series and there is a discrepancy between the different reports it is *The Law Reports* that should normally be followed. There is, nowadays, a wide range of privately-published law reports. Most of these series concentrate upon a particular area of legal developments, e.g. the law relating to industrial relations, or the law concerning road traffic. However, there are two series that publish cases dealing with decisions affecting a wide range of legal issues. These general series, with which most students of law will quickly become familiar, are the *Weekly Law Reports* (W.L.R.) and the *All England Law Reports* (All E.R.).

Each of the modern series, just discussed, reports fully any case contained in its volumes. Everything that the judge or judges said in judgment is to be found in the report. There are, in addition, some sources that provide a short summary of, or extracts from, judgments given. The most up-to-date of these sources are those newspapers that print law reports. *The Times* has contained such reports for the longest time and is regarded as being the most authoritative source of such reports. As well as being in *The Times*, they are now available online on a separate site *(justis.com/the-times-law-reports/)*. Case-note sections published in legal periodicals such as the *New Law Journal* (N.L.J.) or the *Solicitors' Journal* (S.J. or Sol. Jo.) are also a good source of such summaries. Where a full report of a case is available as well as short summaries or extracts it is the full report that should be considered. Extracts or summaries, where full reports are available, are not primary sources of law. They cannot be cited in court. They reflect what the editor of the report thinks are the important parts of a judgment. The judgment as a whole is law. The editor's opinion of the law is merely that, opinion. However such summaries or extracts can be used when there is no full judgment reported elsewhere and they are the only source available.

USING LAW REPORTS

4.4

Every case which is reported in a series of law reports can be referred to by way of the names of the parties concerned in the action. Thus, where a court action is brought by somebody called Harriman in dispute with somebody called Martin, the case can be referred to as *Harriman v Martin*. However, referring to a case in this way is of limited usefulness. The reference does not tell the reader the date of the case nor does it indicate the series of reports in which it is found. It does not even tell us to which case involving a Harriman and a Martin the reader is being referred. There may be several. Thus, in addition to its name, each reported case possesses a unique reference indicator. This normally includes (although not always in the same order):

(1) a reference to the title of the series of law reports in which the report is to be found;
(2) a date (year) reference. Where the date reference is necessary if you are to find the case the date is normally enclosed in square brackets. So me series have individual volume numbers for each year. The date reference is then put in round brackets;
(3) a reference to the volume number (if there is more than one volume of the particular law reports series in the year concerned);
(4) a reference to the page or paragraph number at which the report of the case may be located.

If the case of *Harriman v Martin* is reported in the first volume of the *Weekly Law Reports* for 1962, at p.739, the reference would be [1962] 1 W.L.R. 739. This is sometimes called the citation for the case. If you know this reference or citation, it is possible to go directly to the shelves of the law library which house the volumes containing that reference and to turn directly to the report of the case.

Increasingly people are turning to the web as a source of law reports. This has led to the creation of a system of *neutral citation* for such reports. Under this system, which first began in 2001 courts and tribunals have their own abbreviation and each case is given a unique official number by the courts. Within judgments, each paragraph has its own number.

References for the Supreme Court look like this:	[2009] UKSC 1
References for the House of Lords look like this:	[2006] UKHL 20
References for the Privy Council look like this:	[2006] UKPC 4
References for the Court of Appeal look like this:	
Court of Appeal (Civil)	[2003] EWCA Civ 1
Court of Appeal (Criminal)	[2003] EWCA Crim 1
References for the High Court look like this:	
Chancery Division	[2003] EWHC 123 (Ch)
Patents Court	[2003] EWHC 124 (Pat)
Queen's Bench	[2003] EWHC 125 (QB)
Administrative Court	[2003] EWHC 126 (Admin)
Commercial Court	[2003] EWHC 127 (Comm)
Admiralty Court	[2003] EWHC 128 (Admlty)
Technology and Construction Court	[2003] EWHC 129 (TCC)
Family Division	[2003] EWHC 130 (Fam)

Where it is necessary to refer to a precise passage in a judgment by using a paragraph number the paragraph number is put in square brackets. Where a neutral citation is available it is put first before the more traditional citation to a printed hardcopy version of the judgment.

Some tribunals such as the Employment Appeal Tribunal and the Upper Tribunal also use a system of neutral citation when reporting their cases.

USING ELECTRONIC RETRIEVAL FACILITIES

4.5 If you know only the names of the parties in the case, you will need first to search for the specific citation, whether it be a neutral citation or a more traditional reference to a printed volume. Equally it is not enough to know merely what was said in a particular case in order to know the importance that should be attached to that case. It is also necessary to know whether such an earlier case has been used or referred to subsequently by the judges, or, indeed, whether it has been expressly approved or disapproved of by a later court. If a case is approved by a court that is further up the hierarchy of courts than the court originally giving judgment (and that approval is part of the ratio of that later case) then the case will take on the status of the later decision. Thus a decision of the High Court approved by the Court of Appeal will take on the status of the Court of Appeal. Even if the approval forms part of the obiter within the later judgment this will be significant, indicating the way in which the court is likely to give judgment once the matter becomes central in a decision at that level. Disapproval of a case will be important in a similar fashion. Online electronic resources offer a way of finding citations and then being able to read the relevant report. They also provide a way for finding out how a case has subsequently been treated in later decisions.

"Online" Services

4.6 There are two major, commercially marketed, legal databases which are widely used in universities and by practitioners, Lexis and Westlaw. Both databases cover a number of different jurisdictions and contain not just cases but also legislation and law journals. To use either of these systems effectively requires some training in the way that material is organised and the methods used to search them.

In general both Lexis and Westlaw contain the full text of judgments though the format is somewhat different to that in traditional printed law reports. As well as providing access to a large collection of published legal material Lexis and Westlaw also include unreported cases, i.e. cases that have been decided but which have not yet been published in hardcopy form and in some cases never will be published in that form.

Searching for a case using electronic retrieval systems is generally done using key words. The user asks whether a specific term or set of words is to be found in the database. The user is then given a list of the cases that contain the item that is being searched for and can then look at the cases that have been found. The user will find that on the one hand if they use only very general terms for their search they will be given a very large list of cases to look at, most of which they will find irrelevant to their needs. If on the other hand they use a very precise term the list provided will not contain any case that is relevant but which uses slightly different terminology in its judgment. The skill in using databases like Lexis and Westlaw lies in steering a course between these two extremes.

Cases on the net

4.7 There are many internet sites which discuss law or legal issues or provide material about law. A number of these provide free access to legal materials.

A wide range of material relating to law is available on the British and Irish Legal Information Institute's web site: *https://www.bailii.org/*.

All decisions of the Supreme Court are available at: *https://www.supremecourt.uk/decided-cases/*.

Decisions of the House of Lords are available at: *http://www.publications.parliament.uk/pa/ld/ldjudgmt.htm*.

Privy Council decisions are available at: *http://www.jcpc.uk/decided-cases/index.html*.

FINDING AND UPDATING STATUTES

Statutes are published individually but law libraries and some public libraries have bound collections that include all the statutes for a particular year. Statutes passed since 1988 are available on the internet at: *http://www.legislation.gov.uk/ukpga*. ▶ 4.8

With statutes there are three main problems. Is the statute in force? Has the statute been repealed by Parliament, (i.e. replaced by some other statute)? Has the statute been amended by Parliament, (i.e. had part of its contents altered by Parliament)? The electronic databases that have cases on them normally also have statutes. They will usually contain not only the statutes themselves but also information about whether the statute has been amended or repealed.

USING LIMITED LIBRARY FACILITIES

The problems of finding and using cases and law reports where limited resources are available are significant. Clearly, it will not be possible to find reports of all the cases that you may need, since the available reports may only be found in series which are not at your disposal. By the same token, you may not have access to sufficiently comprehensive reference manuals. You may have access to one of the general series of law reports. This will often be a set of *All England Law Reports*. Many public reference libraries possess a set of these law reports. If this is the case, some searching for cases can be done using the index contained in those volumes, though this will, of course, be time consuming. Alternatively, if you are concerned only with a limited specialist area you may have access to a specialised series of law reports. Whatever your source of available material, however, it is of paramount importance that you familiarise yourself with the specific indexing and cross-referencing system adopted by that source. If you do this, you will be able to use the material at your disposal, limited though it may be by comparison with the resources of a fully-equipped and supported law library, in the most efficient manner. It will also be important to discover whether you can obtain access to some means for updating the material contained in your available sources. Amongst possible sources of updated information might be the general legal periodicals, such as the *New Law Journal* or the *Solicitors' Journal* (both of which have been referred to above). Many public libraries subscribe to one of these, or to other relevant periodicals. Where your needs relate to a specific area, the periodicals available in relation to that area may be of assistance in obtaining up-to-date information. Thus, for example, many human resource management journals contain information about cases decided by the courts in relation to employment law. All of these will probably refer you to sources of information that you do not have but they will also enable you to make the most efficient use of those sources that are available. A further common source of information will be textbooks on the subject about which you are seeking information. The important rule here is to check that you have access to the latest possible edition of the book, and to bear in mind the possibility that case law developments may have overtaken the legal position as it was ▶ 4.9

stated at the time of writing of the book. Most books dealing with the law will contain a statement in the "Foreword" stating the date on which the information given in the book is said to be current. In some instances, you may have access to a casebook. This term is something of a misnomer since casebooks frequently contain not just cases but also statutes and comments on the law. Such books are generally concerned with a specific topic, for example "contract law", and contain edited material relevant to the area. These books can be a very useful source where you have access only to limited library facilities. However, they suffer from several deficiencies. First, the reader relies on the editor of the volume to select the most appropriate material. There is no way in which the quality of the work can be checked. Secondly, the material presented may only be given in part. Again, the reader must trust that the editor has not given misleading extracts. Finally, the reader has no means of updating the material. In some areas of law encyclopaedias are produced. These are similar to casebooks, although they are generally more detailed.

HOW TO USE ENCYCLOPAEDIAS

4.10 Encyclopaedias are not a source of law (although they may contain sources of law). Cases and statutes are sources of law. They are what will be used when judges are deciding what the outcome of a case is to be. However, for some people encyclopaedias will be the only material they have available. Thus it is important to consider how they can be used most effectively. Different examples of encyclopaedias vary in form and content. They do not all contain the same kind of material nor are they ordered in the same way. Therefore it is not possible to give a series of rules saying how encyclopaedias should be used. What follows are points that a reader should consider when first using any encyclopaedia. The first thing to look at is the kind of material that the encyclopaedia contains. One advantage of an encyclopaedia can be that it brings together a wide variety of material about particular subject matter. Thus, you may find the encyclopaedia which you are reading contains all the statutes in a particular area, all the statutory instruments, government circulars and other non- statutory material, references to relevant cases (with some description of their contents) together with some discussion of the application of legal rules in the area. On the other hand the encyclopaedia may contain only some of the material or may extract some of it. Thus, for example, instead of having all of a statute you may find that you have only parts of it. Even if the encyclopaedia claims to be fully comprehensive, remember that it is no more than a claim. The editors of the encyclopaedia may feel that they have included all relevant statutes; others may disagree with them. It is always as important to be aware of what you do not know as what you do know. Relying on an encyclopaedia means that there may be gaps in your knowledge of the particular area of law. However, you may feel it worth relying on the encyclopaedia because it is the only source available. Equally, you may find it quicker to use an encyclopaedia and consider the advantage of speedy access more important than any element of doubt in your knowledge of the area. Most encyclopaedias extract at least some of the material that they cover. That is to say that they contain extracts of a statute, statutory instrument, or whatever, rather than the whole. Here the problem is that, in extracting their material, the editors of the encyclopaedia limit your knowledge of the law. You rely on them to extract that which is relevant and cannot check the matter for yourself. As a source of law, the less comprehensive an encyclopaedia is the less useful it will be. However, the more comprehensive an encyclopaedia is the slower it may be to use. Before using the encyclopaedia you need to consider the kind of question that you are trying to answer. If the question is a very broad and general one about the framework of some area of law you may find an encyclopaedia with less detail easier to use. However, if you are trying to answer a very detailed point, perhaps applying the law to a very precise factual situation, you need the most comprehensive encyclopaedia that you can find. Most encyclopaedias, and increasingly many other books about law, are now issued in looseleaf form. This means that the publisher issues supplements to the encyclopaedia on a regular basis. These supplements, which contain descriptions of changes in the law, are then substituted for the pages that discuss the out-of-date law. The advantage of the looseleaf form over ordinary books is that it means the encyclopaedia is more likely to be accurate. When using looseleaf encyclopaedias before looking up the point of law that interests you always see when it was last updated. You will usually find a page at the front of the first volume of the encyclopaedia that tells you when it was last updated. The technique for finding out about points of law in an encyclopaedia will vary depending upon the encyclopaedia being used. Some are organised according to different areas of law within the subject of the encyclopaedia. Others have different volumes for different kinds of material; one volume for statutes, one for discussion of the law and so forth. Most will have both indexes and detailed contents pages. Most encyclopaedias have a discussion of how they should be used at the beginning of their first volume. Always consult this when first using an encyclopaedia.

FINDING AND USING MATERIAL ON THE LAW OF THE EUROPEAN COMMUNITIES, THE EUROPEAN UNION, AND THE EUROPEAN ECONOMIC AREA

4.11 All basic material in relation to the European Communities, the European Union, and the European Economic Area is published in English. However, some material is not made available in all of the official languages of the European Communities immediately. What is said here refers specifically to English language versions of such material.

The Official Journal of the European Communities is the authoritative voice of the European Communities, and is used to publish daily information. It can be found at: *https://eur-lex.europa.eu/oj/direct-access.html* (the O.J.) is divided into two major parts (the L and C series). There are also separately published notices of recruitment, notices and public contracts and the like, which are published in a Supplement and in Annexes. Twice a year the O.J. issues a Directory of Community legislation in force and other acts of the Community institutions.

LEGISLATION

4.12 The L series (Legislation) contains the text of Community legislation. The series is arranged by Volume, starting in 1958, and by issue number sequentially throughout the issue year. Thus, the text of Council Directive 95/45/EC of 22 September 1994 on the establishment of a European Works Council or a procedure in Community-scale undertakings and Community-scale groups of undertakings for the purposes of informing and consulting employees is to be found in the *Official Journal* of 30 September 1994.

The Volume number for 1994 is Volume 37.
The issue number of the OJ L series for September 30, 1994 is L 254.
The text of the Directive is set out on page 64 and thus the page reference is p.64.
The official reference for the Directive will be OJ No L 254, 30.9.1994, p.64.

INFORMATION AND NOTICES

4.13 The C series (Information and Notices) contains, amongst a host of other items, key extracts (*the operative part*) from judgments of the Court of Justice of the European Communities (the ECJ, sitting in Luxembourg) and the Court of First Instance (which also sits in Luxembourg). Where the language of the particular court being reported is not English, the C series will include *a provisional translation*: the definitive translation being found in the separately published Reports of Cases before the Court. There is also brief coverage of actions brought before the ECJ by Member States against the Council of the European Communities, as well as questions referred to the ECJ by national courts of Member States. Also, to be found in the C series will be Preparatory Acts in the course of being made into legislation by the European Communities. Thus, for example, the *Official Journal* for February 19, 1994 contains the text of an Opinion delivered by the Economic and Social Committee on a proposal for a Council Regulation on substances that deplete the ozone layer.

The Volume Number for 1994 is Volume 37.
The issue of the OJ C series for 19 February 1994 is C 52.
The text of the proposed Decision is item 3 in issue C 52, and so the reference is 03.
The full reference for the Opinion is OJ 94/C 52/03.

OTHER MATERIALS

4.14 Whilst the *Official Journal* is the best official source of information about Community law it should be noted that a wide range of documentation does not find its way into the *Official Journal* and other sources may have to be considered for those wanting a comprehensive list of European materials. In particular, mention should be made of so-called COM documents, which often contain important proposals for future legislation. These are issued by the Commission with a "rolling" numerical reference by sequence of publication during a particular year. Consequently, there is no systematic numbering of such COM Docs a matter which frequently gives rise to criticism about the accessibility of important documentation in the legislative field. By way of example, an important Communication concerning the application of the Agreement on social policy, presented by the Commission to the Council and to the European Parliament on 14 December 1993, is simply designated:

COM(93) 600 final.

Various other series, apart from the COM series, are also to be found in relation to a range of spheres of activity within the European Union. Judgments of the European Court of Justice are reported in two series of law reports. One series is that formally published by the European Union itself the *European Court Reports* (E.C.R.). The other series is the privately produced *Common Market Law Reports* (C.M.L.R.). Both can be found in the normal manner. In addition to these specialised law reports series, an increasing number of judgments delivered by the European Court of Justice are now reported as a normal part of general law report series.

EUROPEAN UNION MATERIALS ON THE INTERNET

4.15 The official internet site of the European Union is found at: *http://europa.eu*. From here it is possible to access all the institutions of the European Union in any of the official languages of the Union.

5

Reading cases and statutes

This chapter will explain how you should use the primary sources for legal rules, cases and statutes. You will find a specimen case report and a specimen statute in each section. In addition, there are further examples of case reports in the exercise section of this book (Cases I and II). Skill in the use of the techniques described here can only be acquired with practice. For this reason the exercises in the book enable you to build a range of experience in handling the material contained in cases and statutes. 5.1

READING A CASE

The contents of law reports are explained here so that you can start to read cases, understand the law which they contain, and make useful notes about them. You will find the court structure, and how cases are decided, explained in Chapter 1. You will find a copy of a case, *R. v Jackson*, on pp.200.00. All specific references in this section will be to that case. The copy is taken from the *All England Law Reports*, which are the most commonly available law reports. However, if you have access to other kinds of hard copy law reports you will find that they look very much the same as the *All England Law Reports*. The techniques discussed here will be just as useful in reading other series of law reports and court transcripts. The different series of law reports and their use has been explained in Chapter 4. 5.2

572 All England Law Reports [1999] 1 All ER

R v Jackson

a

COURT OF APPEAL CRIMINAL DIVISION
ROSE L.J., BUTTERFIELD AND RICHARDS JJ
28 APRIL, 1998

Criminal law—Appeal—Leave to appeal—Practice—Single judge granting leave on some grounds but refusing leave on others—Need for leave of full court to pursue grounds in respect of which leave refused. b

Where, on an application for leave to appeal to the Court of Appeal, Criminal Division, the single judge grants leave on some grounds but specifically refuses leave on others, counsel for the appellant must obtain the leave of the full court if he c wishes to pursue the grounds in respect of which leave has been refused (see p. 574*g*. post).

Notes

For appeal against conviction or sentence following trial on indictment, see 11(2) d *Halsbury's Laws* (4th edn reissue) paras 1352, 1355.

Cases referred to in judgment

R v Bloomfield [1997] 1 Cr App R 135, CA.
R v Chalkley, R v Jeffries [1998] 2 All ER 155, [1998] QB 848, [19983] WLR 146, CA.

e

Appeal against conviction

Stephen Shaun Jackson appealed with leave of the single judge against his conviction on 25 July 1995 in the Crown Court at Croydon before Judge Crush and a jury of theft. The facts are set out in the judgment of the court.

Marc Willers (assigned by the *Registrar of Criminal Appeals*) for the appellant. f
Hugh Davies (instructed by the *Crown Prosecution Service*, Croydon) for the Crown.

ROSE LJ delivered the following judgment of the court. On 25 July 1997 in the Crown Court at Croydon, this appellant was convicted by the jury of theft, on the first count in the indictment. He was acquitted of charges of false accounting on counts 2, 3 and 4. The trial was a retrial, the jury on an earlier occasion having g acquitted in relation to certain counts on the then indictment, but failed to agree in relation to the counts upon which the second jury adjudicated. He appeals against his conviction by leave of the single judge, which was granted in relation to the first of the two matters which Mr Willers, on behalf of the appellant, seeks to canvass before this court. h

For the purposes of this appeal, the facts can be briefly stated. The appellant was the proprietor of a minicab firm. Insurance brokers, Thompson Heath & Bond (South East) Ltd (to whom we shall refer as 'THB') devised a scheme to enable minicab drivers to pay for their motor insurance by instalments. That scheme was underwritten by others.

j

The scheme allowed the premiums to be collected from the minicab drivers on a weekly basis, and passed on to THB each month. THB then paid the underwriters.

It was the Crown's case against the appellant that, while he acted as agent for THB, to collect weekly premiums from the drivers, between February 1991 and March 1994, he failed to declare to THB the full amount that he had collected, a and that he kept a sum of money, in the region of £100,000, for himself and spent much of it on luxury items for his own benefit.

While he was acting in this way, the appellant, it was common ground, devised a form called a Bank 1 form, on which to record payments made by him to THB. At the original trial, the judge had ordered disclosure of Bank 1 forms by the prosecution but, save for one example of such a form, which was in the b appellant's possession at the time of the first trial, no such disclosure had been made. Between the first trial and the retrial, however, those documents, which had apparently been in the possession not of the prosecuting authorities but of THB, were disclosed to the defence and were available to them at the time of the retrial.

A submission was made to the trial judge, Judge Crush, by Mr Willers then, as now, appearing for the defendant, that the second trial should be stayed as an c abuse of the process of the court. The ground of that submission was that it would not be fair to try the appellant a second time, because the Bank 1 forms had not been available during the first trial and, if they had been, the first jury might have acquitted. The learned judge rejected that submission. That rejection forms the ground of appeal in relation to which the single judge gave leave and which Mr d Willers has placed in the forefront of his argument in this court.

Mr Willers accepts that, although the judge at the first trial ordered disdosure and no disclosure took place, that was because the documents had simply not at that stage been found, although they were in the possession of THB.

Mr Willers did not, during the course of the first trial, make any further application, non-disclosure not having been made, either for the jury to be e discharged, or otherwise.

Mr Willers does not suggest that, at the first trial or subsequently, there was any bad faith on the part of the prosecution in relation to the non-disclosure. He submits that, during the cross-examination of Det Sgt James at the second trial, it emerged that he had left with THB the responsibility for looking through the vast f number of documents and passing to the police those which they thought relevant. Although Mr Willers does not suggest that gave rise to bad faith by the officer, he submits that it would have been better had the officer looked through the documents himself.

By the time of the second trial, however, Mr Willers accepts that the defence had all the documentation that they required, including all the Bank 1 forms. But, g he submits, if there was a real possibility of acquittal at the first trial had those forms then been available, it was unfair for the second trial to take place, and the judge should have acceded to the defence application to stay the second trial for abuse of process.

Mr Willers accepted that his submission came to this that, despite the fact that h all the relevant material was before the second jury who convicted, this court, in ruling upon the safety of that conviction, should speculate that the first jury, faced with all the relevant material, might have acquitted; and therefore it was unfair to proceed with the second trial. Mr Willers referred to the decision of this court in *R v Chalkley, R v Jeffries* [1998] 2 All E.R. 155, [1998] QB 848. In the course of j giving the judgment of the court in that case, Auld LJ commented, adversely, on an earlier decision of this court, differently constituted, in *R v Bloomfield* [1997] 1 Cr App R 135, which had attracted some criticism from the editors of the third supplement to *Archbold's Criminal Pleading, Evidence and Practice* (1997 edn) para 7–45. We make that comment because the argument originally advanced in skeleton form on behalf of the appellant relied, in part, on this court's decision in *R v Bloomfield*.

On behalf of the Crown, Mr Davies submits that the safety of the appellant's conviction depends on the evidence at the second trial, which was followed by an admirably succinct summing up by the learned judge, following a trial which, for reasons which are not manifest, had lasted a considerable number of weeks. a

Mr Davies draws attention, in relation to the safety of that conviction, to a number of letters written by the appellant after these apparent defalcations came to light, the first of them, it was common ground, on 21 March 1994 to a man called Andrew Orchard. That letter was written on the day that the defendant left this country, for a period of some seven months in the Canary Islands. The appellant also wrote letters to his sister, Jackie, and to his partner, David. Each of those letter, in various ways, comprises a series of admissions of criminal mis-behaviour of present materiality, coupled with expressions of regret. In the course of the thal, the appellant sought to explain those letters away on the basis of a state of confused mind when he had written them. b c

In our judgment, it is wholly impossible to accept Mr Willers' submission either that the judge was wrong to rule as he did in refusing a stay, or that that refusal gives rise to any lack of safety in this appellant's conviction. It frequently happens that new evidence comes to light between the time of a first trial when a jury disagrees and a second trial. Such evidence may be favourable to the prosecution or to the defence. But the verdict of the second jury does not become unsafe because it was unfair for there to be a second trial. Indeed, pursuing Mr Willers' argument to its logical conclusion, wherever fresh evidence appears between a first and second trial, it would be unfair, at least if the evidence assisted the defence, to have a second trial at all. That is a submission which we roundly reject. The learned judge was, in our view, correct to refuse the stay on the basis of the application made to him. That refusal, in the light of the overwhelming evidence before the second jury, cannot, in any event, be regarded as rendering the verdict of the second jury unsafe. d e

The second matter which Mr Willers sought to canvass related to a criticism of the learned judge's direction in relation to dishonesty and the character of the defence case. It is said that the judge misdirected the jury and failed to put the defence case adequately in relation to the way in which money was spent on luxuries. f

It is fair to say that Mr Willers sought the leave of this court to pursue the interrelated grounds in relation to that aspect of the case, the learned single judge having refused leave to argue those grounds. For the avoidance of doubt, where, in granting leave to appeal on some grounds, the single judge has specifically refused leave to appeal on other grounds, the leave of this court is required before counsel may argue those other grounds. As we have said, Mr Willers sought the leave of this court. We have read the passage in the summing up in the transcript of which he complains. It is to be noted that, in answer to a question from the jury, the judge gave a dear direction as to dishonesty, relevant to this case, in identical terms to that which he had given at the outset of his summing up. g h

Nothing in the passage of the summing up about which complaint is made, in our view, renders it arguable that there was any misdirection. Accordingly, as to that aspect of the case, we refused leave to pursue an appeal on that basis.

For the reasons given, this appeal is dismissed. j

Appeal dismissed.

Carlone Stomberg Barrister.

The case is the criminal law case of *R. v Jackson.* Lawyers pronounce this "Regina (or 'The Queen' or 'King', or 'The Crown') against Jackson". Most criminal cases are written like this. In civil cases, the names of the parties are usually given, as in *Donoghue v Stevenson*, the case being pronounced "Donoghue and Stevenson".

Underneath the name of the case at "**a**" you will see three pieces of information. First, you are told the court in which the case was heard. In this case, it was the Court of Appeal, Criminal Division. It is important to know which court heard a case because of the doctrine of precedent (see pp.100–104 for an explanation of the doctrine of precedent).

The report then gives the names of the judges who took part in the case. This information is used to help evaluate the decision. Some judges are known to be very experienced in particular areas of law. Their decisions may be given extra weight. Finally, you are told when the case was heard and when the court gave its decision. In the House of Lords this process is called "delivering opinions", but in other courts it is known as "giving judgment".

The material in italics, at "**b**" on the first page of the report, is written by the editor of the report. It indicates the subject matter of the case and the issue which it concerned. The subject index at the front of each volume of law reports includes a similar entry under the first words.

The next section, at "**c**", is called the *headnote*. It is not part of the case proper, and is prepared by the law reporter, not by the judges. The headnote should summarise the case accurately giving references to important parts of the court's opinion or judgment and any cases cited. Because it is written when the case is reported, the headnote may stress or omit elements of the case which are later thought to be important. Therefore, care should be taken when using the headnote.

The notes, just below "**d**", direct the reader to appropriate volumes of *Halsbury's Laws of England* and/or *Halsbury's Statutes of England. Halsbury's Laws* provides a concise statement of the relevant law, subject by subject, including references to the main cases and statutes. *Halsbury's Statutes* gives the complete text of all statutes together with annotations that explain them. Although law students and others may need to research the law using *Halsbury* it is not necessary to turn to reference works when reading every case. In most instances, the background law will be sufficiently explained by the judge. In our case of *R. v Jackson* the reference is confined to *Halsbury's Laws.*

At "**e**" there is a list of all the cases referred to by the judges. In relation to each case, a list of different places where the case may be found is given. Where counsel have cited additional cases to which the judges did not refer, this will be given in a separate list under the heading "cases also cited".

At "**e**" to "**f**" you will find a full history of the proceedings of the case. This indicates all the courts that have previously considered the case before the present one. The final sentence of this section indicates where a full account of the facts of the case may be found.

Below "**f**" you will find the names of the counsel (usually barristers but sometimes solicitor-advocates) who appeared in the case. In the case of *R. v Jackson* the barristers on both sides were what are known as "junior counsel". Senior counsel are called "QCs" (Queen's Counsel), or "KCs" (King's Counsel) when the monarch is a King.

The appellant was Jackson, while the Crown (in other words the state) was the respondent. The names of the solicitors who acted for the two parties and instructed the counsel are to be found below "**f**" in the law report. Academics may use this information to obtain further information about the case. Solicitors may use it in order to find out which are the best counsel to instruct for particular kinds of cases.

Not all series of law reports have marginal letters as this one does. When they do, these letters can be used to give a precise reference to any part of the case. Thus, the beginning of Lord Justice Rose's judgment is [1999] 1 All E.R. 572g.

Whilst the matters above provide an introduction to the case, the substance is to be found in the judgments. Every law case raises a question or series of questions to be answered by the judge(s). In civil cases, some of these will be questions of fact (in criminal cases these will be answered by the jury). For example, it may be necessary to know at what speed a car was travelling when an accident occurred. In practice, the answers to these factual questions are very important. Once they have been settled, the legal issues in the case may be simple. However, when it comes to the study of law, it is only the legal questions that matter.

For the judge(s) in a case, therefore, there are two clearly distinguishable processes which have to be gone through when hearing the matter and reaching a judgment. First, there is the process of making "findings of fact". Then, in the light of those findings of fact, there is the process of making "findings on the law". The key questions that are posed to the judge(s) in this context are referred to as "the issues in the case".

Lawyers and students of law are concerned primarily not with the outcome of a case but with the reasoning that the judge gave for the conclusion. The reasoning is important because within it will be found the *ratio decidendi* (often referred to simply as "the ratio"). The ratio is that part of the legal reasoning which is essential for the decision in the case. It is the ratio which is binding under the doctrine of precedent and which is thus part of the law. The ratio and the reasons for the decision are not necessarily the same thing. Not all of the reasons given for the decision will be essential. In courts where there is more than one judge, each may give a separate judgment (as can be seen from the examples in the exercises section of this book). If they do, each judgment will have its own reasons, and thus its own ratio. The judges must agree a conclusion to the case (although they may do so only by majority). However, they do not have to have the same reasons for their decision. If they have different reasons the judgments have different ratios and, thus, the case itself may have no ratio. Lawyers will rarely agree that a case has no ratio at all.

Finding the ratio in a case is crucial. It is also the most difficult part of reading cases, particularly when the case involves several judgments. The ratio is the essence of the case and, thus, may not be found simply by quoting from a judgment. Discovering the ratio involves skills of interpretation—understanding and explaining what judges meant, how they reached their conclusions—in order to see the common ground. Although the ratio is the law, it cannot be divorced entirely from the facts. Facts that are essential for a decision to provide the conditions for the operation of the rules and are, thus, part of the rule itself. Deciding which are essential, as opposed to subsidiary, facts takes skill and practice. Lawyers frequently disagree on exactly what the ratio to a decision is. Some may view it broadly, seeing the decision as having few conditions but laying down a general rule. Others may take a narrower approach, suggesting that only in very limited circumstances would a decision bind a future court. Subsequent cases often help to clarify what the ratio of a previous case is accepted as being. There is a more detailed explanation of the way in which one decides what the ratio of a case is in Chapter 6 below.

The editors of a law report write what they consider the ratio to be in the headnote. They may be wrong. Even if their interpretation is plausible when they write it, a later case may take a different view. For these reasons, statements of law in the headnote cannot be relied on.

If we look at *R. v Jackson* we can see that some of the things that we are told in the judgment are irrelevant for the purposes of constructing the ratio. The case before the Court of Appeal concerns a question relating to "leave to appeal". Thus, for example, the fact that the accused collected money on a weekly basis, rather than monthly, is of no account. Similarly, the fact that he failed to declare to the insurance brokers the full amount that he had collected is not significant for the purposes of the Court of Appeal on the question concerning "leave to appeal". However, we will be aware that, for the original trial judge in the Crown Court, when the charges brought against the accused were of "false accounting", this would have been a very significant matter.

You will see that in the case of *R. v Jackson* Lord Justice Rose (Rose LJ) delivers a judgment that is the "judgment of the court". This therefore reflects the shared views of himself, Lord Justice Butterfield and Lord Justice Richards. Judgments in courts with multiple judges like the Court of Appeal and the Supreme Court are not always like this. Each judge may give their own judgment. Having set out the history of the case (at p.572 g–h), Lord Justice Rose then gives a brief outline of the relevant facts for the purposes of the appeal (at p.572h–573d). This is followed by a summary of the submissions made by the counsel for each party (at p.573d–574c). You will see that counsel are said to have "submitted" certain things and to have "accepted" other matters during the course of their arguments before the Court of Appeal. Having dealt with these matters by way of preliminary presentation, Lord Justice Rose then moves on to the conclusions of the Court of Appeal. It is here that we look for the reasons and the ratio in the case.

The first matter considered (set out at p.574c–e) is the court's view on a proposition put by counsel for the appellant. You will gather that the Court of Appeal has little sympathy for the argument put forward, and in quite strong terms (at p.574e) "roundly rejects" the proposition that "wherever fresh evidence appears between a first and second trial, it would be unfair, at least if the evidence assisted the defence, to have a second trial". This leads the Court of Appeal to the conclusion that (i) the trial judge acted correctly in refusing to "stay" the trial of the accused, and (ii) anyway, given the evidence before the second jury in this case, that the verdict of that second jury could not be regarded as in any way "unsafe" (see p.574e–f). These conclusions are specific to this case, although the first one follows from the view expressed by the court on counsel's (roundly rejected) proposition. The narrow ratio of the case may thus be discovered by looking at that view, which was essential for reaching the eventual decision delivered by the Court of Appeal.

However, it is the "second matter" dealt with by the Court of Appeal that has drawn the attention of the law report editor to this case. At p.574f–g you will see that the court is faced with a question of what permission (or "leave") is required in order for an appeal to be made against particular aspects of a case. The eventual decision of the Court of Appeal (not to allow an appeal to be pursued on the basis of an alleged misdirection in the trial judge's summing up) is set out at p.574j, and the reasons for arriving at this decision are explained at p.574h. In order to reach that decision, the court has had to decide in what circumstances an appeal such as this may or may not be pursued. In this case the Court of Appeal goes further than to pronounce merely in relation to the specific case before it, relating to Jackson, the accused. Here, the court makes a general statement "for the avoidance of doubt", which is intended to clarify the situation for all future cases where this issue arises (set out at p.574g–h). That ratio, indeed, is also the part of the judgment that has been extracted by the editor of the law reports series to form the headnote that we have already looked at (at p.572c).

R. v Jackson contains only a single judgment. That judgment is a short one. If one had a longer judgment (and most judgments are longer) or multiple judgments in the same case, the task of constructing a ratio would be much more difficult. When one has to consider one judgment and its obscurities in the light of other judgments the process of analysing the law becomes even more uncertain. In order to appreciate some of the problems of constructing a ratio in a less straightforward case, therefore, you should apply the techniques discussed here to the law reports contained in the exercises section of this book.

A court must follow the ratio of any relevant case that is binding on it under the doctrine of precedent. Thus, the question arises, when is a case relevant? A case in the same area must be followed unless it can be "distinguished" on the basis of its facts. If the facts of the case cannot be distinguished—if, as it is commonly put, the case is "on all fours"—then it must be followed. The process of distinguishing cases is really just another way of deciding what the ratio of the case is. If the material facts necessary for the operation of the legal rule in the first case are not found in the second, or are different, there is no precedent. Just as lawyers differ about what the ratio to a case is, so they differ about whether a case is binding in a particular situation or not.

That which is not part of the ratio of the case is said to be the *obiter dictum*. This is usually referred to as "the *obiter*". Obiter is said to have "persuasive authority". That which was said obiter in a court such as the House of Lords may be very persuasive indeed for a relatively inferior court such as a County Court. Moreover, remarks made obiter may indicate which way the law is developing, or which kinds of arguments judges find particularly persuasive. Equally, judges are not always very careful about differentiating between ratio and obiter. There is a further explanation of the place of obiter observations in legal reasoning in Chapter 6 below.

The remainder of this section provides some guidance on how to study cases. The first question a student should ask about a case is "Why has this case been set?" The purpose of studying cases is to obtain an understanding of the relevance of the case to the area of law being studied. Some cases will be more important than others. A leading Supreme Court decision will require more time and closer examination than a decision of the High Court that is merely illustrative of a point mentioned in a lecture or included in a problem. Where a case has developed or defined an area of law it is usually helpful to start by reading what the textbook writers say about it. Where more than one case has to be read on the same point of law, they should, if possible, be read in chronological order and each one digested before moving on to the next.

A second question to ask when reading cases is, "How much time is available?" Try to spend more time on important decisions and important judgments, even if you have to rely on a headnote or a textbook when it comes to the others. Do not spend the greater proportion of your time reading cases which have been overruled or which have novel or interesting facts but no new point of law. The headnote is helpful when allocating time. Treat judgments in the same way as you treat cases. Do not waste your time reading judgments that merely repeat something you have already read. Spend more time on the leading judgments than on the others. Again, the headnote will be helpful for this. Some judgments are more clearly written than others. Some judgments are shorter than others. Neither clarity nor brevity necessarily means that the judgment is more important. Choose what you read because it is the best for your purposes, not because it is the easiest!

Notes on any case should start with the case name and any references. They should then include:

(1) a brief statement of the facts of the case;
(2) the history of the case;
(3) the point of law under consideration;
(4) the decision with the reasons for it, together with any names of cases relied upon.

One page should be enough for this basic information.

When reading judgments in order to make notes, look for agreement and disagreement on each of the points relevant to your study. It is often useful to make separate notes on each of the points raised by the case and then see what different judges said about them. In particular, too, do not forget to make it clear in your notes whether a judge was dissenting or not.

HOW TO READ A STATUTE

This section will explain how you should read statutes. The way in which statutes are created is explained on pp.3–4. Looking for a particular legal rule in a statute can be confusing. Some statutes are over 100 pages long, although most are shorter. The language they use often appears complicated and obscure. If you understand the structure of a statute and follow a few simple rules in reading them, statutes will become much clearer. 5.3

A copy of a statute, the House of Lords Act 1999, is reproduced below. All subsequent references here are to this statute.

House of Lords Act 1999 ①

1999 Chapter 34 ②

An Act to restrict membership of the House of Lords by virtue of a hereditary peerage; to make related provision about disqualifications for voting at elections to, and for membership of, the House of Commons; and for connected purposes. ③

[11th November 1999] ④

BE IT ENACTED by the Queen's most Excellent Majesty, by and with the advice and consent of the Lords Spiritual and Temporal, and Commons, in this present Parliament assembled, and by the authority of the same, as follows:—

⑤

1. No-one shall be a member of the House of Lords by virtue of a hereditary peerage. — Exclusion of hereditary peers.

⑥

Exception from section 1.

2.—(1) Section 1 shall not apply in relation to anyone excepted from it by or in accordance with Standing Orders of the House.

(2) At any one time 90 people shall be excepted from section 1; but anyone excepted as holder of the office of Earl Marshal, or as performing the office of Lord Great Chamberlain, shall not count towards that limit.

(3) Once excepted from section 1, a person shall continue to be so throughout his life (until an Act of Parliament provides to the contrary).

(4) Standing Orders shall make provision for filling vacancies among the people excepted from section 1; and in any case where—

(a) the vacancy arises on a death occurring after the end of the first Session of the next Parliament after that in which this Act is passed, and
(b) the deceased person was excepted in consequence of an election,

that provision shall require the holding of a by-election.

(5) A person may be excepted from section 1 by or in accordance with Standing Orders made in anticipation of the enactment or commencement of this section.

(6) Any question whether a person is excepted from section 1 shall be decided by the Clerk of the Parliaments, whose certificate shall be conclusive.

Removal of disqualifications in relation to the House of Commons.

3.—(1) The holder of a hereditary peerage shall not be disqualified by virtue of that peerage for—

(a) voting at elections to the House of Commons, or
(b) being, or being elected as, a member of that House.

(2) Subsection (1) shall not apply in relation to anyone excepted from section 1 by virtue of section 2.

Amendments and repeals.

4.—(1) The enactments mentioned in Schedule 1 are amended as specified there.

(2) The enactments mentioned in Schedule 2 are repealed to the extent specified there.

Commencement and transitional provision.

5.—(1) Sections 1 to 4 (including Schedules 1 and 2) shall come into force at the end of the Session of Parliament in which this Act is passed.

(2) Accordingly, any writ of summons issued for the present Parliament in right of a hereditary peerage shall not have effect after that Session unless it has been issued to a person who, at the end of the Session, is excepted from section 1 by virtue of section 2.

(3) The Secretary of State may by order make such transitional provision about the entitlement of holders of hereditary peerages to vote at elections to the House of Commons or the European Parliament as he considers appropriate.

(4) An order under this section—

(a) may modify the effect of any enactment or any provision made under an enactment, and
(b) shall be made by statutory instrument which shall be subject to annulment in pursuance of a resolution of either House of Parliament.

Interpretation and short title.

6.—(1) In this Act "hereditary peerage" includes the principality of Wales and the earldom of Chester.

(2) This Act may be cited as the House of Lords Act 1999.

SCHEDULES

SCHEDULE 1

AMENDMENTS

Peerage Act 1963 (c.48)

1. In section 1(2) of the Peerage Act 1963 (disclaimer of certain hereditary peerages) for the words from "has" to the end there shall be substituted the words "is excepted from section 1 of the House of Lords Act 1999 by virtue of section 2 of that Act".

Recess Elections Act 1975 (c.66)

2. In section 1 of the Recess Elections Act 1975 (issue of warrants for making out writs to replace members of the House of Commons whose seats have become vacant), in—

   (a) subsection (1)(a), and

   (b) paragraph (a) of the definition of "certificate of vacancy" in subsection (2),

   for the words "become a peer" there shall be substituted the words "become disqualified as a peer for membership of the House of Commons".

SCHEDULE 2

REPEALS

Chapter	Short title	Extent of repeal
1963 c.48.	The Peerage Act 1963.	In section 1(3), paragraph (b) and the word "and" immediately preceding it. Section 2. In section 3, in subsection (1)(b), the words from "(including" to "that House)" and, in subsection (2), the words from "and" to the end of the subsection. Section 5.

Statutes are available online at a number of different websites (see, for example, *http://www.statutelaw.gov.uk/*, *http://www.legislation.gov.uk/ukpga* and *http://www.bailii.org/*). These are open-access online databases. Commercial services such as Lexis and Westlaw also have statutes online. In the present day online services is one of the ways that you are most likely to get access to a statute. The other way, as a student, that you may read a statute is in a hard-copy collection of statutes in a particular area of law that has been commercially published. In the case of both hard-copy collections and online services statutes are sometimes published in an annotated form. This means that the statute has an accompanying explanatory text that tells you what the statute means. If you use an annotated statute remember that only the words of the statute are definitive. The explanatory text, although it may be helpful in understanding the statute, is only ever the opinion of the author.

THE DIFFERENT PARTS

5.4 ① This is the *short title* of the Act, together with its year of publication. When you are writing about a statute, it is normal to use the short title and year of publication to describe the statute. Sometimes, when a statute is referred to constantly, the short title is abbreviated. Thus, the Matrimonial Causes Act 1973 is often referred to as "the MCA 1973". If you work in a particular area of law, you will quickly learn the standard abbreviations for that area.

② This is the official *citation* for the statute. Each Act passed in any one year is given its own number. This is known as its *chapter number*. Thus you can describe a statute by its chapter number and year. The citation "1999 Chapter 34" could only mean the House of Lords Act 1999. "Chapter" in the official citation may be abbreviated to "c.", as in the top right hand corner of your copy of the statute. This form of official citation began in 1963. Before that, statutes were identified by the "regnal year" in which they occurred, followed by their chapter number. A regnal year is a year of a monarch's reign. Thus, "30 Geo 3 Chapter 3" refers to the Treason Act 1790, which was passed in the 30th year of King George III's reign. It is much easier to remember and use the short title of an Act rather than its official citation.

③ This is the *long title* of the Act. The long title gives some indication of the purpose behind the Act. It may be of some use in deciding what the Act is all about. However, the long title may be misleading. For example, the long title of the Parliament Act 1911 indicates that the Act is part of a process of abolishing the House of Lords—although, over 100 years later, that institution is still in existence, even though the House of Lords Act 1999 has introduced restrictions upon membership of the institution by virtue of a hereditary peerage. Long titles are sometimes vague and may conflict with the main body of the Act. In the event of such a conflict, the legal rule is that expressed in the main body of the Act.

④ This indicates when the *royal assent* was given and the House of Lords Bill 1999 became an Act. Statutes become law on the date when they receive the royal assent *unless the Act says otherwise*. The statute itself may say that it becomes law on a fixed date after the royal assent, or it may give a Government Minister the power to decide when it becomes law. When a Minister brings a statute into effect after the date on which it has been passed a "commencement order" must be made. This is a form of delegated legislation. Statutes do not have a retrospective effect unless the Act expressly says so.

⑤ This is known as the *enacting formula*. It is the standard form of words used to indicate that a Bill has been properly passed by all the different parts of the legislature.

⑥ By each section you will find a short explanation of the content of that section. These *marginal notes* may help you to understand the content of the section if it is otherwise unclear.

The main body of the statute that follows is broken up into numbered *sections*. Each section contains a different rule of law. When you refer to a rule of law contained in a statute, you should say where that rule of law is to be found. This enables others to check your source and to see whether or not they agree with your interpretation of the law. Instead of writing "section", it is usual to abbreviate this to "s.". Thus, "section 1" becomes "s.1". Sections are often further subdivided. These sub-division are known as *subsections*. When you wish to refer to a subsection, you should add it in brackets after the main section.

In larger statutes, sections may be grouped together into different *Parts*. Each Part will deal with a separate area of law. Looking for the correct Part will help you to find the particular legal rule that you want.

Some statutes have one or more *Schedules* at the end. The content of these varies. Some contain detailed provisions that are not found in the main body of the act. Others are merely convenient reminders and summaries of legal rules, and changes to legal rules, found elsewhere in the Act.

In the House of Lords Act 1999, for example, there are two Schedules. The first Schedule says which sections of previous statutes have been changed (amended) by the 1999 Act. This Schedule sets out the detailed effect of the amendments, which are given their legal effect by virtue of s.4(1) of the Act. The second Schedule sets out which sections of a previous statute have been repealed by the 1999 Act. Those repeals are given their legal effect by virtue of s.4(2) of the Act.

Example

Q. How many people are excepted from s.1 of the House of Lords Act 1999? A. 90 people at any one time. See s.2(2) House of Lords Act 1999.

References to Schedules are often abbreviated as "Sched.". Where a Schedule is divided up, the divisions are known as *paragraphs*, and can be abbreviated as "para.".

USING A STATUTE

Your use of statutory material will vary. Sometimes you will be referred to a particular section or sections of a statute in a case, article, or book that you are reading. In other instances, a new statute will be passed which you need to assess as a whole in order to see how it affects those areas of law in which you are interested. In either case, when first reading statutory material, you may be able to gain some help in deciding what it means from commentaries.

5.5

Commentaries are explanations of the law written by legal academics or practitioners. Annotated statutes, which were discussed earlier, are one useful source of such commentaries. You may also find such commentaries in books and articles on the area of law in which the statute falls. Always remember that a commentary represents only one author's opinion of what the statute says. In the case of a very new statute there will probably be no commentary. Therefore, you will need to be able to read a statute yourself, so that you can assess the value of other people's opinions and form your own view when there is no other help available.

When reading a statute, do not begin at the beginning and then work your way through to the end, section by section. Statutes do not necessarily use words to mean the same things that they do in ordinary conversation. Before you can decide what a statute is about you need to know if there are any special meanings attached to words in it. These special meanings can be found in the Act, often in sections called *definition* or *interpretation sections*. These are frequently found towards the end of the Act. For example, in the House of Lords Act 1999, there is a guide in s.6(1) to the interpretation of the expression "hereditary peerage" when used in the context of the Act. An Act may have more than one definition section. Sometimes, Parliament, when laying down a particular meaning for a word, will say that the specified meaning will apply in all statutes in which that word appears. Unless a statute specifically says this, however, you should assume that a definition in a statute applies only the use of the word in that statute.

You are now in a position to decide what new legal rules the statute creates. Some people begin this task by reading the long title of the Act to give themselves some idea of the general aim of the statute. Although this can be helpful, as we saw above in the section on the different parts of the Act, it can also be misleading.

Statutes should be read carefully and slowly. The general rule is that a statute means precisely what it says. Each word is important. Because of this, some words that we use loosely in ordinary conversation take on special significance when found in a statute. For example, it is important to distinguish between words like "may" and "shall", one saying that you *can* do something and the other saying that you *must* do something. Conjunctives, such as "and", joining things together, must be distinguished from disjunctives, such as "or", dividing things apart.

So far, the emphasis has been upon closely reading the particular statute. You should also remember that the statute should be read in the context of the general Acts, rules and principles of statutory interpretation discussed in Chapter 7.

One further thing to remember when reading a statute is that the fact that it has been printed does not mean that it is part of the law of the land. It may have been repealed. It may not yet be in force. Re-read pp.34–35 if you cannot remember how to find out if a statute has been repealed. Go back and read about the royal assent on p.50 if you cannot remember how to find out if a statute is in force.

STATUTORY INSTRUMENTS

5.6 ▶ What statutory instruments are, the way in which they are created, and the purposes that they have, are discussed on p.4.

Statutory instruments should be read in the same way as statutes. However, whilst statutes make relatively little reference to other sources, statutory instruments, because of their purpose, make very frequent reference either to other statutory instruments or to their parent statute. The legislative power has been given only for a limited purpose, the statutory instrument is a small part of a larger whole. For this reason, you will find it much more difficult to understand a statutory instrument if you do not have access to the surrounding legislation. Before reading a statutory instrument, it is vital that you understand the legislative framework into which it fits.

Exercise 1

STATUTES I

Start by re-reading the appropriate parts of Chapters 5 and 7 and then look at the Laser Misuse (Vehicles) Act 2018 and answer the questions below. When answering the questions, make sure you include the correct statutory references. Answers to Section A for each exercise can be found in Appendix III.

5.7

ELIZABETH II c. 20

Laser Misuse (Vehicles) Act 2018

2018 CHAPTER 9

An Act to make provision creating new offences of shining or directing a laser beam towards a vehicle or air traffic facility; and for connected purposes. [10th May 2018]

BE IT ENACTED by the Queen's most Excellent Majesty, by and with the advice and consent of the Lords Spiritual and Temporal, and Commons, in this present Parliament assembled, and by the authority of the same, as follows:—

1 Offence of shining or directing a laser beam towards a vehicle

(1) A person commits an offence if—
- (a) the person shines or directs a laser beam towards a vehicle which is moving or ready to move, and
- (b) the laser beam dazzles or distracts, or is likely to dazzle or distract, a person with control of the vehicle.

(2) It is a defence to show—
- (a) that the person had a reasonable excuse for shining or directing the laser beam towards the vehicle, or
- (b) that the person—
  - (i) did not intend to shine or direct the laser beam towards the vehicle, and
  - (ii) exercised all due diligence and took all reasonable precautions to avoid doing so.

(3) A person is taken to have shown a fact mentioned in subsection (2) if—
- (a) sufficient evidence is adduced to raise an issue with respect to it, and
- (b) the contrary is not proved beyond reasonable doubt.

(4) A person who commits an offence under this section is liable—
- (a) on summary conviction in England and Wales, to imprisonment for a term not exceeding 12 months, to a fine or to both;

(b) on summary conviction in Scotland, to imprisonment for a term not exceeding 12 months, to a fine not exceeding the statutory maximum or to both;
(c) on summary conviction in Northern Ireland, to imprisonment for a term not exceeding six months, to a fine not exceeding the statutory maximum or to both;
(d) on conviction on indictment, to imprisonment for a term not exceeding five years, to a fine or to both.

(5) In relation to an offence committed before the coming into force of section 154(1) of the Criminal Justice Act 2003, the reference in subsection (4)(a) to 12 months is to be read as a reference to six months.

(6) A mechanically propelled vehicle which is not moving or ready to move but whose engine or motor is running is to be treated for the purposes of subsection (1)(a) as ready to move.

(7) In relation to an aircraft, the reference in subsection (1)(b) to "a person with control of the vehicle" is a reference to any person on the aircraft who is engaged in controlling it, or in monitoring the controlling of it.

(8) In relation to a vessel, hovercraft or submarine, the reference in subsection (1)(b) to "a person with control of the vehicle" is a reference to the master, the pilot or any person engaged in navigating the vessel, hovercraft or submarine.

2 Offences relating to air traffic services

(1) A person commits an offence if—
(a) the person shines or directs a laser beam—
(i) towards an air traffic facility, or
(ii) towards a person providing air traffic services, and
(b) the laser beam dazzles or distracts, or is likely to dazzle or distract, a person providing air traffic services.

(2) It is a defence to show—
(a) that the person had a reasonable excuse for shining or directing the laser beam towards the facility or person, or
(b) that the person—
(i) did not intend to shine or direct the laser beam towards the facility or person, and
(ii) exercised all due diligence and took all reasonable precautions to avoid doing so.

(3) A person is taken to have shown a fact mentioned in subsection (2) if—
(a) sufficient evidence is adduced to raise an issue with respect to it, and
(b) the contrary is not proved beyond reasonable doubt.

(4) A person who commits an offence under this section is liable—
(a) on summary conviction in England and Wales, to imprisonment for a term not exceeding 12 months, to a fine or to both;
(b) on summary conviction in Scotland, to imprisonment for a term not exceeding 12 months, to a fine not exceeding the statutory maximum or to both;

(c) on summary conviction in Northern Ireland, to imprisonment for a term not exceeding six months, to a fine not exceeding the statutory maximum or to both;

(d) on conviction on indictment, to imprisonment for a term not exceeding five years, to a fine or to both.

(5) In relation to an offence committed before the coming into force of section 154(1) of the Criminal Justice Act 2003, the reference in subsection (4)(a) to 12 months is to be read as a reference to six months.

(6) In this section—

"air traffic facility" means any building, structure, vehicle or other place from which air traffic services are provided;

"air traffic services" has the meaning given by section 98(1) of the Transport Act 2000.

3 Interpretation

In this Act—

"aircraft" means any vehicle used for travel by air;

"laser beam" means a beam of coherent light produced by a device of any kind;

"vehicle" means any vehicle used for travel by land, water or air;

"vessel" has the meaning given by section 255(1) of the Merchant Shipping Act 1995.

4 Extent, commencement and short title

(1) This Act extends to England and Wales, Scotland and Northern Ireland.

(2) This section and section 3 come into force on the day on which this Act is passed.

(3) Section 1 comes into force, so far as extending to England and Wales and Scotland, at the end of the period of two months beginning with the day on which this Act is passed.

(4) Section 1 comes into force, so far as extending to Northern Ireland—

(a) in relation to aircraft, vessels, hovercraft and submarines, at the end of the period of two months beginning with the day on which this Act is passed;

(b) in relation to other vehicles, on such day as the Secretary of State may by regulations made by statutory instrument appoint.

(5) Section 2 comes into force at the end of the period of two months beginning with the day on which this Act is passed.

(6) Different days may be appointed under subsection (4)(b) for different purposes.

(7) This Act may be cited as the Laser Misuse (Vehicles) Act 2018.

Section A

1. To where does this Act apply?
2. Is the Act part of the civil or criminal law?
3. What is the long title of this Act?
4. A lorry has its engine on but the handbrake is applied and the driver is eating a sandwich. Can the Act apply to the lorry?
5. Does the Act apply to aircraft?

Section B

1. How would you find out why this Act has been passed?
2. Having consulted the resources that you have identified in your answer to question 6, why do you think this Act was passed?
3. Suresh pointed a laser at a moving car. Has he committed an offence under the Act?
4. In England and Wales what punishment can follow from conviction under the Act?
5. Is the Act in force?

Exercise 2

STATUTES II

5.8 Read the Stalking Protection Act 2019 and answer the questions. When answering the questions make sure you include the correct statutory references. Answers to Section A for each exercise can be found in Appendix III.

Stalking Protection Act 2019

2019 CHAPTER 9

An Act to make provision for orders to protect persons from risks associated with stalking; and for connected purposes. [15th March 2019]

BE IT ENACTED by the Queen's most Excellent Majesty, by and with the advice and consent of the Lords Spiritual and Temporal, and Commons, in this present Parliament assembled, and by the authority of the same, as follows:—

Stalking protection orders

1 Applications for orders

(1) A chief officer of police may apply to a magistrates' court for an order (a "stalking protection order") in respect of a person (the "defendant") if it appears to the chief officer that—
- (a) the defendant has carried out acts associated with stalking,
- (b) the defendant poses a risk associated with stalking to another person, and
- (c) there is reasonable cause to believe the proposed order is necessary to protect another person from such a risk (whether or not the other person was the victim of the acts mentioned in paragraph (a)).

(2) A stalking protection order is an order which, for the purpose of preventing the defendant from carrying out acts associated with stalking—
- (a) prohibits the defendant from doing anything described in the order, or
- (b) requires the defendant to do anything described in the order.

(3) A chief officer of police for a police area in England and Wales may apply for a stalking protection order only in respect of a person—
- (a) who resides in the chief officer's police area, or
- (b) who the chief officer believes is in that area or is intending to come to it.

(4) A risk associated with stalking—

(a) may be in respect of physical or psychological harm to the other person;
(b) may arise from acts which the defendant knows or ought to know are unwelcome to the other person even if, in other circumstances, the acts would appear harmless in themselves.

(5) It does not matter—
(a) whether the acts mentioned in subsection (1)(a) were carried out in a part of the United Kingdom or elsewhere, or
(b) whether they were carried out before or after the commencement of this section.

(6) See section 2A of the Protection from Harassment Act 1997 for examples of acts associated with stalking.

2 Power to make orders

(1) A magistrates' court may make a stalking protection order on an application under section 1(1) if satisfied that—
(a) the defendant has carried out acts associated with stalking,
(b) the defendant poses a risk associated with stalking to another person, and
(c) the proposed order is necessary to protect another person from such a risk (whether or not the other person was the victim of the acts mentioned in paragraph (a)).

(2) A magistrates' court may include a prohibition or requirement in a stalking protection order only if satisfied that the prohibition or requirement is necessary to protect the other person from a risk associated with stalking.

(3) Prohibitions or requirements must, so far as practicable, be such as to avoid—
(a) conflict with the defendant's religious beliefs, and
(b) interference with any times at which the defendant normally works or attends an educational establishment.

(4) A prohibition or requirement has effect in all parts of the United Kingdom unless expressly limited to a particular locality.

(5) It does not matter—
(a) whether the acts mentioned in subsection (1)(a) were carried out in a part of the United Kingdom or elsewhere, or
(b) whether they were carried out before or after the commencement of this section.

(6) Subsection (7) applies where a magistrates' court makes a stalking protection order in relation to a defendant who is already subject to such an order (whether made by that court or another).

(7) The court may not include any prohibition or requirement in the new stalking protection order which is incompatible with a prohibition or requirement in the earlier stalking protection order.

3 Duration of orders

(1) A stalking protection order has effect—

(a) for a fixed period specified in the order, or
(b) until a further order.

(2) Where a fixed period is specified it must be a period of at least 2 years beginning with the day on which the order is made.

(3) Different periods may be specified in relation to different prohibitions or requirements.

4 Variations, renewals and discharges

(1) The defendant or a relevant chief officer of police (see section 14(1)) may apply to a magistrates' court for an order varying, renewing or discharging a stalking protection order.

(2) Before making a decision on an application under subsection (1), the court must hear—
(a) the defendant, and
(b) any relevant chief officer of police who wants to be heard.

(3) On an application under subsection (1) the court may make any order varying, renewing or discharging the stalking protection order that the court considers appropriate.

(4) But the court may not—
(a) in renewing or varying an order, impose an additional prohibition or requirement unless satisfied that it is necessary to do so in order to protect a person from a risk associated with stalking;
(b) discharge an order before the end of 2 years beginning with the day on which the order was made without the consent of the defendant and—
(i) where the application was made by a chief officer of police, that chief officer, or
(ii) in any other case, the chief officer of police who applied for the stalking protection order and (if different) the chief officer of police for the area in which the defendant resides, if that area is in England or Wales.

5 Interim stalking protection orders

(1) This section applies where an application for a stalking protection order (the "main application") has not been determined.

(2) A magistrates' court may make an order (an "interim stalking protection order") in respect of the defendant on an application—
(a) made at the same time and by the same chief officer of police as the main application, or
(b) if the main application has already been made, made by the chief officer of police who made that application.

(3) The court may, if it considers it appropriate to do so, make an interim stalking protection order—
(a) prohibiting the defendant from doing anything described in the order, or
(b) requiring the defendant to do anything described in the order.

(4) Prohibitions or requirements must, so far as practicable, be such as to avoid—

(a) conflict with the defendant's religious beliefs, and
(b) interference with any times at which the defendant normally works or attends an educational establishment.

(5) A prohibition or requirement has effect in all parts of the United Kingdom unless expressly limited to a particular locality.

(6) An interim stalking protection order—
(a) has effect only for a fixed period specified in the order, and
(b) ceases to have effect, if it has not already done so, on the determination of the main application.

(7) The defendant or the chief officer of police who applied for an interim stalking protection order may apply to a magistrates' court for an order varying, renewing or discharging the interim stalking protection order.

(8) On an application under subsection (7), the court may make any order varying, renewing or discharging the stalking protection order that the court considers appropriate.

6 Content of orders

A stalking protection order and an interim stalking protection order must specify—
(a) the date on which the order is made;
(b) whether it has effect for a fixed period and, if it does, the length of that period;
(c) each prohibition or requirement that applies to the defendant;
(d) whether any prohibition or requirement is expressly limited to a particular locality and, if it is, what the locality is;
(e) whether any prohibition or requirement is subject to a fixed period which differs from the period for which the order has effect and, if it is, what that period is.

Appeals and enforcement

7 Appeals

(1) A defendant may appeal to the Crown Court against—
(a) the making of a stalking protection order,
(b) the making of an interim stalking protection order,
(c) the making of an order under section 4 on an application by a chief officer of police, or
(d) the refusal to make an order under section 4 on an application by the defendant.

(2) A chief officer of police who applied for a stalking protection order, an interim stalking protection order or an order under section 4 may appeal to the Crown Court against—
(a) the refusal to make a stalking protection order,
(b) the refusal to make an interim stalking protection order, or
(c) the refusal to make an order under section 4 on an application by the chief officer.

(3) A relevant chief officer of police (see section 14(1)) may appeal to the Crown Court against the making of an order under section 4 on an application by the defendant.

(4) On any such appeal, the Crown Court may make—

(a) such orders as may be necessary to give effect to its determination of the appeal, and

(b) such incidental or consequential orders as appear to it to be appropriate.

8 Offence of breaching stalking protection order etc

(1) A person who, without reasonable excuse, breaches a stalking protection order or an interim stalking protection order commits an offence.

(2) A person guilty of an offence under this section is liable—

(a) on summary conviction, to imprisonment for a term not exceeding 12 months or to a fine or both, or

(b) on conviction on indictment, to imprisonment for a term not exceeding 5 years or to a fine or both.

(3) In relation to an offence committed before section 154(1) of the Criminal Justice Act 2003 comes into force, the reference in subsection (2)(a) to 12 months is to be read as a reference to 6 months.

(4) If a person is convicted of an offence under this section, it is not open to the court by or before which the person is convicted to make an order under subsection (1)(b) of section 12 of the Powers of Criminal Courts (Sentencing) Act 2000 (conditional discharge).

(5) In proceedings for an offence under this section, a copy of the original stalking protection order or interim stalking protection order, certified by the designated officer for the court which made it, is admissible as evidence of its having been made and of its contents to the same extent that oral evidence of those things is admissible in those proceedings.

Notification requirements

9 Notification requirements

(1) A person subject to—

(a) a stalking protection order (other than one which replaces an interim stalking protection order), or

(b) an interim stalking protection order,

must, within the period of 3 days beginning with the date of service of the order, notify to the police the information set out in subsection (2).

(2) The information is—

(a) the person's name and, where the person uses one or more other names, each of those names;

(b) the person's home address.

(3) A person who—

(a) is subject to a stalking protection order or an interim stalking protection order, and

(b) uses a name which has not been notified under this section,

must, before the end of the period of 3 days beginning with the date on which that happens, notify to the police that name.

(4) A person who—

(a) is subject to a stalking protection order or an interim stalking protection order, and

(b) changes home address,

must, before the end of the period of 3 days beginning with the date on which that happens, notify to the police the new home address.

(5) The requirements imposed by this section do not apply to a person who is subject to notification requirements under Part 2 of the Sexual Offences Act 2003.

(6) Subsection (7) applies where—

(a) a person is subject to a stalking protection order or an interim stalking protection order,

(b) at the time the order is made, the requirements imposed by this section do not apply to the person as a result of subsection (5),

(c) the person ceases on a subsequent day ("the final day") to be subject to the notification requirements mentioned in that subsection, and

(d) the order remains in effect on the final day.

(7) The requirements imposed by this section apply to the person as from the final day, but as if the reference in subsection (1) to the date of service of the order were a reference to the final day.

10 Method of notification and related matters

(1) A person whose home address is in England or Wales gives a notification under section 9(1), (3) or (4) by—

(a) attending at a police station in the person's local police area, and

(b) giving an oral notification to a police officer, or to any person authorised for the purpose by the officer in charge of the station.

(2) A person who does not have a home address in England or Wales gives a notification under section 9(1), (3) or (4) by—

(a) attending at a police station in the local police area in which the magistrates' court which last made a stalking protection order or an interim stalking protection order in respect of the person is situated, and

(b) giving an oral notification to a police officer, or to any person authorised for the purpose by the officer in charge of the station.

(3) In relation to a person giving a notification under section 9(4), the references in subsections (1) and (2) to the person's home address are references to—

(a) the person's new home address if the person gives the notification after changing home address, or

(b) the person's old home address if the person gives the notification before changing home address.

(4) A notification given in accordance with this section must be acknowledged—
 (a) in writing, and
 (b) in such form as the Secretary of State may direct.

(5) When a person gives notification under section 9(1), (3) or (4), the person must, if requested to do so by the police officer or person mentioned in subsection (1)(b), allow that officer or person to—
 (a) take the person's fingerprints,
 (b) photograph any part of the person, or
 (c) do both of these things.

(6) The power in subsection (5) is exercisable for the purpose of verifying the identity of the person.

11 Offences relating to notification

(1) A person commits an offence if the person—
 (a) fails, without reasonable excuse, to comply with section 9(1), (3) or (4), or with section 10(5), or
 (b) notifies to the police, in purported compliance with section 9(1), (3) or (4), any information which the person knows to be false.

(2) A person guilty of an offence under this section is liable—
 (a) on summary conviction, to imprisonment for a term not exceeding 12 months or to a fine or both, or
 (b) on conviction on indictment, to imprisonment for a term not exceeding 5 years or to a fine or both.

(3) A person commits an offence under subsection (1)(a) on the day on which the person first fails, without reasonable excuse, to comply with section 9(1), (3) or (4).

(4) The person continues to commit the offence throughout any period during which the failure continues.

(5) But the person may not be prosecuted more than once in respect of the same failure.

(6) Proceedings for an offence under this section may be commenced in any court having jurisdiction in any place where the person charged with the offence resides or is found.

(7) In relation to an offence committed before section 154(1) of the Criminal Justice Act 2003 comes into force, the reference in subsection (2)(a) to 12 months is to be read as a reference to 6 months.

Guidance

12 Guidance

(1) The Secretary of State must issue guidance to chief officers of police about the exercise of their functions under this Act.

(2) The Secretary of State may, from time to time, revise the guidance issued under subsection (1).

(3) The Secretary of State must arrange for any guidance issued or revised under this section to be published in such manner as the Secretary of State considers appropriate.

General

13 Procedure

(1) An application to a magistrates' court under any provision of this Act is to be by complaint.

(2) Section 127 of the Magistrates' Courts Act 1980 (time limits) does not apply to a complaint under any provision of this Act.

14 Interpretation

(1) In this Act—

"acts" includes omissions;

"chief officer of police" means—

(a) the chief constable of a police force maintained under section 2 of the Police Act 1996 (police forces in England and Wales outside London);
(b) the Commissioner of Police of the Metropolis;
(c) the Commissioner of Police for the City of London;
(d) the chief constable of the British Transport Police;
(e) the chief constable of the Ministry of Defence Police;

"defendant" has the meaning given by section 1(1);

"home address", in relation to a person, means—

(a) the address of the person's sole or main residence in the United Kingdom, or
(b) if the person has no such residence, the address or location of a place in the United Kingdom where the person can regularly be found and, if there is more than one such place, such of those places as the person may select;

"interim stalking protection order" has the meaning given by section 5(2);

"local police area", in relation to a person, means—

(a) the police area in which the person's home address is situated,
(b) in the absence of a home address, the police area in which the home address last notified is situated (whether that notification was in accordance with the requirements imposed by section 9 or in accordance with notification requirements under Part 2 of the Sexual Offences Act 2003), or
(c) in the absence of a home address and of any such notification, the police area in which the magistrates' court which last made a stalking protection order or an interim stalking protection order in respect of the person is situated;

"magistrates' court", in relation to a defendant under the age of 18, means youth court;

"photograph" includes any process by means of which an image may be produced;

"relevant chief officer of police", in relation to an application for an order under section 4 or to an appeal under section 7, means—

(a) the chief officer of police for the area in which the defendant resides,

(b) a chief officer of police who believes that the defendant is in, or is intending to come to, that chief officer's police area, and

(c) the chief officer of police who applied for the stalking protection order to which the application or appeal relates;

"stalking protection order" has the meaning given by section 1(1).

(2) In this Act, references to a "risk associated with stalking" are to be read in accordance with section 1(4).

15 Extent, commencement and short title

(1) This Act extends to England and Wales only.

(2) This section comes into force on the day on which this Act is passed.

(3) The other provisions of this Act come into force on such day as the Secretary of State may by regulations made by statutory instrument appoint.

(4) This Act may be cited as the Stalking Protection Act 2019.

Section A

1. What is the short title of this Act?
2. The Act says that a chief officer of police can apply for a stalking protection order. Where does it say this and who is a chief officer of police?
3. Anne has had a stalking protection order made against her. She does not feel that this is fair. Is there anything that she can do against about this?
4. Anne breaches the stalking protection order made against her. What is the punishment for such a breach?
5. When making a stalking protection order does the magistrates' court have to pay any attention to the circumstances of the defendant?

Section B

1. Where does this Act extend to?
2. What are interim stalking protection orders? Why do you think the Act makes it possible to apply for them?
3. In order to make a stalking protection order, the magistrates' court must think, amongst other things, that the defendant poses a risk associated with stalking to another person (s.1(1)(b)). What legally is a risk associated with stalking?
4. What do you think are the potential advantages and disadvantages of stalking protection orders?
5. What reforms to the Stalking Protection Act 2019 do you think are necessary?

Exercise 3

CASES I

5.9 Begin by re-reading the appropriate parts of Chapters 4 and 5. After you have read *O'Dwyer v O'Dwyer* answer the questions below. When noting your answers to the questions, you should include reference(s) to the appropriate points in the judgment from which you have drawn your information. Answers to Section A questions are found in Appendix III.

Neutral Citation Number: [2019] EWHC 1838 (Fam)

Case No: 2018/0078

IN THE HIGH COURT OF JUSTICE
FAMILY DIVISION

Royal Courts of Justice
Strand, London, WC2A 2LL

Date: 12/07/2019

Before :

MR JUSTICE FRANCIS

- -

Between :

John Thomas O'Dwyer	**Applicant**
- and -	
Cindy Lea O'Dwyer	**Respondent**

- -
- -

Valentine Le Grice QC (instructed by **Fletcher Day Solicitors**) for the **Applicant**
Nicholas Wilkinson (instructed by **Seymours + Solicitors**) for the **Respondent**

Hearing dates: 19th December 2018

- -

Approved Judgment

I direct that pursuant to CPR PD 39A para 6.1 no official shorthand note shall be taken of this Judgment and that copies of this version as handed down may be treated as authentic.

....

MR JUSTICE FRANCIS

This judgment was delivered in private. The judge has given leave for this version of the judgment to be published on condition that (irrespective of what is contained in the judgment) in any published version of the judgment the anonymity of the children and members of their family must be strictly preserved. All persons, including representatives of the media, must ensure that this condition is strictly complied with. Failure to do so will be a contempt of court.

Mr Justice Francis :

1. This is my Judgment in respect of an appeal by John O'Dwyer (to whom I shall refer in this Judgment as "the husband") against an order made by His Honour Judge O'Dwyer in the Central Family Court in March 2018 following a draft judgment which was circulated on 19 December 2017.

2. At the hearing below and on appeal before me, the husband was represented by Valentine Le Grice QC and the Respondent Cindy Lea O'Dwyer (to whom I shall refer as "the wife") was represented by Nicholas Wilkinson of counsel. The appeal hearing took place on the 19 December 2018. Tragically, only a few days later, and completely unexpectedly, Mr Le Grice collapsed and died. Much has been said and will be said by others elsewhere but I cannot commence this Judgment without first paying tribute to one of the great, and greatly admired, family lawyers of his generation, and extending our deepest sympathy to the loved ones left behind.

Delay

3. This case has been beset by delay. The original hearing took place on 24, 25 and 26 July 2017. The case overran and so there were two further days on 20 and 21 November 2017. The Judge circulated a draft Judgment on 19 December 2017 and he asked for any suggested amendments to be provided to him by 8 January 2018. Although these amendments were provided, albeit a few weeks late, the Judge has never circulated a perfected Judgment.

4. Mr Wilkinson, for the wife, sent a draft order to Mr Le Grice on the 12 January 2018. After some reminders, Mr Le Grice returned an amended draft order on 6 February 2018. Counsel were unable to resolve the parties' remaining differences and agreed that it would be necessary to have a further hearing. This further hearing took place on 7 March 2018. Mr Le Grice sought permission to appeal on behalf of the husband but this was refused by the Judge. No perfected Judgment was handed down. Mr Le Grice emailed the Judge's clerk enquiring about the final Judgment on 15 March, 20 March and 26 March 2018. On 5 April 2018, Mr Le Grice's clerk hand-delivered a letter for the Judge at the Central Family Court which enquired about a final Judgment, enclosed a further copy of the agreed amendments and repeated an earlier offer to carry out the amendments. No reply was received to that letter.

5. Thus it is that we have neither a final version of the Judgment nor an agreed order, still less a sealed order. For the purposes of this appeal I treat the draft Judgment dated 19 December 2017 as the Judgment and I treat the draft order prepared by counsel as the order under appeal.

6. The failure to produce a sealed order led to considerable difficulties in the husband's solicitors issuing their notice of appeal. Mr Wilkinson, for the wife, contends that the notice of appeal should have been issued within 21 days of the decision, in this instance being either the draft Judgment or the draft order. It is, of course, the case that pursuant to rule 30.4(2)(b) FPR 2010, the husband had 21 days from the date of the Judge's decision to lodge an appellant's notice. Mr Wilkinson initially contended that the imposed time limits should have been adhered to and that, as no application has been made by the husband for permission to vary the time limit for appeals, permission should not be granted. However, I was told by Mr Le Grice, and accept,

that the court office would not issue, and therefore would not date or seal, the husband's notice of appeal without there being in place an order which was under appeal. Accordingly, it seems to me that it would be unfair and prejudicial to the husband to hold the relevant time limits against him in circumstances where those acting for him have done all they reasonably can to progress the application for permission to appeal. Upon hearing Mr Le Grice's explanation in full, the wife did not maintain her objection in this regard. I anticipate that these are extremely unusual circumstances, it being mercifully rare to have a situation where the Judge fails to perfect either his Judgment or his order. In the unlikely event that this should ever happen again then I suggest that, if repeated attempts to persuade the judge to finalise his order fail, the matter is taken up with the office of the President of the Family Division.

7. Baker J (as he then was) considered the notice of appeal on paper and on 8 August 2018 he ordered that the application for permission to appeal against the periodical payments order included in the order of HH Judge O'Dwyer dated 7 March 2018 was to be listed for an oral hearing with the appeal to follow immediately if permission was granted. He listed the appeal for one day, plus half a day's pre-reading. As soon as I saw the papers in this case on 18 December 2018 it was apparent to me that it would be impossible for this case to be heard and a Judgment delivered in one day. I have a bundle containing almost 400 pages as well as a bundle of 19 authorities from Mr Wilkinson and 5 authorities from Mr Le Grice. Further authorities were handed up during the course of the hearing. My options on 19 December 2018 were either (a) to adjourn this case for a proper listing or (b) to hear it but reserve Judgment. Neither of these options was satisfactory but it seemed to me that, given the history of delay referred to above, adjourning it for what would have been very many months would have been contrary to the interests of justice. My delay in delivering this reserved Judgment, whilst advertised clearly to the parties, has been a consequence of a full diary throughout this year to date. Whilst I accept that in this case the time estimate was initially made by Baker J (who disagreed with the longer time estimate suggested by Mr le Grice) , there is a general duty on counsel and solicitors to inform the court if it is obvious that the time estimate is incorrect. Failure to do so is likely to result in the case not being heard and this plainly could have substantial costs implications.

The order under appeal

8. Paragraph 21 of the draft order of Judge O'Dwyer provides:

> *"The respondent shall pay to the applicant maintenance pending suit until the date of decree absolute and afterwards periodical payments. Payment shall be at the rate of £150,000 per annum, payable monthly in advance by standing order. Payment shall start on 1 February 2018, with credit for payments made, and shall end on the 1st to occur of:*
>
> *a. the death of either the applicant or the respondent;*
>
> *b. the applicant's remarriage;*
>
> *c. a further order; or*

d. the respondent's 66th birthday on 8 November 2022;

after which the applicant's claims for periodical payments and securec periodical payments shall be dismissed, and it is directed that:

i. upon the expiry of this term, the applicant shall not be entitled to make any further application in relation to the marriage for an order under the matrimonial causes act 1973 section 23(1)(a) or (b) for periodical payments or secured periodical payments;

ii. pursuant to matrimonial causes act 1973 section 28(1A), the applicant may not apply for an order to extend this term;

iii. upon the expiry of the term, the applicant shall not be entitled on the respondent's later death to apply for an order under the Inheritance (Provision for Family and Dependants) Act 1975, section 2, provided that the respondent does not die before the order is otherwise terminated and any application shall be subject to the provisions at paragraph 5.e above.For the avoidance of doubt, the applicant may not apply for an orderto extend this term."

9. The husband sought a stay of the periodical payments order. An extant appeal does not, of course, operate as a stay unless the court orders a stay. However, the matter came before me as a paper exercise. The wife is a US citizen living in Texas, with no assets in the UK against which an order for the return of overpaid periodical payments, if made, can be enforced, apart from a modest property in Newcastle under Lyme. In circumstances where the wife had received £870,000 in January 2018, £500,000 in April 2018 and a final lump sum payment of £700,000 shortly thereafter, it was obvious that the wife would have sufficient funds for her own needs between the date of any stay and the date of my Judgment. I ordered that the husband should make the periodical payments into an account in the name of his solicitors, or a joint account between the firms, as he elected, on the basis that the sums are to be held until the outcome of the appeal is known. I understand that the husband has complied with this.

10. On 19 December 2018, when I reserved Judgment, I granted permission to appeal and, if needed, permission to appeal out of time. I indicated to the parties then that, whilst I had not made my decision because I wanted to consider the papers and the authorities with care and with more time than I had been allowed at court, I recognised that the husband's appeal had a real prospect of success.

Relevant factual background

11. The parties were married in March 1988 and have four grown up children. The husband is 62 and the wife is 60. They separated in March 2016. The wife, who is an American citizen, returned to live in the United States.

12. For many years the husband ran a business as a McDonald's franchise. This is now operated partly through a limited company and partly as a sole proprietorship. By the time of the final hearing, with the assistance of expert valuations, the parties agreed

that the business had a gross value of £6.4 million. The parties also agreed that there should be set off against this the sum of £3.89 million in respect of what has been referred to as the "McDonald's reimaging programme". As I understand it, this is necessary investment in various capital items. It was also agreed that the business would be subject to a modest CGT charge of £251,000, the husband qualifying for Entrepreneur's Relief. Thus the **agreed** net value of the business was £2.409 million.

13. Although the business was 90% owned by the husband, the parties sensibly identified that this was a paradigm sharing case, given the length of the marriage and the full contributions that they had each, in their different ways, made. On behalf of the wife, Mr Wilkinson prepared a schedule of assets and liabilities totalling £5,865,478. In addition to the business referred to above, the schedule identified UK properties, US properties and miscellaneous bank accounts. Mr Wilkinson's schedule asserted that the parties should therefore each exit the marriage with £2,932,739. The judge correctly dealt with these assets in paragraphs 12 to 26 of his draft judgment.

14. At one point before Judge O'Dwyer, Mr Wilkinson had contended on behalf of the wife that she should receive the value of the business when the husband ceased to operate it and sold it. She had contended that the business would be worth a great deal more at that stage. The judge found that fairness can be done to the parties by properly recording the division of the business at this stage and also recording that the value as per the expert report does not reflect the full extent of the income stream which the husband derives from it.

15. Accordingly, Mr Wilkinson's figures were adopted by the judge (subject to one or two tiny and inconsequential amendments) and the husband has now paid the relevant lump sums to the wife such that the parties each have the figure identified by Mr Wilkinson's schedule and agreed by the Judge, i.e. a sum just short of £3 million. No one seeks to complain about, still less to appeal, the capital distribution ordered by the Judge.

The order for periodical payments

16. Accordingly, this appeal relates only to the order for periodical payments. Mr Le Grice forcefully asserts on behalf of the husband that, particularly following the decision of the Court of Appeal in *Waggott v Waggott* [2018] 2FLR 406, the sharing of an income stream is unprincipled and that payments should be ordered only to meet needs or, possibly in some very rare cases, compensation. Compensation has (sensibly in my judgment) never been argued in this case. Nevertheless, in paragraph 23(d) of his skeleton argument Mr Wilkinson referred to "relationship generated disadvantage", a phrase which seems to me to be synonymous with compensation.

17. It is clear that the Judge approached the periodical payments order by reference principally to the sharing principle. In paragraph 41 of his Judgment, he said, *"as a result of the joint enterprise of the parties the reality is that the business has been producing and will produce an income of approaching £1 million per year".* In paragraph 42 the judge said, *"from that the parties live well. Why after divorce should only Mr O'Dwyer continue to live well upon it when clearly it is the product of matrimonial endeavour?"* Mr Le Grice asserts that in asking this question the judge fell into error. In paragraph 43 of the draft Judgment, the judge said, *"it is clear that the business itself produces these incomes and of course although Mr O'Dwyer*

should have credit for the management of the business to a significant figure [sic] however the ownership of these franchises is much valued asset [sic] for the income stream. I identify that they are matrimonial property. I identify that their value is not only the capital value at this point but also the income that they will produce over the coming years."

18. The sentence , *"I identify that they are matrimonial property"* lies at the heart of this appeal. There has for some years been debate as to whether part of Baroness Hale's speech in *Miller;McFarlane* suggested that an earning capacity could be a matrimonial asset subject to a sharing claim. The preponderance of authority has been significantly against such an outcome. Any remaining doubts as to whether an income stream is an asset which can be shared, save for the purposes of paying for needs or compensation, was clearly dispelled by the judgment of the Court of Appeal in *Waggott*. The Judgment of the court in *Waggott* was handed down on 7 April 2018 and so would not have been before Judge O'Dwyer. In paragraph 121 of *Waggott*, Moylan LJ posed the following question: *"is an earning capacity capable of being a matrimonial asset to which the sharing principle applies and in the product of which, as a result, an applicant spouse has an entitlement to share?"*. The judge answered his question by saying, *"in my view, there are a number of reasons why the clear answer is that it is not"*. This answer was clear and unequivocal. Moylan LJ said that: *"any extension of the sharing principle to post-separation earnings would fundamentally undermine the court's ability to effect a clean break. In principle..... the entitlement to share would continue until the payer ceased working (subject to this being a reasonable decision), potentially a period of many years. If the court was seeking to effect a clean break this would, inevitably, require the court to capitalise its value which would conflict with what Wilson LJ said in Jones v Jones"*.

19. Moylan LJ went on to say: *"looking at its impact more broadly, it would apply to every case in which one party had earnings which were greater than the other's, regardless of need. This could well be a very significant number of cases. Further, if this submission was correct, I cannot see how this would sit with Baroness Hale's observation in Miller that, even confined to in general, it can be assumed that the marital partnership does not stay alive the purpose of sharing future resources unless it is justified by need or compensation"*.

20. In paragraph 128 of his judgment, Moylan LJ said: *"in my view Miller and the subsequent decisions referred to above, in particular Jones and Scatliffe, do not support the extension of the sharing principle to an earning capacity. The sharing principle applies to marital assets, being 'the property of the parties generated during the marriage otherwise than by external donation' (Charman). An earning capacity is not property and .... it results in the generation of property after the marriage."*

21. In paragraph 131, Moylan LJ said: *"in my view it is clear from Miller and Charman alone that, as a matter of principle, the court applies the need principle when determining whether the sharing award is sufficient to meet that party's future needs."*

22. Applying the very clear dicta enunciated in *Waggott*, I agree with Mr Le Grice's submission that it is now settled law that income cannot be shared. An award of periodical payments (absent rare compensation cases) must be based on properly

analysed arithmetic reflecting need, albeit that the judge is still left with a significant margin of discretion as to how generously the concept of need should be interpreted.

23. Mr Wilkinson disagrees with the submission that Judge O'Dwyer's decision cannot be sustained in the light of *Waggott*. In his skeleton argument Mr Wilkinson provided a list of distinctions that could be drawn between the two cases. Whilst he did not seek to rely on each point as a freestanding issue, and argues that they should be taken as a whole, I shall address that list. First, when addressing the question of fairness, he seeks to draw a distinction between the 12 year marriage in that case and the 30 year marriage in this case. I reject that submission as being plainly wrong and inconsistent with the clear analysis of the law by Moylan LJ in *Waggott*. It is not possible to discern from any part of Moylan LJ's clear Judgment that an earning capacity in a long marriage is to be treated differently from one in a short or medium length marriage.

24. Secondly, says Mr Wilkinson, this case is to be distinguished from *Waggott* because the income here is paid out as profit from a family partnership of McDonald's franchises built up over the 30 year marriage, subject to the Judge's finding that the husband should have credit for the management of the business to reflect post-marital endeavour. I also reject this submission, which in reality forms part of the previous point dealt with in the foregoing paragraph. The clear enunciation of the law, and the reasons for it, do not permit the sharing of an income for sharing's sake in the circumstances of the instant case. The court has a statutory duty to secure a clean break if this can be done. This is one of the principal reasons why the parties had the business valued. As at the date of the lump sum payment, the wife received half of the agreed value of the business.

25. Thirdly, Mr Wilkinson contends that the court was concerned with fixed term profits from a family partnership being prepared for sale as opposed to an earning capacity. I agree that it would have been possible for the judge, had he thought it right to do so in the exercise of his discretion, to award the wife a capital sum in respect of her half of the business together with some form of balancing payment in the event that the business sold for a substantially different amount than the agreed value. It will be a rare case when it is appropriate to do this, having regard to the statutory steer towards a clean break. Alternatively, in rare cases the Judge can adjourn the lump sum claims if it is thought appropriate to do so, for example when ascertaining value is extremely difficult. In my judgment the Judge was correct to decide that he needed to resolve the case now. In paragraph 43 of his Judgment, the Judge referred to the business producing "*these incomes*". The Judge referred to the income stream as "*matrimonial property*".

26. Somewhat incomprehensibly, with the greatest of respect to a very experienced judge, the judge then said, "*this approach also leads to a true determination of the reasonable needs of the wife*". In my judgment there is a disconnect between the income stream and the reasonable needs of the wife. It was the Judge's task to assess the reasonable needs of the wife and then to assess whether the capital provided to her was sufficient. Only if he found that the capital remaining in the wife's hands, after providing for her reasonable housing and other assessed capital needs, was insufficient to provide for her income needs could he then go on to consider an award of periodical payments. If he reached this stage, the Judge would then have a broad

discretion both as to the assessment of need and as to the issue of amortisation. I turn to this below.

27. Fourthly, Mr Wilkinson asserts that in the instant case the wife would be suffering a considerable relationship generated disadvantage if the income is not shared. Mr Wilkinson refers to the fact that in *Waggott* there was no compensation claim. This defence is bound to fail since there was no suggestion of a compensation claim in the instant case and one was not articulated by the Judge.

28. Fifth, Mr Wilkinson says that in *Waggott* the wife received a share of the husband's bonuses, as recognition of the fact that they related to matrimonial enterprise. The issue of bonuses has arisen in many cases. If a bonus is earned during the marriage but not paid out until after the marriage has ended then there is every reason to treat it as matrimonial property in the true sense. Sharing bonuses that were generated or earned after the marriage ended would usually be possible only by reference to the principles of needs and compensation. As I have already said, the instant case is not a compensation case and there are almost no examples of successful compensation claims in the reported cases.

29. Sixth, Mr Wilkinson says that the husband in *Waggott* was only 53 whereas the husband here is 61, so that the proximity of the sale is much closer and the 4 year period of profits to be generated by the business pending sale more defined. In my judgment, Mr Wilkinson here is confusing income and capital. The capital value of the business was shared by the payment of the lump sum. Moylan LJ could not have been clearer that future income is not an asset to be shared. I do not find it possible to read into Moylan LJ's judgment that a distinction can in some way be made between a man of 53 and a man of 61 or, more properly put, I cannot accept from the judgment that age is of itself material to the principle that the Judge was discussing.

30. Next, Mr Wilkinson correctly identifies that in *Waggott*, the first instance court failed to give proper weight to the clean break principle. I agree that in this case the judge imposed a five-year term with a section 28(1)(A) bar. However, I cannot read into the judgment in *Waggott* that even a short period of sharing of income can be justified other than by reference to the doctrines of need and compensation.

31. Eighth, Mr Wilkinson says that in *Waggott*, the court found that the wife's capital should not be preserved and the approach taken was too narrow with no consideration of part deployment of capital. Mr Wilkinson says that in the instant case the Judge adopted a more broad approach and found that the wife's capital should only be preserved during the five-year maintenance term, whilst the family business continued to pay out £1 million per annum of profits. Again, I go back to the fundamental principles enunciated by Moylan LJ. The fact is that in the instant case the parties had agreed the value of the business as at the date of the hearing. The parties agreed that the husband would continue to operate the franchise as he always had.

32. Furthermore, central to all of these defences to the appeal raised by Mr Wilkinson is the Judge's finding, at paragraph 38 of the draft judgment, that there was insufficient evidence to support a contention that the business will be worth greatly more once the re-imaging programme has been effected. Mr Wilkinson has not sought to challenge this finding on appeal and the wife has not raised a Respondent's Notice in respect of this (or any other) issue.

33. Mr Wilkinson ends his defence on this point by saying that, factually, *Waggott* was a very different case from the instant case but that the legal approach adopted by the Judge was in line with the judgment in *Waggott* and within the ambit of his discretion. I agree that the two cases are factually different but it is clear that in the passages to which I have referred, as well as other passages to which I have not referred, that Moylan LJ was purposefully setting out general guidance rather than dealing with facts very specific to that case. I note that Sir James Munby, then president of the Family Division and MacDonald J both agreed with him.

34. Accordingly, in my judgment, the judge was plainly wrong to identify the income stream of the business as matrimonial property.

The consequence of my finding that the Judge applied the wrong test

35. I have already identified what I referred to as the disconnect in the judge saying that the income stream is matrimonial property and that this approach leads to a true determination of the reasonable needs of the wife. It is clear that, in selecting the figure of £150,000 per annum by way of periodical payments, the judge intended that the wife should preserve her own capital during the period of the term order. I accept that to the wife there may seem to be an unfairness in the fact that she has to start living on her capital straightaway (whether or not amortised), whereas the husband does not. That, it seems to me, is the inevitable and direct consequence of the fact that an earning capacity is not subject to the sharing principle.

36. In spite of the fact that the Judge plainly alighted upon this figure for periodical payments by reference to the sharing principle, he nevertheless also sought to justify it by reference to needs. The Judge said: "*as to the level of periodical payments I have considered the wife's outgoings. In the main they are reflective of the standard of living of these parties however in the light of a net income available to Mr O'Dwyer in the region of £400,000, I am satisfied that the level of periodical payments of £150,000 per annum is appropriate*". In the exercise of his broad discretion, the Judge was absolutely entitled to be generous to the wife in terms of assessment of her maintenance requirement by reason of the fact that the husband will be enjoying a substantial income. However, a judge is not entitled simply to take a round number without reference to any arithmetic, and in particular (a) the recipient's needs; (b) the income that the recipient's capital will generate and (c) whether or not the recipient's capital should be amortised; and, if so (d) from what date the recipient's capital should be amortised. Parties who conduct these cases up and down the land, often without the benefit of legal advice, need to know how judges alight upon a particular figure for periodical payments. Otherwise, discretion gives way to a risk of disorder or even chaos with people not knowing how or whether to settle.

37. The starting point must be to establish how much capital the wife will have once she has purchased a home for herself. In paragraph 27 of his judgment, the judge said: "*Mr O'Dwyer, while seeking to retain the FMH allocates housing of only $600,000 to Mrs O'Dwyer's needs*". Mr Le Grice says that, whilst the husband might retain the former matrimonial home, it was never his case that he needed to retain it. In my judgment, the Judge was entitled to note that the husband aspired to living in the

former family home. In paragraph 27 of his Judgment, the Judge described the wife's chosen properties as "approaching the grandiose". The cheapest of these three, described by Mr LeGrice as properties that "might be described as approaching the grandiose" had an asking price of $1.090 million. Using the exchange rate employed by the parties of $1.33 to the pound, this equates to about £820,000. The Judge complained that both parties had presented unrealistic indications of appropriate properties. The Judge then allocated a total housing fund to the wife of $1.5 million including cost of acquisition. This amounts to £1.128 million. I have some sympathy with the husband complaining, through Mr Le Grice, that the Judge on the one hand complains that the wife produces unrealistic properties and then allocates a sum for property which is in the range which he had previously described as grandiose. However, as a Judge hearing an appeal, it is not my function to tinker with the numbers taken by an experienced Judge after a long hearing where he has had the benefit of oral evidence. Whilst I agree that the figure allocated to the wife for housing seems quite high, it is not in my judgment plainly wrong and I therefore work with the figure taken by the Judge.

38. The Judge found that, after deducting £1.2 million to cover the costs of a car, currency fluctuations and other expenses, the wife would have £1.776 million. The parties have since agreed that the Judge was in error when arriving at this figure and that the correct figure is £1,732,739. I must infer that the Judge meant to include in the list of items totalling £1.2 million the £1.128 million allocated to her for the purposes of purchasing a property. In respect of that figure, the judge said, *"that sum, given the maintenance level for the next five years, would be entirely preserved and should grow"*. In my judgment the Judge fell into error here. The Judge does not give any reasons why the wife should not spend the income generated by her capital. I infer that the words "should grow" refer to the ordinary investment growth, rather than the fact of saving from the periodical payments, however there is some confusion here since the judge later commented that the wife *"may wish to effect some savings"*. The Judge failed to address the issue of amortisation.

39. If the wife is left with £1,732,739, it is necessary to attribute an income to that figure. One can argue endlessly about the appropriate rate of return but it seems to me that time and again the assumptions in *At A Glance* are used and I use them for the purposes of this case. At paragraph 136 in *Waggott*, Moylan LJ saw clear advantages in adopting the *Duxbury* assumptions, and whilst of course I have a discretion to depart from them it seems to me that I should follow the lead so clearly given by him. I therefore work on the basis of a return of 3.75%. This equates to an income of £64,978 (or $84,471). This figure would be taxable in the wife's hands in the United States. In paragraph 34 of his skeleton argument in support of this appeal, Mr Le Grice set out tables with US tax calculations which were not challenged. Applying his figures, I round the wife's net income down to about £52,000 (or $67,600).

40. If I were to amortise all of the wife's capital from day one (and working on the basis that the wife was aged 59 when the Judge heard the case), it produces about £100,000 net per annum. I appreciate that there is inevitable rounding of these numbers and that the wife will be investing her money principally in the United States.

41. Whether or not a spouse should be required to amortise their capital will be case specific. It is my view that, in a bigger money case, after a long marriage where contributions are likely to have been equal, if different, if the economically stronger

party (here the husband) has a very substantial income, it is fair to determine that the economically weaker should not have to amortise their capital for a period of time. In *Waggott*, Moylan LJ made clear that there should be flexibility in respect of the extent to which capital should be amortised. In my judgment, there is every reason in the present case not to amortise the wife's capital during the remaining years when the husband will enjoy very substantial income. It seems to me that this will also give proper effect, post *Waggott*, to the Judge's assessment of fairness. I note that, in paragraph 134 of his Judgment in *Waggott*, Moylan LJ referred to *"the range of options from full amortisation to an assumed rate of return"* and said that *"it is difficult to see how a definitive outcome can, in fairness, be mandated for all cases"*. It is clear that the Judge left a substantial element of discretion in this respect. I am satisfied that in this case, after a long marriage with full contributions, where the husband has a large income from a business developed during the marriage, it is fair not to amortise the wife's capital for the remaining years of the husband's employment. In my judgment this strikes the correct balance between NOT sharing income, which is proscribed, and applying my discretion in the wife's favour as respects amortisation.

42. Accordingly, I find that the wife's net return from capital is the sum of £52,000 referred to above.

43. The wife made many presentations of her budget, and the figures "kept changing", as Mr Le Grice asserted. I am troubled by the absence of any proper analysis of the wife's budget. It is clear to me that it is the judicial function to analyse the budgets put forward, albeit that a detailed analysis of every item is not required. A judge must always, of course, be alive to forensic manoeuvrings by experienced family lawyers.

44. In her Form E, the wife assessed her needs at " not less than £10,000 per month". I am told that, at the last minute, the wife produced a budget of £15,000 per month. It is clear that there was extensive cross-examination of the wife on her various budgets. The transcript shows that the Judge intervened even to the extent of asking about the price of a litre of milk, the sprinkler systems in the wife's garden and the cost of toll roads, which make the lack of analysis in the Judgment all the more surprising.

45. I have considered whether I should remit the case to the Judge for him to carry out the analysis of budget that is absent from his Judgment. In the light of the delay referred to above I am certain that this course would simply add further to the already unacceptable delay and that such a course would be unfair to all. Mr Le Grice submitted that £75,000 a year would be a generous assessment". Mr Wilkinson asserted that the Judge did carry out an assessment, a submission which I have already explained that I cannot accept. I am alive to the fact that I have criticised the Judge for just alighting on a number without a proper analysis and that I must take care not to repeat that mistake. I am entitled to assume, and do so, that the wife's asserted figure in her Form E was carefully thought through. By any standard, £120,000 a year is a substantial net income, and there was clear evidence that her cost of living in Texas is lower than in England. I propose to adopt that figure. It is considerably higher than the figure contended for by Mr Le Grice but I bear in mind that there is significant judicial discretion in the assessment of need and that the Judge made his assessment after a long hearing, albeit, at least in part, on what I have found to be a flawed basis.

46. On the basis that I have assessed the wife's net return on capital is £52,000 per annum, in my judgment the correct figure for periodical payments should have been £68,000, and not the £150,000 ordered by the Judge in paragraph 21 of the Order. I propose to substitute the figure of £68,000 for the figure determined by the Judge. I am not going to interfere with the term set out in that paragraph. I accept that the term could have been different, but I do not think it appropriate, in an appeal, to substitute my discretion for that of the Judge who heard the case.

47. The Order will be amended accordingly and I shall of course hear any submissions in respect of costs, I suggest that these are presented electronically as soon as possible, in order to obviate the need for a further hearing. The parties will need to agree on the figure to be paid to the wife from the accumulated sum and the amount to be returned to the husband.

Section A

1. Which court was this case heard in? Why does this matter?
2. What was the subject-matter of this case?
3. Why was the maintenance payment awarded at the particular amount set?
4. What was held to be wrong with the way in which maintenance payments had been calculated?
5. Why should maintenance be paid in this case?

Section B

1. How did counsel seek to rebut the arguments made about relevant binding authority?
2. The judgment talks about the need to establish a "clean break" after a divorce. How would you find out what, legally, is meant by a clean break in these circumstances?
3. Why is a clean break after a divorce thought to be desirable?
4. Did the judge in case think that fairness will result of earning capacity is not subject the sharing principle?
5. Do you think that the treatment of the parties in this case is fair?

Exercise 4

CASES II

Re-read the appropriate parts of Chapters 4 and 5 before attempting the questions below. Remember to note which part of the judgment you are referring to when giving your answers. The answers for Section A are found in Appendix III.

5.10

Hilary Term
[2019] UKSC 17
On appeal from: [2018] EWCA Civ 170

JUDGMENT

Stocker (Appellant) *v* Stocker (Respondent)

before

Lord Reed, Deputy President
Lord Kerr
Lady Black
Lord Briggs
Lord Kitchin

JUDGMENT GIVEN ON

3 April 2019

Heard on 24 January 2019

Appellant	*Respondent*
David Price QC	Manuel Barca QC
Jonathan Price	Claire Overman
(Instructed by David Price Solicitor Advocate)	(Instructed by SA Law LLP)

LORD KERR: (with whom Lord Reed, Lady Black, Lord Briggs and Lord Kitchin agree)

1. "He tried to strangle me." What would those words convey to the "ordinary reasonable reader" of a Facebook post?

Background

2. The respondent to this appeal, Ronald Stocker, is the former husband of the appellant, Nicola Stocker. Their marriage ended in acrimony in 2012. Mr Stocker subsequently formed a relationship with Ms Deborah Bligh. On 23 December 2012 an exchange took place between Mrs Stocker and Ms Bligh on the Facebook website. In the course of that exchange, Mrs Stocker informed Ms Bligh that her former husband (now Ms Bligh's partner) had tried to strangle her. It is now clear that the date on which this is alleged to have occurred is 23 March 2003.

3. Mrs Stocker also said that her husband had been removed from the house following a number of threats that he had made; that there were some "gun issues"; and that the police felt that he had broken the terms of a non-molestation order. These statements and the allegation that Mr Stocker had tried to strangle her were the basis on which he took proceedings against her for defamation.

4. The allegations about threats, gun issues and the breach of a non-molestation order are relevant to provide context to the statement that Mr Stocker had tried to strangle Mrs Stocker. They paint a picture of acute marital conflict and on that account set the scene for any reader of the Facebook post. That reader would know that Mrs Stocker's statement that her former husband had tried to strangle her was made against the background that this had been, towards the end of its life, a most disharmonious marriage.

The proceedings in the High Court

5. Mr Stocker issued proceedings against his former wife, claiming that the statement that he had tried to strangle her was defamatory of him. He claimed that the meaning to be given to the words "tried to strangle me" was that he had tried to kill her. Mrs Stocker denied that the words bore that meaning. She claimed that, in the context of domestic violence, the words do not impute an intention to kill. What they would be understood to mean, she said, was that her husband had violently gripped her neck, inhibiting her breathing so as to put her in fear of being killed.

6. Mr Stocker also claimed that the statement that he had uttered threats and breached a non-molestation order was defamatory and was to be taken as implying that he was a dangerous and thoroughly disreputable man. Mrs Stocker refuted this. She said that it was not reasonable to infer that she had suggested that her husband was dangerous on account of his having been arrested a number of times. It is to be observed, however, that in the defence filed on her behalf, Mrs Stocker averred that the statement that her husband was dangerous and disreputable was justified. It seems likely that this was by way of alternative plea. In any event, for reasons that will later appear, this is immaterial because of the rule concerning the substantial truth of the statements made by the alleged defamer.

7. At the start of the defamation proceedings, Mitting J, the trial judge, suggested that the parties should refer to the Oxford English Dictionary's definition of the verb, "strangle". This provided two possible meanings: (a) to kill by external compression of the throat; and (b) to constrict the neck or throat painfully. The judge was asked by counsel for the appellant, Mr Price QC, to consider how the words, "tried to strangle" had been used in different contexts. Mr Price also sought to introduce legal definitions of the word "strangle". These do not appear to have been taken into account by Mitting J and he did not refer to them in his judgment.

8. Mr Stocker gave evidence that, on the occasion when the altercation which led to his wife accusing him of trying to strangle her took place, he had been standing on a stool or a chair while she was adjusting the length of a pair of his trousers. She had pricked him with a pin. He had sworn at her. She swore back at him and he placed his hand over her mouth to prevent her raised voice from waking their sleeping son. The judge rejected this account, saying, at para 43:

> "I do not accept [Mr Stocker's] account that he merely put one hand over [Mrs Stocker's] mouth while he was standing on the stool or chair. His hand would have been at his thigh level. He could not have exerted more than momentary pressure on her

> mouth, from which she could instantly have escaped. Nor could he have left the reddening marks on her neck or throat which I am satisfied were seen by the police. I do not, however, believe that he threatened to kill her or did anything with his hands with that intention. I do not believe that he was capable even in temper of attempted murder. The most likely explanation about what happened is that he did in temper attempt to silence her forcibly by placing one hand on her mouth and the other on her upper neck under her chin to hold her head still. His intention was to silence, not to kill."

9. This finding implicitly rejects Mrs Stocker's account of the incident also. She had said that her husband had dismounted from the chair, had pushed her against a small sofa, put his hands around her neck and squeezed, causing her to believe that he would kill her. The judge accepted that some two hours after the incident, red marks on Mrs Stocker's neck had been seen by police officers but he came up with a theory as to how those had come about which neither party had proposed.

10. It is of course open to a trial judge, after considering all the evidence, to reach his or her own conclusions or to draw inferences which neither party has advanced or espoused. But there must be a sound basis for doing so. In this case, the judge accepted the police evidence that there were red marks on Mrs Stocker's neck. Mr Stocker had agreed during a police interview that it was possible that he had put his hand around his wife's neck and, implicitly, that this had caused the red marks that were found there. He had also said that he had dismounted from the chair or stool on which he had been standing; had followed Mrs Stocker over to a chair and that it was possible that he had put his hand around her neck. Unsurprisingly, he was content to go along with a suggestion put to him by a police officer that he had not "maliciously grabbed her around the throat or tried to assault her".

11. At no point did Mr Stocker claim that he had grasped his wife by the throat in order to secure his hand covering her mouth or to prevent her from wrenching free from his grasp. Nor did he suggest that he could not have prevented her from shouting simply by placing his hand over her mouth. It is to be noted that he had admitted to police that he had alighted from the stool or chair. If that statement was accurate and truthful, he was therefore on the same level as his wife. Yet, the judge rejected Mr Stocker's evidence that he had simply put his hand over his wife's mouth. Mitting J considered that a further hand (on the neck) was needed to secure the grip on Mrs Stocker's mouth. This conclusion seems to have been premised on Mr Stocker remaining on the chair. (And, in fairness to the judge, it seems that Mr Stocker so claimed in evidence.)

12. If other considerations had not supervened, there might well have been an issue as to whether it was open to the judge to reach the conclusion which he did, particularly because that conclusion is more benevolent to Mr Stocker than any version of the facts which he could reasonably have advanced. It seeks to explain the red marks on a basis which Mr Stocker has never argued for. In the event, however, it is unnecessary to deal with that matter because of the conclusions that I have reached on other issues and, since it had not been argued that the judge's finding on this point was one which he should not have made, I say nothing more about it.

13. The judge began his discussion about the meaning to be given to the statements said to be defamatory by referring to the well-known case of *Jeynes v News Magazines Ltd* [2008] EWCA Civ 130 and cited the eight propositions made in that case by Sir Anthony Clarke MR in para 14. The judge also quoted the supplementary qualification to those propositions provided by Sharp LJ in *Rufus v Elliott* [2015] EWCA Civ 121, para 11. (Both authorities will be considered below.)

14. Having considered these judicial pronouncements, Mitting J said that he did not understand that either authority indicated that, in order "to confirm the meaning in ordinary usage of a single English word", it was impermissible to refer to "an authoritative English dictionary such as the Oxford English Dictionary." He then referred to the two dictionary definitions which I have set out at para 7 above and continued at para 36:

> "If the defendant had said 'he strangled me', the ordinary reader would have understood her to have used the word in the second sense for the obvious reason that she was still alive. But the two Facebook comments cannot have been understood to refer to 'trying' to strangle her in that sense because, as she said, the police had found handprints on her neck. These could only have been caused by the painful constriction of her neck or throat. If understood in that sense, she could not have been taken to have said that the defendant had tried to strangle her because he had succeeded. The ordinary reader would have understood that the defendant had attempted to kill her by external compression of her throat or neck with his hands and/or fingers."

15. It is clear from this passage of his judgment that the trial judge had confined the possible meaning of the statement, "he tried to strangle me" to two stark alternatives. Either Mr Stocker had tried to kill his wife, or he had constricted her neck or throat painfully. In the judge's estimation, the fact that Mrs Stocker had said that her husband "tried" to strangle her precluded the possibility of her statement being taken to mean that he had constricted her neck painfully.

16. This approach produces an obviously anomalous result. If Mrs Stocker had said, "he strangled me", she should be understood to have meant that her husband had constricted her neck or throat painfully, on account of her having survived to tell the tale. But, because she said that he had "tried" to strangle her (in the normal order of things and in common experience a less serious accusation), she was fixed with the momentous allegation that her husband had tried to kill her. On this analysis, the use of the verb, "to try" assumes a critical significance. The possible meaning of constricting the neck painfully was shut out by what might be regarded as the adventitious circumstance that Mrs Stocker had said that her husband had "tried" to strangle her rather than that he had strangled her.

17. This anomalous result was the product of confining the meaning of the words exclusively to two dictionary definitions. If "tried to strangle" did not fit with the notion of trying to constrict the neck or throat painfully (because of the prosaic fact that Mrs Stocker was still alive), the only possible meaning was that Mr Stocker had tried to kill.

18. On the remainder of the claimed defamatory meaning the judge's reasoning was closely allied to that on the first part. In the passage of his judgment which immediately succeeded that quoted at para 14 above, he said at para 36:

> "That understanding [that her husband had tried to kill Mrs Stocker] would have informed the ordinary reader about the meaning of the remaining comments. They were that he had been arrested on at least two other occasions for 'gun issues' and for breach of a non-molestation order and possibly on a third for 'threats'. In addition, he would have understood her to assert that the police believed that he had broken the terms of the non-molestation order; in other words, that there was a basis beyond mere suspicion for doing so."

19. The judge then dealt with an argument made on behalf of Mrs Stocker that all that she had done was to state that Mr Stocker had been arrested on more than one occasion and that this was not itself a defamatory statement. Of these claims, the judge said this at para 37:

> "I agree that in principle the statement that a person has been arrested is not necessarily defamatory. But these statements, taken together, go well beyond that. They justify the claimant's pleaded case that the reasonable inference to draw from the statement was that the defendant was dangerous, at least to any woman with whom he lived or had lived, that he was a man

> who tried to kill on one occasion, had been arrested for an offence involving firearms on another, and had given the police reason to believe that he had broken a non-molestation order made against him. To describe him thus was defamatory."

20. The meaning attributed by the judge to the statement that the claimant had been arrested, in the context of the other statements, therefore was that Mr Stocker was a man who was dangerous to any woman with whom he had lived or might live.

21. Mrs Stocker had pleaded that her statements were substantially true and that she was therefore entitled to rely on the defence of justification. The judge dealt with that plea in para 54 of his judgment:

> "The defendant has proved some justification for the words which she used in the Facebook postings. The claimant did commit an offence against her on 23 March 2003, at least common assault. He was arrested three times. There were 'gun issues'. He had made threats, though not of immediate violence against her. But she has not met the sting of the postings that the claimant was a dangerous man. The impression given by the postings to the ordinary reader was a significant and distorting overstatement of what had in fact occurred."

The Court of Appeal

22. At para 17 of her judgment, Sharp LJ in the Court of Appeal said this about the use of dictionaries as a means of deciding the meaning to be given to a statement alleged to be defamatory:

> "The use of dictionaries does not form part of the process of determining the natural and ordinary meaning of words, because what matters is the impression conveyed by the words to the ordinary reader when they are read, and it is this that the judge must identify. As it happened however no harm was done in this case. The judge told counsel during the course of submissions that he had looked at the OED definitions and what they said, so the parties had the opportunity to address him about it; the judge, as he then said, merely used the dictionary definitions as a check, and no more; those definitions were in substance the rival ones contended for by the parties, and in the event, the judge's ultimate reasoning, not dependent on dictionaries, was sound."

23. The suggestion that the judge told counsel "in the course of submissions" that he had looked at the dictionary definition may mislead. On the first day of the trial, before any evidence had been given, counsel for Mr Stocker, Mr Barca QC, had suggested to Mitting J that no time would be saved by asking him to deliver a preliminary ruling on meaning. The judge replied that he had "a preliminary opinion about it" which he was willing to disclose. Shortly thereafter, he suggested that counsel should look at the Oxford English Dictionary definitions and said, "You might from that gain the primary and secondary definition and fit it (sic) into the context of a message that he 'tried' to do something". All of this occurred before the judge heard any argument about meanings. This suggests that, contrary to Sharp LJ's view, the judge was not using the dictionary definitions as a cross-check. Plainly, he regarded those definitions as comprehensive of the possible meanings of the statement, "he tried to strangle me".

24. Sharp LJ's statement that Mitting J merely used the dictionary definitions as a check may have been based on his comment in para 36 of his judgment that the authorities do not "prohibit reference to an authoritative English dictionary such as the Oxford English Dictionary to confirm the meaning in ordinary usage of a single English word". I do not construe this statement as signifying that the judge was using the dictionary definitions as a cross-check and, indeed, neither in his judgment nor in his exchanges with counsel, does he ever use the expression, "check". Given that Mitting J had consulted the dictionary before the trial began and commended consideration of it to counsel, it seems to me plain that, far from using the definitions as a check, what the judge did was to regard the two definitions as the only possible meanings which he could consider or, at the very least, the starting point for his analysis, rather than a cross-check or confirmation of the correct approach.

25. Therein lies the danger of the use of dictionary definitions to provide a guide to the meaning of an alleged defamatory statement. That meaning is to be determined according to how it would be understood by the ordinary reasonable reader. It is not fixed by technical, linguistically precise dictionary definitions, divorced from the context in which the statement was made.

26. Moreover, once the verb, "strangle" is removed from its context and given only two possible meanings before it is reconnected to the word, "tried" the chances of a strained meaning are increased. The words must be taken together so as to determine what the ordinary reasonable reader would understand them to mean. Mitting J examined the word "strangle" in conspicuous detail before considering it in conjunction with the word, "tried". Having determined that "strangle" admitted of only two possible meanings, he then decided that "tried" could be applied to only one of these. Underpinning his reasoning is the unarticulated premise that "to try" is necessarily "to try and fail". Since Mr Stocker had not failed to constrict his wife's throat, the judge concluded that the only feasible meaning of the words was that he

had tried (and failed) to kill her. But that is not how the words are used in common language. If I say, "I tried to regain my breath", I would not be understood to have tried but failed to recover respiratory function.

27. On the meaning found by the judge at para 37 of his judgment (that Mr Stocker was dangerous to any woman with whom he lived), Sharp LJ at para 21 of her judgment said:

> "The judge's reference to the respondent's dangerousness was merely his overall characterisation of the impression the [comments made by Mrs Stocker on Ms Bligh's Facebook wall] conveyed, *in the light of the discrete meanings he had found them to bear (the respondent had tried to kill etc). This was not a freestanding meaning therefore detached from the meanings complained of,* nor was this a characterisation which founds an appeal that the judge was wrong; indeed to my mind, in the light of the meanings found by the judge, this overall characterisation of what was alleged was self-evidently correct." (Emphasis added)

28. Plainly, the Court of Appeal considered (as did, indeed, the judge) that that meaning was dependent, to some extent at least, on the correctness of Mitting J's conclusion as to the meaning to be given to the words, "tried to strangle me". The passage quoted was in reaction to Mr Price's argument that the judge was wrong to have fastened on that meaning when it had not been advanced by Mr Stocker. Sharp LJ had observed of this argument that the judge was not bound to accept either party's contention on meaning; his task was "to identify the single meaning of the words complained of within the relevant area of contention". For reasons that will appear, it is important to note the two aspects of Sharp LJ's reasoning: first that the judge was entitled to fix on a meaning which had not been advanced by either party; and, secondly, that his choice of meaning was influenced by his findings in relation to the first defamatory meaning - that Mrs Stocker's words "he tried to strangle me" were to be taken as meaning that her husband had tried to kill her.

29. Sharp LJ then turned to the question of justification. She referred to an argument advanced on behalf of Mrs Stocker that the judge had failed to advert to section 5 of the Defamation Act 1952 (which has now been replaced by section 2(3) of the Defamation Act 2013):

> "In an action for libel or slander in respect of words containing two or more distinct charges against the plaintiff, a defence of justification shall not fail by reason only that the truth of every charge is not proved if the words not proved to be true do not

materially injure the plaintiff's reputation having regard to the truth of the remainingcharges."

30. At para 25, Sharp LJ said:

"I can see why an issue in relation to section 5 might arise for consideration if the judge was wrong to conclude that the comments alleged the respondent had tried to kill the appellant by strangling her. In my view however, the failure of the principal argument on meaning deprives the argument on section 5 of any force that it might have had. The judge found in short that there was a real and substantial difference between the allegations made and those proved; and in my view he was entitled to reach that view on the evidence he heard. Having carefully appraised the evidence of justification and dealt with the essential points relating to that defence, the judge put the matter in this way. Though the appellant had proved some justification for the words she used, the allegations made in the comments were a significant and distorting overstatement of what had in fact occurred. His views were similarly expressed during the course of submissions. It is true that the judge found as a fact that during the course of an argument, the respondent had committed common assault at least, by placing his hand over the appellant's mouth and putting his hand under her chin, to stop her speaking. However there is a material difference in gravity between such conduct, however unpleasant it may be, and an attempt to kill by strangulation; and it was plainly open to the judge to find, as he did, that what the appellant had proved in this and other respects, fell short by some measure of establishing a successful defence of justification, by reference to section 5 or otherwise."

31. Again, it is to be noted that the finding of Mitting J about the meaning to be given to the words, "he tried to strangle me" was pivotal to the conclusion that section 5 could not be prayed in aid by Mrs Stocker. It is clear that, if it had been held that Mitting J was wrong to fix on the meaning of those words that he did, a markedly different view as to the applicability of section 5 would have been warranted.

The single meaning rule

32. Section 11 of the Defamation Act 2013 abolished the statutory right to trial by jury (in section 69(1) of the Senior Courts Act 1981). Under the previous dispensation, the judge would determine which meanings the allegedly defamatory words were capable of bearing and exclude those which she or he considered they were not capable of bearing. The judge would then put to the jury the various possible meanings and, with appropriate directions, invite the jury to decide which of those adumbrated meanings was the one to be attributed to the words said to be defamatory.

33. The almost complete abolition of jury trial meant that the task of choosing a single meaning fell to the judge alone. The exercise of choosing a single immutable meaning from a series of words which are capable of bearing more than one has been described as artificial - see, in particular, Diplock LJ in *Slim v Daily Telegraph Ltd* [1968] 2 QB 157, 172C. But the single meaning rule has had its robust defenders. In *Oriental Daily Publisher Ltd v Ming Pao Holdings Ltd* [2013] EMLR 7, Lord Neuberger of Abbotsbury, sitting as a judge of the Hong Kong Court of Final Appeal, said at para 138 that the criticism of the rule's artificiality and (implicitly) its irrationality was misplaced. He suggested that the identification of a single meaning to be accorded a statement arose "in many areas of law, most notably … the interpretation of statutes, contracts and notices" - para 140.

34. Whether the analogy between a single defamatory meaning and a sole meaning to be given to a contractual term, statutory provision or notice is apt (which I take leave to doubt), it is clear that the single meaning approach is well entrenched in the law of defamation and neither party in the present appeal sought to impeach it. And, whatever else may be said of it, it provides a practical, workable solution. Where a statement has more than one plausible meaning, the question of whether defamation has occurred can only be answered by deciding that one particular meaning should be ascribed to the statement.

35. It is then for the judge to decide which meaning to plump for. Guidance as to how she or he should set about that mission was provided in *Jeynes* (mentioned in para 13 above). At para 14, Sir Anthony Clarke MR set out the essential criteria:

> "(1) The governing principle is reasonableness. (2) The hypothetical reasonable reader is not naïve, but he is not unduly suspicious. He can read between the lines. He can read in an implication more readily than a lawyer and may indulge in a certain amount of loose thinking, but he must be treated as being a man who is not avid for scandal and someone who does

> not, and should not, select one bad meaning where other non-defamatory meanings are available. (3) Over-elaborate analysis is best avoided. (4) The intention of the publisher is irrelevant. (5) The article must be read as a whole, and any 'bane and antidote' taken together. (6) The hypothetical reader is taken to be representative of those who would read the publication in question. (7) In delimiting the range of permissible defamatory meanings, the court should rule out any meaning which, 'can only emerge as the produce of some strained, or forced, or utterly unreasonable interpretation …' (see Eady J in *Gillick v Brook Advisory Centres* approved by this court [2001] EWCA Civ 1263 at para 7 and Gatley on Libel and Slander (10th ed), para 30.6). (8) It follows that 'it is not enough to say that by some person or another the words *might* be understood in a defamatory sense.' *Neville v Fine Arts Co* [1897] AC 68 per Lord Halsbury LC at 73."

36. Sharp LJ added a rider to the second of these criteria in *Rufus v Elliott* when she said at para 11:

> "To this I would only add that the words 'should not select one bad meaning where other non-defamatory meanings are available' are apt to be misleading without fuller explanation. They obviously do not mean in a case such as this one, where it is open to a defendant to contend either on a capability application or indeed at trial that the words complained of are not defamatory of the claimant, that the tribunal adjudicating on the question must then select the non-defamatory meaning for which the defendant contends. Instead, those words are 'part of the description of the hypothetical reasonable reader, rather than (as) a prescription of how such a reader should attribute meanings to words complained of as defamatory': see *McAlpine v Bercow* [2013] EWHC 1342 (QB), paras 63 to 66."

37. Clearly, therefore, where a range of meanings is available and where it is possible to light on one meaning which is not defamatory among a series of meanings which are, the court is not obliged to select the non-defamatory meaning. The touchstone remains what would the ordinary reasonable reader consider the words to mean. Simply because it is theoretically possible to come up with a meaning which is not defamatory, the court is not impelled to select that meaning.

38. All of this, of course, emphasises that the primary role of the court is to focus on how the ordinary reasonable reader would construe the words. And this highlights the court's duty to step aside from a lawyerly analysis and to inhabit the world of the typical reader of a Facebook post. To fulfil that obligation, the court should be particularly conscious of the context in which the statement was made, and it is to that subject that I now turn.

Context

39. The starting point is the sixth proposition in *Jeynes* - that the hypothetical reader should be considered to be a person who would read the publication - and, I would add, react to it in a way that reflected the circumstances in which it was made. It has been suggested that the judgment in *Jeynes* failed to acknowledge the importance of context - see *Bukovsky v Crown Prosecution Service* [2017] EWCA Civ 1529; [2018] 4 WLR 13 where at para 13 Simon LJ said that the propositions which were made in that case omitted "an important principle [namely] ... the context and circumstances of the publication ...".

40. It may be that the significance of context could have been made more explicitly clear in *Jeynes,* but it is beyond question that this is a factor of considerable importance. And that the way in which the words are presented is relevant to the interpretation of their meaning - *Waterson v Lloyd* [2013] EWCA Civ 136; [2013] EMLR 17, para 39.

41. The fact that this was a Facebook post is critical. The advent of the 21st century has brought with it a new class of reader: the social media user. The judge tasked with deciding how a Facebook post or a tweet on Twitter would be interpreted by a social media user must keep in mind the way in which such postings and tweets are made and read.

42. In *Monroe v Hopkins* [2017] EWHC 433 (QB); [2017] 4 WLR 68, Warby J at para 35 said this about tweets posted on Twitter:

> "The most significant lessons to be drawn from the authorities as applied to a case of this kind seem to be the rather obvious ones, that this is a conversational medium; so it would be wrong to engage in elaborate analysis of a 140 character tweet; that an impressionistic approach is much more fitting and appropriate to the medium; but that this impressionistic approach must take account of the whole tweet and the context in which the ordinary reasonable reader would read that tweet.

> That context includes (a) matters of ordinary general knowledge; and (b) matters that were put before that reader via Twitter."

43. I agree with that, particularly the observation that it is wrong to engage in elaborate analysis of a tweet; it is likewise unwise to parse a Facebook posting for its theoretically or logically deducible meaning. The imperative is to ascertain how

a typical (ie an ordinary reasonable) reader would interpret the message. That search should reflect the circumstance that this is a casual medium; it is in the nature of conversation rather than carefully chosen expression; and that it is pre-eminently one in which the reader reads and passes on.

44. That essential message was repeated in *Monir v Wood* [2018] EWHC (QB) 3525 where at para 90, Nicklin J said, "Twitter is a fast moving medium. People will tend to scroll through messages relatively quickly." Facebook is similar. People scroll through it quickly. They do not pause and reflect. They do not ponder on what meaning the statement might possibly bear. Their reaction to the post is impressionistic and fleeting. Some observations made by Nicklin J are telling. Again, at para 90 he said:

> "It is very important when assessing the meaning of a Tweet not to be over-analytical. ... Largely, the meaning that an ordinary reasonable reader will receive from a Tweet is likely to be more impressionistic than, say, from a newspaper article which, simply in terms of the amount of time that it takes to read, allows for at least some element of reflection and consideration. The essential message that is being conveyed by a Tweet is likely to be absorbed quickly by the reader."

45. And Nicklin J made an equally important point at para 92 where he said (about arguments made by the defendant as to meaning), "... these points only emerge as a result of close analysis, or someone pointing them out. An ordinary reasonable reader will not have someone by his/her side making points like this."

46. A similar approach to that of Nicklin J had been taken by Eady J in dealing with online bulletin boards in *Smith v ADVFN plc* [2008] EWHC 1797 (QB) where he said (at paras 13 to 16):

> "13. It is necessary to have well in mind the nature of bulletin board communications, which are a relatively recent development. This is central to a proper consideration of all the matters now before the court.
>
> 14. ... Particular characteristics which I should have in mind are that they are read by relatively few people, most of whom will share an interest in the subject-matter; they are rather like contributions to a casual conversation (the analogy sometimes being drawn with people chatting in a bar) which people simply note before moving on; they are often uninhibited, casual and ill thought out; those who participate know this and expect a certain amount of repartee or 'give and take'.
>
> ...
>
> 16. People do not often take a 'thread' and go through it as a whole like a newspaper article. They tend to read the remarks, make their own contributions if they feel inclined, and think no more about it."

Further discussion

47. It will be clear from what I have said already that, in my view, Mitting J fell into legal error by relying upon the dictionary definition of the verb "to strangle" as dictating the meaning of Mrs Stocker's Facebook post, rather than as (as Sharp LJ suggested) a check. In consequence, he failed to conduct a realistic exploration of how the ordinary reader of the post would have understood it. Readers of Facebook posts do not subject them to close analysis. They do not have someone by their side pointing out the possible meanings that might, theoretically, be given to the post. Anyone reading this post would not break it down in the way that Mitting J did by saying, well, strangle means either killing someone by choking them to death or grasping them by the throat and since Mrs Stocker is not dead, she *must* have meant that her husband tried to kill her - no other meaning is conceivable.

48. In view of the judge's error of law, his decision as to the meaning of the Facebook post cannot stand, and this court must either determine the meaning for itself, or if that is not possible, remit the case for a rehearing. It is entirely appropriate in this case for us to take the former course, determining the meaningourselves.

49. I return to the ordinary reader of the Facebook post. Such a reader does not splice the post into separate clauses, much less isolate individual words and contemplate their possible significance. Knowing that the author was alive, he or she would unquestionably have interpreted the post as meaning that Mr Stocker had grasped his wife by the throat and applied force to her neck rather than that he had tried deliberately to kill her.

50. Ironically, perhaps, this conclusion is reinforced by the consideration that only one meaning is to be attributed to the statement. Taking a broad, overarching view, and keeping in mind that only one meaning could be chosen, the choice to be made between the meaning of the words being that Mr Stocker grasped his wife by the neck or that he tried to kill her is, in my opinion, a clear one. If Mrs Stocker had meant to convey that her husband had attempted to kill her, why would she not say so explicitly? And, given that she made no such allegation, what would the ordinary reasonable reader, the casual viewer of this Facebook post, think that it meant? In my view, giving due consideration to the context in which the message was posted, the interpretation that Mr Stocker had grasped his wife by the neck is the obvious, indeed the inescapable, choice of meaning.

51. I emphasise again that it is a legal error on the part of the judge that has opened the door to a redetermination of the meaning of Mrs Stocker's words. This is not a case of the appellate court giving precedence to its view of meaning over that legitimately reached by the judge. To the contrary, it is the court's recognition that the meaning determined by the judge was reached via a route which was impermissible and having then to confront the question what me aning should properly be attributed to the relevant words. It is nevertheless appropriate to say something generally about the role of the appellate court in appeals concerning the meaning of avowedly defamatory words chosen by a trial judge.

The role of the appellate court

52. The question of when it was appropriate for an appellate court to substitute its view for that of a trial judge on the meaning of a claimed defamatory statement was addressed at some length in *Bukovsky*. At para 30 Simon LJ set out the competing contentions of counsel as to how this issue should be approached:

> "... [Counsel for the appellant] submitted that the relevant test on an appeal on meaning was whether the decision of the lower court was wrong: see CPR rule 52.11(3)(a), now CPR rule 52.21(3)(a). In contrast, [counsel for the respondent] submitted that this court should only reject the meaning found by the

judge if it was 'clear' that some other meaning applied. A passage in *Duncan & Neill* ... at para 33.03 describes both arguments in relation to the determination of meaning (a different approach is adopted in a determination made under paragraph 4 of CPR Practice Direction 53 that a statement is capable or incapable of bearing a particular meaning). I have added the letters A and B to para 33.03 so as to distinguish the two approaches:

> '[A] A determination of the actual meaning of a statement is a determination of fact that an appeal court is bound to overturn if the judge's determination was 'wrong'. Since determination of meaning is often based on the consideration of a single document, an appellate court, it might be said, is as well placed as the first instance judge to decide the issue and should simply substitute its own view if it disagrees with the judge.'

> '[B] On the other hand, it might be said, determination of meaning is nevertheless an exercise that involves the evaluation and weighing of various parts of a statement, such that an appeal court should normally accord a degree of deference to the first instance judge and interfere only when 'quite satisfied' that a judge's determination of meaning was wrong and that some other meaning clearly applied. It appears that this more deferential approach is the one likely to be adopted.'"

53. At para 31, Simon LJ observed that proposition B had been supported by a number of judgments of the Court of Appeal, including that of Sir Thomas Bingham MR in *Skuse v Granada Television Ltd* [1996] MLR 278, 287, where he said:

> "The Court of Appeal should be slow to differ from any conclusion of fact reached by a trial judge. Plainly this principle is less compelling where his conclusion is not based on his assessment of the reliability of witnesses or on the substance of their oral evidence and where the material before the appellate court is exactly the same as was before him. But even so we should not disturb his finding unless we are *quite satisfied* he was wrong." (Emphasis added)

54. As Simon LJ noted, however, when the Court of Appeal came to state its conclusion in *Skuse*, it merely said that it was "satisfied" that the natural and ordinary meaning which the judge gave to the material complained of was wrong. The "satisfied/quite satisfied" dichotomy featured again in *Cruddas v Calvert* [2013] EWCA Civ 748; [2014] EMLR 5, para 18 Longmore LJ summarised the claimant's argument thus:

> "[Counsel for the claimants] relied heavily on a supposed principle that the meaning of words was a jury question (and thus a question of fact) and that the judge was the best person qualified to reach the right conclusion which should not be 'second guessed' by this court."

55. He then referred to *Skuse v Granada Television Ltd* and to *Cammish v Hughes* [2012] EWCA Civ 1655; [2013] EMLR 13, where Arden LJ had said at para 31:

> "As to the test that this court should apply, although this court has the same documents as were available to the judge, and the meaning depends on documents, we apply the dictum of Sir Thomas Bingham MR, [in *Skuse*]. The determination of meaning does not depend solely on the documents, but on an evaluation of those words in their context. In those circumstances, we consider that we should not depart from the judge's meaning unless it is *clear that some other meaning applies*." (Emphasis added)

56. Longmore LJ in *Cruddas* acknowledged the force of the submission that the Court of Appeal should not second guess the judge and said at para 19:

> "19. There is, of course, considerable force in this argument. On the other hand, imputations of criminal conduct are extremely serious and, if an appellate court thinks that an article just does not bear that imputation, it should say so. It is an important aspect of the law of libel that it should be open to a defendant to justify a lesser defamatory meaning than that alleged by a claimant if that is the right meaning to be given to the article."

57. He concluded by saying that if, in order to come within Sir Thomas Bingham's eighth principle in the *Skuse* case, he had to, he would say that he was not merely satisfied but "quite satisfied". For my part, the difference in this context

between being satisfied and being quite satisfied, if it can be discerned at all, is so ephemeral, so elusive a concept as to be of scant utility. Ultimately, the court in *Bukovsky* elected to steer a middle course between what Simon LJ had described as options A and B. At para 39, Simon LJ said:

> "It seems to me that the better approach is for this court to adopt a position somewhere between *Duncan & Neill's* propositions A and B. It should proceed cautiously before substituting its own views on meaning and only do so when satisfied that the judge is wrong, not least because meaning is very often a matter of impression, because experienced defamation judges are well practised at applying the relevant tests for determining meaning and because it is plainly undesirable for the Court of Appeal to approach the issue on appeal simply on the basis that they might have formed a different view from the judge."

58. Of course, a reviewing court should be slow to disturb a finding of a trial judge as to the meaning of a claimed defamatory statement. This is mainly because it is a finding of fact, whereas the construction of a written contract is a question of law. It is well settled, outside the field of defamation, that an appellate court will not interfere with a finding of fact by a first instance judge merely because it takes a different view of the matter. The degree of restraint which the appellate court will exercise will depend upon whether the judge had the advantage of seeing and hearing the witnesses, whether the finding is an inference based upon the review of a large mass of primary factual material, and whether the finding is in the nature of an evaluation involving mixed fact and law. The following passage from the judgment of Lord Reed in *McGraddie v McGraddie* [2013] UKSC 58; [2013] 1 WLR 2477, paras 3-4 sufficiently covers the ground:

> "3. The reasons justifying that approach are not limited to the fact, emphasised in *Clarke's* case and *Thomas v Thomas*, that the trial judge is in a privileged position to assess the credibility of witnesses' evidence. Other relevant considerations were explained by the United States Supreme Court in *Anderson v City of Bessemer* (1985) 470 US 564, 574-575:
>
> > 'The rationale for deference to the original finder of fact is not limited to the superiority of the trial judge's position to make determinations of credibility. The trial judge's major role is the determination of fact, and with experience in fulfilling that role comes expertise.

> Duplication of the trial judge's efforts in the court of appeals would very likely contribute only negligibly to the accuracy of fact determination at a huge cost in diversion of judicial resources. In addition, the parties to a case on appeal have already been forced to concentrate their energies and resources on persuading the trial judge that their account of the facts is the correct one; requiring them to persuade three more judges at the appellate level is requiring too much. As the court has stated in a different context, the trial on the merits should be 'the 'main event' … rather than a 'try-out on the road'' … For these reasons, review of factual findings under the clearly erroneous standard - with its deference to the trier of fact - is the rule, not the exception.'

…

4. Furthermore, as was stated in observations adopted by the majority of the Canadian Supreme Court in *Housen v Nikolaisen* [2002] 2 SCR 235, para 14:

> 'The trial judge has sat through the entire case and his ultimate judgment reflects this total familiarity with the evidence. The insight gained by the trial judge who has lived with the case for several days, weeks or even months may be far deeper than that of the Court of Appeal whose view of the case is much more limited and narrow, often being shaped and distorted by the various orders or rulings being challenged.'"

59. As to whether the appellate task needs to be described as one requiring caution, as Simon LJ suggested, I am doubtful. I would prefer to say that it calls for disciplined restraint. Certainly, the trial judge's conclusion should not be lightly set aside but if an appellate court considers that the meaning that he has given to the statement was outside the range of reasonably available alternatives, it should not be deterred from so saying by the use of epithets such as "plainly" or "quite" satisfied. If it was vitiated by an error of law then the appellate court will have to choose between remitting the matter or, more usually in this context, determining the meaning afresh. But if the appellate court would just prefer a different meaning within a reasonably available range, then it should not interfere.

60. This discussion is academic in the present case for I am of the view that Mitting J's use of the dictionary definitions to confine the possible meanings of the Facebook post involved an error of law and, on that account the Court of Appeal needed to approach the question of meaning afresh. Since it did not do so, that task falls to this court, with the consequence which I have described.

Justification

61. In light of my conclusion as to the correct meaning to be given to the words, "tried to strangle me", section 5 of the Defamation Act 1952 must occupy centre stage. It is beyond dispute that Mr Stocker grasped his wife by the throat so tightly as to leave red marks on her neck visible to police officers two hours after the attack on her took place. It is not disputed that he breached a non-molestation order. Nor has it been asserted that he did not utter threats to Mrs Stocker. Many would consider these to be sufficient to establish that he was a dangerous and disreputable man, which is the justification which Mrs Stocker sought to establish. Mitting J considered that the meaning of the statement that the claimant was arrested on numerous occasions, in the context of the other statements, was that he represented a danger to any woman with whom he might live. I see no warrant for adding that dimension to the actual words used by Mrs Stocker in her various Facebook postings.

62. Even if all her allegations were considered not to have been established to the letter, there is more than enough to satisfy the provision in section 5 of the 1952 Act that her defence of justification should not fail by reason only that the truth of every charge is not proved, having regard to the truth of what has been proved.

Conclusion

63. I would allow the appeal, and subject to any submissions which the parties might wish to make, order that the costs of the appeal and the hearings before the lower courts be borne by the respondent.

Section A

1. The parties to this case were once married. Is this therefore a family law case?
2. At first instance, the judge suggested that the Oxford English Dictionary should be consulted in order to ascertain what the word "strangle" meant. Why did the Supreme Court think that this was the wrong thing to do?
3. What problems might there be if you do not use dictionaries to determine what words mean?
4. If you do use dictionaries to decide what words mean what problems might this create?
5. What is meant by "justification" in this judgment?

Section B

1. Write a short statement giving the ratio in this case.
2. Lord Kerr gives the only judgment in this case. This is not uncommon. When this happens, what then is the benefit of having more one judge hearing the case?
3. Why does Lord Kerr think that it is important that the alleged defamatory remarks were made on Facebook?
4. What arguments do you think there are that would oppose Lord Kerr's view of the way in which Facebook is used?
5. Does defamation ever cause significant harm?

6 Legal Reasoning in Judgments

THE HIERARCHY OF PRECEDENT

6.1 As we noted in Chapter 1 there is a hierarchy of courts with respect to precedents. Judgments of the Supreme Court are binding on all courts below it. However, because of a 1960 House of Lords Practice Statement, judgments of the Supreme Court are not binding on itself. The Supreme Court will normally follow its own previous judgments in order to ensure consistency and predict- ability in the operation of the legal system but it is not legally obliged to do so. However, it may be possible to persuade the court that social circumstances have changed so that what it previously held to be the law is no longer good law. Equally it may be possible to persuade the court that its previous judgment was simply badly reasoned.

Judgments of the Court of Appeal, the court below the Supreme Court, are not binding on the Supreme Court. They are binding on all courts below the Court of Appeal. The Court of Appeal is said normally to be bound by its own previous decisions but there are a considerable and increasing number of exceptions to this general rule. In the past several judges in the Court of Appeal have argued that the Court of Appeal should not be bound by its own previous decisions. They have suggested that the reasons for allowing the House of Lords to depart from its own previous decisions are equally valid when applied to the Court of Appeal. In addition to this in practice in many areas of law people cannot afford to take their cases to the Supreme Court; requiring the Court of Appeal to follow its own previous decisions therefore means that law cannot develop quickly enough in the light of changing social circumstances. The court below the Court of Appeal is the High Court. Decisions of the High Court do not bind the Court of Appeal or the Supreme Court. They do bind all courts below the High Court. Decisions of the High Court, however, do not bind the High Court itself.

None of the courts below the High Court create precedents in the same way. Whilst their decisions are binding on the parties to the case they do not create rules of law that are binding on other courts in new cases.

		Importance in Precedence
Supreme Court (formerly House of Lords)	→	Binds courts below but not itself
Court of Appeal	→	Binds courts below and normally binds itself
High Court	→	Binds courts below but not itself
Crown Court	→	Binds no-one
County Court	→	Binds no-one
Family Court	→	Binds no-one

RATIO AND OBITER

Even when a previous case is binding within the hierarchy of the courts, different parts of the judgment have to be treated in different ways. Lawyers distinguish two parts of a judgment: (a) the *ratio decidendi* and (b) that which is *obiter dicta* (*obiter dictum* in the singular). These two terms, ratio decidendi and obiter dicta, are commonly shortened to *ratio* and *obiter*. Put most simply, the ratio in a judgment is that part of reasoning in the judgment which is necessary in order to reach the conclusion that the judge arrived at. It is this that is *binding* on other courts in the hierarchy. Obiter dicta is a term that describes the remainder of the judgment. Examples of things that will usually be obiter dictum include reflections in a judgment on the historical development of a particular area of law or consideration of what decision the court would have made if the facts of the case had been different. Remarks in a judgment that are obiter are not binding on future courts. Thus, for example, in principle a magistrates' court could choose not to follow parts of a judgment from the Supreme Court that were merely obiter dicta, even though the Supreme Court is higher in the hier- archy of courts. However things that are obiter dicta in a judgment cannot

6.2

simply be ignored; they are said to be *persuasive*. In the absence of a binding ratio the court may be influenced by obiter, particularly if that obiter is something that was said in a judgment in one of the higher courts within the legal system such as the Supreme Court or the Court of Appeal.

The basic distinction between ratio and obiter is clear enough. Three things are, however, more difficult. The first is deciding what the ratio of any particular case in fact is. The second is understanding exactly what is meant by saying that obiter is persuasive. The third is deciding to what degree, if at all, the judges actually follow the rules about ratio and obiter when they are arriving at their judgments. All these matters are areas of considerable controversy.

Judges do not, in their own judgments, say which part of the judgment is ratio and which part is obiter. The reader has to decide what the ratio is for themselves. However the decision is not simply a subjective one. What *you* are trying to do is to predict what future *courts* will say the ratio of a past case is. If you can do this then you can predict what the courts will think the case tells them to do. In turn if you can do this you have more chance of saying what judgments future courts will produce. Because this is what you are trying to do it does not matter what you think the ratio is. If your view differs from that of the courts you will not know what the courts are going to do. You need to know what the courts will think. Equally, however, you do not know which judge will be deciding a case in the future. Thus what you are trying to do is to predict what an unknown judge in the future decides is the ratio of a past case. If you are to do this then it would seem that there have to be rules for determining the ratio that both you and the judge follow. If you use the same rules as the judge, and if you both use them correctly, you will arrive at the same answer.

Whilst there is general agreement between many academics and judges about the broad nature of the rules that surround the notions of ratio and obiter there is much disagreement about the detail. One starting point, however, is the observation that legal reasoning in the English courts is usually pragmatic in its nature. This means that the courts do not start with some general statement of legal principle but, instead, tend to begin with the facts of the case before them and then try to say what legal rules apply to those facts. Of course not all the facts in a case are important. The fact that the contract was made on a Friday will not usually matter. Whether or not somebody who is alleged to have conducted an assault was wearing a blue tracksuit or a red one might matter in terms of identifying the culprit but it will not affect how legal rules are applied. Legal reasoning thus begins with the facts of the case but it begins only with what some people have called the *material* facts of the case. These facts are, very roughly, the facts that are central to the law in the case. The question then is how do we determine what are the material facts of a case. What rules help us decide?

The facts of the case are the facts stated in, or sometimes to be implied from, the judgment. It does not matter if the judge is plainly mistaken about those facts. If a judge makes a mistake about the facts of a case that might mean that the case will be taken to a higher appellate court. However, for the purpose of determining the legal rules that flow from the judgment, the facts are as the judge states them. If the judge says that a fact is material then it is so. Judges rarely do this. They usually talk about the facts in the case in their judgments but they often include many that are not material. There are certain presumptions about which are and which are not material facts. Facts about where something happened, when it happened and who it happened to, for example, are rarely material facts. However, the rules run out when it comes to deciding exactly what is a material fact and what is not. A material fact is a fact that is central to the reasoning of the case, central to the line of argument that leads to the conclusion that the judge reached, but it is difficult to be more precise than that. The ratio is then the rule that arises as the result of the judge's reasoning about these material facts.

A ratio in a previous case only binds a court if it is addressing the same legal issue that arises in the new case. The fact that the Supreme Court has decided something about the law of murder will not usually matter if the current case before the court, whichever court it is, is about theft. In order to decide whether there is a binding precedent for a new case before the court it is necessary first to decide what the ratio of a previous case is and then to decide whether or not the previous case and the present case are sufficiently analogous. In deciding this, the notion of material facts is again said to be useful. Are the material facts in the two cases the same or similar? If so there will be a binding precedent. Deciding whether or not a previous case is sufficiently analogous with a new one so as to make a binding precedent is, in itself, a difficult task. Judges will sometimes draw a distinction, sometimes a very fine distinction, between two apparently similar cases. They are then said to *distinguish* the previous case.

All parts of a judgment need to be read because even obiter, although not binding, are persuasive. However, what persuasive means in this context is not entirely clear. "Persuasive" in ordinary conversation means something like "provides good reasons". However persuasive in the context of legal reasoning seems to mean something rather different. The higher the court the dicta comes from the more persuasive it is taken to be. This could be for several reasons. First higher courts are appellate courts. Lower courts might find their judgments taken on appeal to those higher courts. Dicta from the higher courts might indicate how the higher courts will treat a particular issue when it becomes central to a case before it. Secondly the higher the court, in principle, generally the better and more experienced the judges should be. Obiter from such judges ought to have some kind of authority which stems from the knowledge of those who produce the dicta. Neither argument, however, is entirely convincing. Many, perhaps most, cases are not appealed even when they could be because of pressure of time or money. Why, then should lower courts worry about the prospect of appeal? More importantly, if cases are appealed, the appellate courts may change their minds about an issue, particularly when it becomes central to the trial and the argument that counsel puts forward. Obiter remarks are a far from perfect guide to what the authors of those dicta will decide in the future. Equally, even experienced judges make mistakes. A ratio that is clearly incorrectly argued is nevertheless a binding ratio. Is incorrectly argued obiter from a higher court still "persuasive"? It seems that it is but, then, what the word persuasive means is a little mysterious.

Everyone would accept that when the higher courts pass judgments they refer to previous cases. There are very few judgments of any length in the law reports that do not have copious references to past judgments. The traditional view is that the rules described above in chapter one about the hierarchy of the courts and the distinction between ratio and obiter described above in this chapter are sufficiently clear and sufficiently rigid so as to mean that most judicial decisions can be predicted before they are made. It is not just that there are legal rules. There are also rules and principles about how judges make law by referring to past cases and how they interpret statutes. Judges are bound by them. Thus, if you know what they are and if you read enough previous judgments, on most occasions, because of this, you will know what the court is going to decide. However many academics now view such a statement with some scepticism.

We have seen above that, even in a very elementary explanation of the notion of precedent, there are gaps in the rules that surround the notions of ratio and obiter. At the points where these gaps exist, the rules do not tell judges what they must decide. Choice or discretion is given to the judiciary. How large these gaps are is a matter for debate. However they are certainly there. When thinking about how precedent works we also need to take account of the fact that judges make many decisions each year. They make far more than they did in the past. This has created a great mass of previous judgments often offering a range of alternative views about the law in any one area. In trying to decide which precedents are applicable, in distinguishing or not distinguishing previous cases, the judiciary are also faced with choices. Here again the rules that are said to guide them might be thought to be vague and imprecise. Finally many modern judges and an even greater number of academics believe that some judicial decisions involve, at least in part, consideration of policy issues. Legal decisions sometimes involve decisions about things other than legal rules. Rules about ratio, obiter and the hierarchy of the courts are of little assistance in these instances. Here again judges are faced with discretion and choice.

To suggest that the traditional rules of precedent are of limited assistance in explaining how judges reach their decisions is not to argue that judicial behaviour is wholly unpredictable. Equally such a suggestion does not involve arguing that judicial decisions are mere personal whims or that cases that are found in the law reports are inconsequential when looking at legal rules. Instead it is to argue that judicial use of past cases is often more subtle than has previously been thought. Sometimes judges do talk about ratio and obiter in their judgments in the way described above. However this is infrequent. Even when they do not overtly refer to the rules above they may still be following them. Nevertheless what may be as important is a need that judges feel to justify their new decisions by references to what other judges have previously decided. In doing this they are seeking to show that their decisions are in keeping with the spirit of the legal system; they are not just their own individual preferences for what the law ought to be. This constrains what they can decide. Previous case law contains a wealth of views about the law but it does push thought in particular directions and thus makes some decisions more likely than others.

The legislature plainly makes new legal rules. The traditional notion is that common law rules do not alter to meet the requirements of society (or "public opinion"); it is the role of the legislator to remedy this through statutory intervention with specific legislation, and not for the judges to create new rules. The legislature makes law; the judiciary merely apply it. However, many academics and an increasing number of judges would now argue that the judiciary sometimes do more than simply apply existing law; that in looking for rules of law in previous cases the judiciary subtly change the rules, consciously or otherwise, so that they produce the conclusions that they seek. If this is correct the judiciary are, in this sense, just as much legislators as Parliament.

FURTHER READING

6.3 ▶ F. Cownie, A. Bradney and M. Burton, *English Legal System in Context,* 6th edn, Oxford University Press, (2013), Chapter 5.

R. Cross and J. Harris, *Precedent in English Law,* 4th edn, Oxford University Press, (1991).

P. Goodrich, *Reading the Law: Critical Introduction to Legal Method and Techniques*, Wiley Blackwell, (1986), particularly Chapter 6.

7
Statutory Interpretation

JUDGES AND STATUTES

7.1 The traditional view, which has been accepted since at least the nineteenth century, is that the judiciary are bound by and, legally, must apply legislation, whether it is primary legislation or secondary legislation, no matter what its content. This is known as the *doctrine of parliamentary sovereignty*. This principle has the advantage that it separates clearly the role of the legislature, which is democratically elected to pass laws, and the judiciary, whose job it is to use their technical expertise to apply those laws. This, in turn, relates to a political concept, known as *the separation of powers*, under which the legislature, the executive and the judiciary have different but complementary roles in the political running of the country.

When the doctrine of parliamentary sovereignty is applied to the job of the judiciary one potential problem with this approach to the judicial role is that a statute might be passed that does something that is fundamentally objectionable. It might, for example, take away part of the population's right of access to the courts. A political principle, known as *the rule of law,* says, amongst other things, that everybody should be subject to the law and that the law should treat people equally. Many people see this as being fundamental to the maintenance of a liberal democracy. However the doctrine of parliamentary sovereignty in its traditional form does not guarantee that there will be adherence to the rule of law. If Parliament passes a statute saying all people with red hair will no longer have the right to vote the doctrine of parliamentary sovereignty says that the judges should enforce that law. Given that there is no written constitution for the UK, guaranteeing people's rights, this does not seem to be entirely satisfactory.

Not everyone is now convinced that, if a statute was passed that contravened the rule of law, judges should necessarily apply it. Some judges have argued that, at the very least, if a statute takes away the fundamental rights of the population as a whole, or a group of people in the country, it has to do so in very clear language before it could be enforced in the courts. Parliament has to make it plain that they intend to deny people rights that morally the population might think that they ought to have. The majority of people, including the majority of judges, still adhere to the traditional notion of parliamentary sovereignty. However, some people, including some judges, think this principle is too simplistic for the modern era. There should be some limits to what legislation Parliament can pass and expect the judiciary to apply. How we decide what those limits are is a difficult matter. Nevertheless we ought to agree that judges should not enforce every conceivable statute. However, even people who take this view think that judges should normally apply primary or secondary legislation whatever it says, even if, privately, they disapprove of its content.

Even if you do take the view that judges should always apply legislation you have to accept that sometimes an Act or piece of delegated legislation may be unclear or ambiguous. In some cases the difficulty will be resolved by applying one of the general Interpretation Acts. These are Acts that give a definition of words commonly found in legislation. Thus, for example, one Interpretation Act, the Interpretation Act 1978, says that where a piece of legislation uses the word "he" or "she" this should be taken to mean "he or she" unless it is plain from the context that this should not be so. Some Acts have their own interpretation section, in which certain important words or phrases used in the Act are defined. However, if a difficulty cannot be resolved by such an Act or section, if the ambiguity or lack of clarity remains, it is for the judiciary to decide what the legislation means.

THE PRINCIPLES OF STATUTORY INTERPRETATION

7.2 In order to discover the way in which legislation should be applied, the judges have developed a complex network of principles for statutory interpretation, which are designed to assist in the proper application of the law. Although these principles are often called rules they are not rules in the strictest of senses. If you drive above 70 miles per hour, if caught and convicted, you will be punished. The rule is clear and when it is to be applied is clear. The principles of statutory interpretation are much more unclear. There is no definitive source for what any one of these principles actually says. When they should be applied is also a matter of constant debate. This is not to say that they have no substance at all. Judges sometimes talk about them explicitly when they are passing judgment. They are part of the language which many people use when they analyse what judges do. However some people would argue that these so-called principles cloak, in part or whole, what judges do when they interpret statutes. When we look at statutory interpretation, they would argue, we should put the emphasis on the word "interpretation". Judges may talk about these principles of statutory interpretation in their judgments, they would suggest, but what judges actually do is to make personal choices about how to read a statute. Their individual choices are influenced by things like their education and the legal culture in which they work. They are not simply personal whims. For this reason their choices are to some degree predictable. However, for some people, judicial decisions about how to interpret a statute are not really influenced by the principles of statutory interpretation discussed below.

The traditional starting point for statutory interpretation is *the literal rule*. The judiciary ought to look at the statute and apply its words literally. This principle accords with the traditional doctrine of parliamentary sovereignty. Parliament decided what the law should be and expressed their wishes through the language of the statute. The courts must interpret those words literally. However, although the literal rule seems to offer an easy solution to the problem of statutory interpretation, in practice its application raises many difficulties. First words often, and perhaps even usually, have a number of different meanings. We may not be familiar with all of these meanings. In ordinary conversation we use only a limited range of meanings. However, if you look at the 20 volumes of the Oxford English Dictionary, the complexity of the English language immediately becomes apparent. It is also the case that sometimes words have ordinary, everyday meanings and also technical meanings. Equally words are usually read as parts of phrases or sentences. Rules of grammar tell us how to read such groupings but rules of grammar are not precise and are subject to debate.

On the face of it the literal rule seems to take away choice from the judiciary when they interpret legislation. They should just follow the words that Parliament used. But in many instances, and some would argue in almost all instances, language gives us a choice of meanings, with there being more than one literal meaning that could be followed. We have to choose between meanings, to choose between ordinary and technical meanings or to decide which rules of grammar apply to the construction of the particular phrase in the statute before us.

There is no doubt that in the past the literal rule had substantial support from the judiciary. They cited the literal rule as a reason for their judgments. In doing so they denied that they exercised any discretion when they passed judgment. However whether it actually adequately described their practices is another matter. In the present day both most academics and judges, because they acknowledge the complexities of language, will be uncomfortable with the idea that the literal rule will usually be of much assistance in deciding how to interpret a statutory provision. It may be used sometimes but usually it is too simplistic a principle to help when trying to work out what a statute means.

The second principle of statutory interpretation that can be used is *the golden rule* or *the purposive approach*. Following this approach the courts should look at a statute as a whole. Where there is more than one meaning that could be put to a particular provision, and where one of those meanings would lead to an "absurdity or inconvenience" in the context of the interpretation of the statute taken as a whole, then the courts should choose the other meaning, even if grammatically it seems to be the less appropriate choice. It is argued that such an approach, even when it involves not following the literal meaning of the words chosen by Parliament, complies with the traditional notion of parliamentary sovereignty because it could not have been Parliament's intention to write a statute that contained a clear absurdity. In more modern language, when interpreting statutes courts ought to have an eye to the purpose of that statute. This approach does acknowledge that judges play a role in creating law, even when they are interpreting legislation, because they are making choices about what meanings they should apply. However, following this approach, their choice is constrained by the idea that they are making choices that would best fit with what must have been the intention of Parliament when they passed the statute. The choices they make are not personal decisions about what policy they think ought to underlie the law. Moreover the judges are still following the language of the statute.

The final broad principle that is applied to statutory interpretation is *the mischief rule*. The mischief rule still adheres to the traditional notion of parliamentary sovereignty. However the mischief rule says that sometimes Parliament's choice of language in a statute is so poor that any sensible interpretation of the statutory provisions as they have been laid down will not lead to the desired change in the law that was clearly the intention of Parliament. In such cases, following the mischief rule, the courts may be forced to read a statute as though it said something other than what it actually says so as to reach the result that Parliament intended. The statute says X but the courts will read it as though it says Y. One problem in applying this principle lies in knowing how the courts will be sure what the intention of Parliament with respect to an individual statute was. Since the 1990s the courts have increasingly looked to Hansard, the record of what is said in Parliament, to seek to ascertain the intention of statutes. As with the previous principle of statutory interpretation there is no straightforward clash between this principle and the traditional notion of parliamentary sovereignty. The courts are still said to be following the intention of Parliament. However this principle does give the courts considerable discretionary powers to create what is in effect new statutory language. Some will question how far such choices really reflect the court's knowledge of what Parliament actually intended, notwithstanding the contrary evidence of the language they used.

One final important influence on statutory interpretation is the Human Rights Act 1998. The 1998 Act incorporated many of the rights found in the European Convention on Human Rights into domestic law meaning that, in addition to the right that everyone has to take a case to the European Court of Human Rights, they are now enforceable within the domestic courts. When the courts are interpreting a statute they are now required, under the Human Rights Act, to interpret a statute, "so far as possible", so that it accords with the Convention rights. Once again this requirement does not contradict the traditional notion of parliamentary sovereignty. The courts must look at the language of a statute and see whether it can be interpreted in a way that is in keeping with the Convention. This might involve an interpretation that is more strained than it otherwise would be. However Parliament, in the 1998 Act, has told them that is what they should do. Moreover, although there can be a strained interpretation of a statutory provision, the courts must still follow the language of the statute. Where it is not possible to interpret a statute so that it accords with Convention rights the courts can issue a *declaration of incompatibility*. Where this has been done that statute is still valid law but Parliament and others have been alerted to the fact that the provisions of a statute are incompatible with people's Convention rights. In practice Parliament will amend the legislation so that it does not breach people's Convention rights, although this may take some time, but it is not legally bound to do this.

FURTHER READING

7.3 F. Cownie, A. Bradney and M. Burton, *English Legal System in Context*, 6th edn, Oxford University Press, (2013), Chapter 6.

R. Cross, J. Bell and G. Engle, *Cross: Statutory Interpretation*, 3rd edn, Oxford University Press, (1995).

P. Goodrich, *Reading the Law: Critical Introduction to Legal Method and Techniques*, Wiley Blackwell, (1986), particularly Chapter 4.

8
Reading research materials

Chapter 4 explained that one way to answer questions about law was to use research methods taken from the social sciences and humanities. Because this kind of research is the only way in which some questions about law can be answered, it is important that those interested in law can understand it.

8.1

In order to understand research into law you have to understand how and why it is written in the particular way that it is. Once you can understand the structure of the material, you will be able to see whether or not it helps to answer the questions in which you are interested.

Haphazard approaches to research are likely to be unsuccessful, the information gathered being too unrepresentative of the world at large and, therefore, too inaccurate for any conclusions to be drawn safely. Good research is done systematically. Research methods are highly developed. There are three sources of information about how and why the law operates: records, people and activities. There are also three principal methods used in socio-legal research. The researcher may read records, interview people (or send questionnaires), or observe activities.

RECORD READING

8.2

Information is recorded for a wide range of purposes; the information contained depends on the primary purpose of the recording, which is not usually research. For example: applicants in legal proceedings must file an application—the information required depends on the nature of the case; the police must record specific details when people are arrested or detained in custody; courts keep records of each case so they can manage individual cases. Organisations of all sorts keep administrative data about the work they do to establish the productivity of staff, the use of other resources and plan their services. Both case and administrative data can provide the basis for research about aspects of the operation of law.

The researcher has to collect the information required by extracting it from existing records or obtaining access to a database. All the information which could be useful for a particular study may not be available—records may not be complete and the database may not include all the required information.

INTERVIEWS AND QUESTIONNAIRES

8.3

Interviews are conducted in person, either face-to-face or by telephone. Questionnaires are given, sent or made available via the web for the respondents to complete. It is important, in so far as is possible, to ask the same questions in the same way each time so as to get comparable information. Questions may be "open", allowing the respondent to reply in his or her own words, or be "closed", requiring selection of the answer from a choice given by the interviewer. The style and wording of the question is selected to fit the data sought. Whatever the questions, the interview must be recorded. This may be done by using a digital recorder or by the interviewer noting the replies. Interviews are most useful for finding out what reasons people have for what they have done and for exploring their feelings. If questions are asked about the future, the answers can only indicate what respondents currently think they would do. It has also been established that recollection of past events may be inaccurate, particularly about dates, times and the exact sequence of events. Interview and questionnaire design requires considerable skill, as does interviewing itself, if it is to reflect the respondent's views rather than those of the researcher.

OBSERVATION

8.4 The observer attends the event and records what occurs there. The observer may be an outsider; for example, a person watching court proceedings from the public gallery. Alternatively, the observer may be a person actually taking part in the events being described; for example, a police officer researching into the police force. Observation needs to be done systematically and accurately in order to avoid bias. Observers cannot record everything that they see. They must be careful that they do not record only what they want to see and neglect that which is unexpected and, perhaps, thereby unwelcome. One great difficulty in noting observations lies in deciding what to note down and what to omit. What seems unimportant at the time the notes were taken may take on a greater significance when a later analysis is made. It is important that the observer's record is contemporaneous, otherwise the data is weakened by what has been forgotten.

CHOOSING RESEARCH METHODS

8.5 For any particular piece of research, one method may be more suitable than another, because of the nature of the data sources or the approach that the researcher wishes to take. If, for example, you want to research into the reasons litigants have for taking a case to court, there is little point in reading statements of claim because these may have been prepared by lawyers and are likely to reflect the legal requirements rather than the motivation for seeking redress via the courts. Here, the best place to start would be to interview (or send a questionnaire to) litigants. No single method can be said to provide the truth about every situation; some would argue that no method can provide the truth about any situation, for no one truth exists. Each method provides information based on the perceptions of the people who provide it, the record keepers, the interviewers or the observers.

Choice of research method depends not only on what information is sought but also on practicalities. The researcher may not be given access to records or permitted to carry out interviews. Professional bodies and employers are not always willing to let their members of staff participate in research. This may be because they consider the research unethical (perhaps requiring them to divulge information given in confidence), because they are too busy, because they do not see the value of the research or because they wish to conceal the very information in which the researcher is interested.

For many research studies more than one method is used to obtain a complete picture. However, practical matters, including budget and time limits, may mean that not every avenue of enquiry is pursued. What is important is that the methods chosen are appropriate to the subject of study, the approach of the researcher and the conclusions drawn.

SAMPLING

Looking at every case is not normally practical in research. Instead, the researcher takes a sample of cases. Thus, one may interview some lawyers or some defendants or observe, or read records at some courts. If a completely random sample is taken, then it should have the characteristics of the population as a whole. A sample of judges should, for example, include judges of the different ages, backgrounds and experience to be found amongst the judiciary. However, if a characteristic is very rare a sample may not contain any example of having that characteristic. The size of the sample and method of sampling must be chosen to fit with the study. In a study of attitudes of clients to lawyers there is clearly no point in interviewing only successful clients. The number of people refusing to take part in a study is also important. Researchers will try to obtain a high response rate and also attempt to find out if those who refuse are likely to be different in any material way from those who agree to participate in the study.

8.6

RESEARCH FINDINGS

The account of any research will usually include some background information about the subject, the purpose of the study (the questions to be answered) and the methods used. Findings presented in words should cause no difficulty to the reader, but numbers may be quite confusing. Where comparisons are made, it is usually thought better to use *proportions* or *percentages* rather than actual numbers unless the numbers are very small. It is then important to be clear what the percentage represents: for example, was it 20 per cent of all plaintiffs or 20 per cent of successful plaintiffs. Some researchers do not give the actual figures, but prefer to use words such as "some", "most" or "the majority". This is not very helpful, since a word like "majority" can mean anything from 51 per cent to 99 per cent. If the numbers in a study are very small the use of percentages or proportions can itself be misleading. If a researcher looks at 10 people in their study and says 50 per cent of their sample said X this might look more impressive than saying five people said X.

8.7

There is a variety of ways of presenting figures so as to make them clearer. Tables (lists of figures) are commonly used because they make it easier to compare two or more categories or questions. Graphic presentation, using bar charts (histograms), pie charts or graphs, can create a clear overall impression of a complex set of figures.

Figure 1 below is a bar chart. It shows clearly the different numbers of offenders starting different types of probation orders for knife possession each quarter from 2008. Two main types of order were used, and the use of each declined over the period 2008–2012. This chart tells us nothing about the use of imprisonment for knife possession.

Figure 1

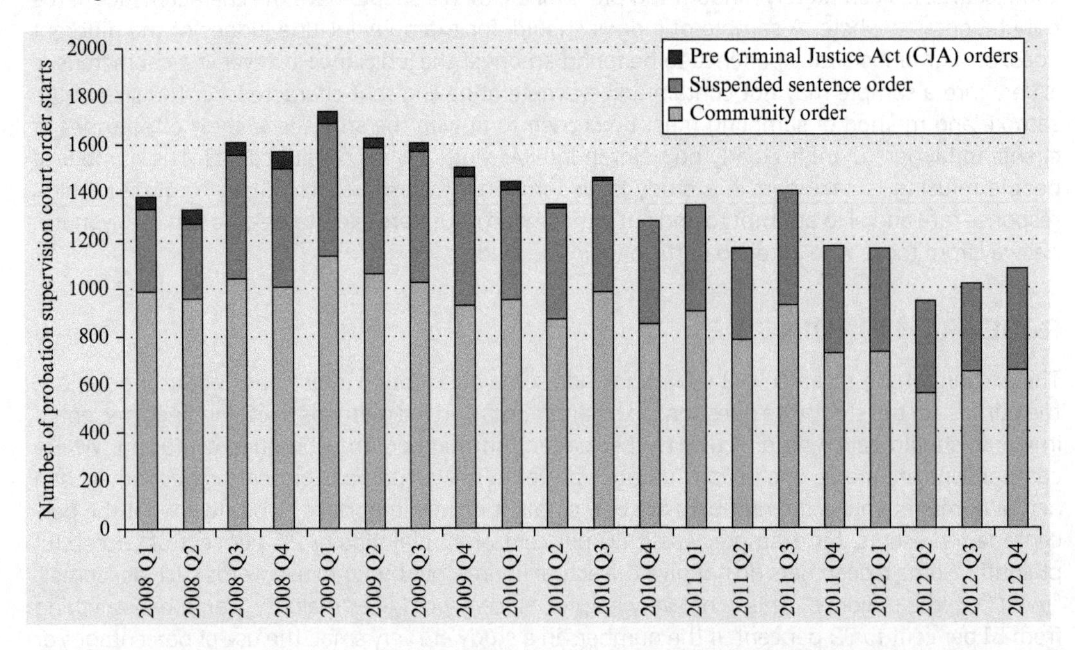

Figure 2 is a pie chart. The whole circle represents 100 per cent of the particular group. The segments represent different percentages. In this example, the exact percentages represented in the different segments have been printed on to the chart. This is not always done. Different circles represent the sentences of those with and without previous convictions for knife possession.

Figure 2

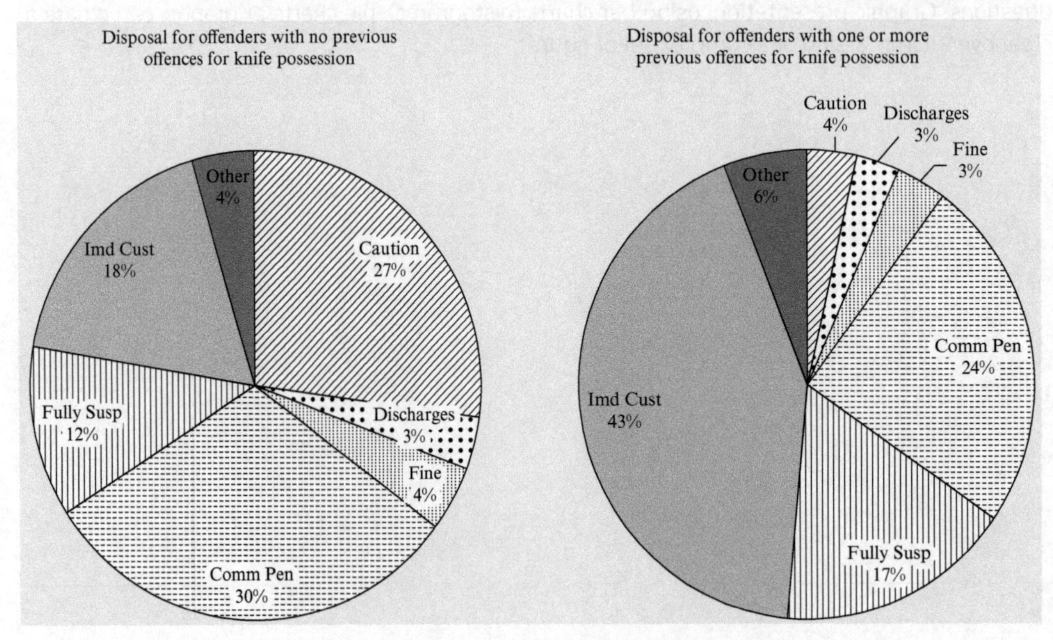

Figure 3 is a graph. This is probably the best way of showing a trend over time. The graph is designed to show the number of people in prison for knife possession between 2007 and 2012. The middle portion of the graph (2009–2010) contains no data. An explanation states that "due to technical problems relating to the supply of statistical data, it is not possible to provide figures" for this period.

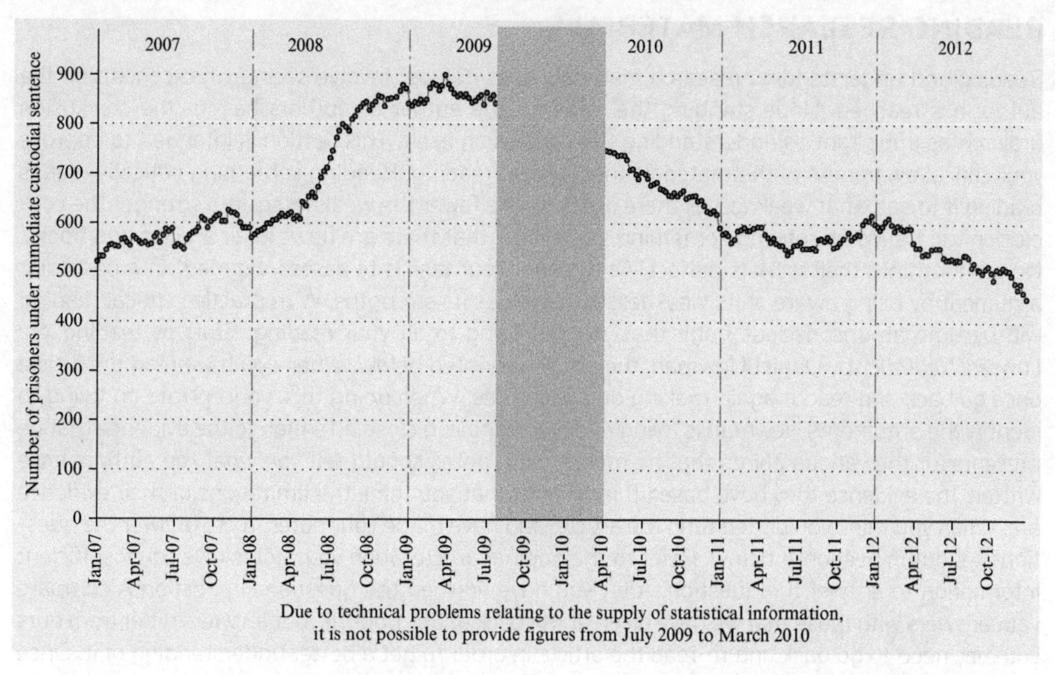

Figure 3

As well as graphs and tables, most researchers will state the conclusions that they have drawn from the material and summarise the main findings of the study. It is crucial that the data should establish no more and no less than is stated in the conclusions. Some researchers make great claims for their data, whilst others do not draw out all the answers that it could provide. To avoid being persuaded by poor reasoning, look at the data and see what conclusions seem appropriate, then read the explanation given, and compare it with what you originally thought. A critical approach to any empirical research should always consider the following three questions. First, are the methods chosen appropriate? This includes both, "have the right questions been asked" and "have the right people (people who should know about the topic) been asked". There many have been better sources of information available to the researcher, but were the ones used good enough for this study? Secondly, is the sample big enough and has it been properly drawn? Thirdly, does the data justify the conclusions that have been drawn? If it does not, can you see any other conclusions that it would justify?

Research often leaves as many questions raised as answers provided. Further studies may be indicated, interesting new areas that need to be explored. Studying this type of material will, hopefully, increase your interest and insight into the operation of law. It will not provide you with all the answers.

Exercise 5

READING RESEARCH MATERIALS

8.8 ▶ Reading and understanding research materials does not just involve seeing what conclusion the author has reached. Understanding the evidence the author or authors has for the conclusion drawn is as important as understanding the conclusion itself. This section is intended to improve your critical awareness of the materials that you are reading. Reading something critically means reading it to see what weaknesses there are in it. The fewer the weaknesses the stronger the conclusion will be. When reading something, remember that there are flaws in all articles and books. No author thinks their work is perfect. As a reader your task is to assess the merit of a particular argument by being aware of its weaknesses as well as its strengths. With practice critical reading will become an unconscious habit that you will bring to all your reading. Start by reading *Are Lawyers Neurotic?* by Daniel Newman, the article reprinted below. When you have read the article once go back and read it again making detailed notes. When doing this, concentrate on trying to identify the arguments Newman is trying to develop, paying close attention to the evidence that he presents for the various points that he makes. Your notes should tell you what the authors have written, the evidence they have based this on and what you think the limitations of their evidence are. When you think you understand the article, and have made your notes, try to answer the questions set out in Section A below. Refer to the original article when your notes give you insufficient information to answer the question. After you have finished the questions in Section A compare your answers with those that we have given at the back of this book. If your answers differ from ours you may need to go back and re-read the article in order to get a better understanding of it. Once you are sure you understand the answers to Section A go on and complete the questions that are set out in Section B.

INTERNATIONAL JOURNAL OF THE LEGAL PROFESSION, 2018
VOL. 25, NO. 1, 3–29
https://doi.org/10.1080/09695958.2017.1359612

Are lawyers neurotic?

Daniel Carl Newman

Cardiff Law School, Cardiff University, Cardiff, UK

ABSTRACT
This paper reports on an ethnographic exploration of the lawyer–client relationship focusing on the attitudes held by legally aided lawyers to their criminal clients. The study combines formal interviews with participant observation in a mixed methodology approach designed to give voice to the lawyers taking part as well as allow the researcher to provide their own perspective. The research produced two quite contradictory viewpoints as lawyers claimed to hold positive attitudes of their clients in interview while presenting negative attitudes under observation. To reconcile this difference, the author suggests considering psychoanalytic literature on self-image, which can be applied to show that the lawyers may have been displaying signs of Freudian defence mechanisms and, ultimately, presented as neurotic in their practise.

Introduction

This paper explores the lawyer–client relationship under criminal legal aid by considering whether lawyers in England and Wales might be understood as neurotic in their attitudes towards clients. The reason for pursuing this line of enquiry on lawyers' mental states is not to claim that individual lawyers suffered with neuroses but to provide an analytical schema that might help illuminate why lawyers under research might say one thing about clients in interview and quite another when observed during their everyday practise.[1] It is important to understand how lawyers perceive their clients because the state of the lawyer–client relationship can be held up as a key indicator of procedural justice in the English criminal courts. This research is premised on the notion that access to justice requires access to lawyers (Young & Wall, 1996).[2] The principle of the equality of arms means the criminal justice system presupposes roughly equal resources and expertise on both sides of the equation. The self-referential nature of the legal system, with its complex web of technical language and internal rules, acts to overwhelm and alienate defendants (McBarnet, 1981). In order that those suspected and accused of crimes can comprehend what is going on and, thus, properly take part in their own cases, Cain (1983) highlights that they need a lawyer to act as translator. The court system removes the defendant from the criminal process in significant ways: they become definitively a

CONTACT Daniel Carl Newman ✉ NewmanDC@Cardiff.ac.uk

client, losing the ability to be active players as they are rendered reliant upon lawyers.[3] They are locked into a process of what Ericson & Baranek (1982) term 'legal dependency'.

With access to lawyers of such importance that it might be considered a human right to have a lawyer facilitate understanding of the criminal justice system (Luban, 2014),[4] it becomes imperative that research ensures legal aid lawyers practise active defence and appear fully committed to their client, always putting their clients' interests first. This is the approach Smith (2013) labels 'zealous advocacy' whereby the lawyer acts as a loyal partisan to their client, with the lawyer giving themselves fully to their client and all they represent. The adversarial advocacy model is perhaps one of the most commonly used means of attaining ethical practice by ensuring that lawyers work to give voice to their clients (Parker & Evans, 2007). Access to lawyers in and of itself cannot be properly considered enough to produce access to justice in any meaningful sense of the word. Rather, the lawyer–client relationship must properly function to ensure that lawyers serve their clients to the best of their abilities and display a commitment to their client that is beyond reproach whatever the eventual result of a case. It is procedural justice that is crucial here and lawyers should be understood to take on an important role in realising defendant desires to feel they have been fairly and decently treated during the course of a case (Tyler, 1988). Mather *et al.* (1995) have said that lawyers are like taxi drivers taking passengers (clients) to their destination, meaning it is vital that each side can properly communicate so that they both know where they want to go. Sarat & Felstiner's (1988) work went a step further, suggesting that lawyers often controlled the destination as well as the route; lawyers generally make up their own minds about the course of action to be taken and spend much time persuading their clients. Indeed, Sarat & Felstiner (1995) found that lawyer and client interests are fundamentally at odds, meaning lawyers focus on ensuring what the lawyers think important predominates. The aforementioned studies concerned divorce in the USA but, as a more general point, it has been suggested that "the production of justice might be defined as a dimension of the relationship of lawyers to clients" (Felstiner, 2001: 191). The exchange of knowledge that is the lawyer–client relationship makes justice about a social interaction (Suseno *et al.*, 2006). Reducing justice to this exchange between the two means it is imperative to pay due attention to the social side of the lawyer–client relationship. This paper addresses that social relationship by looking at the attitudes lawyers hold towards their clients with these attitudes duly conceived of as the foundation that underpins the whole structure of doing access to justice. Lawyers do not necessarily need to like their clients to believe that they deserve representation and/or to provide competent representation but, if lawyers do not like their clients, it raises interesting questions about the nature of the lawyer–client relationship that are best brought out into the open and worked through.

The issue of attitudes, then, presents an invaluable aid through which to engage with the data obtained through lawyer–client research. The ethnographic data in this research, however, have not produced a simple, unified picture of the issue of attitudes in the lawyer–client relationship. Instead, two apparently contradictory narratives arose. In formal interviews, lawyers presented positive attitudes when talking about their clients; however, participant observation showed lawyers displaying negative attitudes when discussing clients. In this paper, both accounts are offered individually. Material is presented to allow an appreciation of typical statements made by lawyers, first, in interview, and then at work. Thereafter these are drawn together into a critical debate reflecting on why there was such divergence and considering what impact this may have had on the lawyer–client relationship. The paper raises the question of whether the practise of these lawyers was displaying symptoms of neuroses. A loose appropriation of Freud (and, later, Jung) is offered, albeit one that is intended to say more about approaches to practise than individual psychology, as ideas from psychoanalytic theory are used as a heuristic device to promote new ways of thinking about the lawyer–client relationship. This echoes Shiner's (2010) study on police practice, wherein a psychoanalytic reading of self-image was offered to critique Hoyle's (1998) previous research. For Shiner, appropriating psychoanalysis provides a means to move beyond conventional socio-legal study with its focus on internal mental processes as well as the usual social activity. In Shiner's paper, an analysis of the psychological processes underpinning what the officers actually say provides a greater contextualisation of the statements and actions, through conceiving of the findings in terms of 'organisational defence mechanisms' rather than simply social processes.

There is a rich potential for overlap between psychoanalysis and the law, as deftly outlined by Goldstein (1968: 1053):

> Psychoanalysis endeavours to provide a systematic theory of human behaviour. Law, both as a body of substantive decisions and as a process for decision-making, has been created by man to regulate the behaviour of man. Psychoanalysis seeks to understand the workings of the mind. Law is mind-of-man-made.

Accordingly, there has been legal scholarship drawing on the insight provided by Freudian theory into the ideologies that underpin systems of law (Caudill, 1991), exploring key Freudian tenets such as motivation, aggression and symbolism in legal principles (Schoenfeld, 1973) or considering the impact of Freud's pleasure principle on the regulation of morality (Cornell, 1997). Frank (2009) has applied Freudian psychoanalysis to lawyers, equating the legal practitioner's apparent need to perpetuate the myth that law is precise and coherent to a child's quest for security and authority in their father. Beyond this, in general, there is a large literature on law and psychology with several journals devoted to that field alone but Freudian theory has not been previously applied to legal practice. There has been little attention paid to ways Freudian theory can shine a light on the lawyer–client relationship. The value of Freudian theory in this paper is to allow the prospect of a more multifaceted, profound analysis with which to augment existing knowledge around the lawyer–client relationship. Such understandings have previously gone unheeded in work on the legal profession so there seems worth in applying them here. The deliberately relaxed usage of neuroses in this argument is purely about stimulating debate and not offering a diagnosis. As such, the paper offers an attempt at an embryonic explanatory framework revolving around self-image that is intended to open a dialogue and initiate discussion. Before outlining the results, however, the paper considers the methods and methodology of the study.

Giving voice to lawyers

This research is based on a 12-month ethnographic fieldwork split evenly between three law firms specialising in legally aided criminal defence.[5] Social relationships such as those between lawyers and clients are best understood by empirical social research that allows us to capture the reality of these interactions. Traditionally, empirical social research on the lawyer–client relationship has been somewhat lacking – whether due to the difficulty of gaining access to the legal profession or the lack of social research training for legal scholars (Hillyard, 2002). There has, then, long been a need for socio-legal research to shed light on the lawyer–client relationship (Abel, 1988). In the 1990s, two studies answered the call for social enquiry into the lawyer–client relationship with *Standing Accused* by McConville *et al.* (1994) and *The Reality of Law* by Travers (1997b) becoming iconic pieces of research. Although more recent socio-legal research has produced excellent insight into the lawyer–client relationship,[6] these two studies remain held up as key reference points, in no small part due to their scale: offering substantial ethnographic fieldwork of a kind that it is rare to gain funding or consent to undertake. Ethnography provides insight into the richness of social life that illuminates the lawyer–client relationship. At least it should, but wider understanding has been clouded by the way these studies produced seemingly contradictory results. McConville *et al.* revealed lawyers with little but contempt for their clients showing wanton disrespect, while Travers talked about a profession that admired clients and dedicated their lives to supporting them. In part, this divergence results from the epistemologies underpinning the studies.

A disagreement over methodology led to a heated exchange between the two research teams, wherein Travers (1997a) outlined his interpretivist analytical framework in opposition to the structuralism of McConville *et al.*[7] McConville *et al.* were accused of offering research that simply reflected their own values and ignored the perspectives of those they studied, with out of context examples deployed to support a chosen line of attack. These authors hit back and criticised Travers' research for refusing to challenge the outlooks of those he studied, running the real possibility of a work that naïvely takes their views and self-justifications at face value. McConville *et al.* sought a larger sample of firms to produce generalisable results, although this meant they stayed with some firms for very short periods, while Travers studied one firm for a significant length of time, allowing for thick description, but, as a result, had difficulty arguing the wider applicability of his data. My research followed these studies; I adopted ethnography in an attempt to reconcile the discrepancy between the two and help further understanding of the lawyer–client relationship in England and Wales.

To bridge the gap between structuralism and interpretivism I combined insights from both, splitting the 12 months between three firms. With four months at each, I spent the amount of time that Travers was at one firm in three firms, making my results more generalisable. At the same time, the dozens of firms studied by McConville *et al.* means my results are not as generalisable but they do allow some wider applicability with the added bonus of offering thick description of different firms. As such, the research contains both local knowledge lawyers themselves would recognise (to satisfy the interpretivist) and more general critique that allows me to engage in wider debates (to satisfy the structuralist). In addition to time considerations, the research was divided up into two phases at each firm: an initial three months of participant observation, shadowing the lawyers as they went about their daily practise in cafes, offices, police stations, meeting rooms and courts; and a final month of formal exit interviews with 35 practitioners, allowing the lawyers to reflect on their practise. The former are more easily shaped by me as researcher than the latter, with my notebooks full of the events as I saw them in contrast to tape-recorded interviews allowing lawyers to speak on the record. The observation was kept separate from the interviews to further balance structuralist and interpretivist concerns. These were formal exit interviews rather than informal exchanges or concurrent interviews to keep distance between the two components and use this space to properly give lawyers the ability to describe their practise in their own words as removed from my influence as possible.

It follows that the results offered in this paper are organised into two sections where representative data from the research are presented to highlight the data as I found them. The interviews are offered first, then the observation. These accounts are presented relatively free of critical engagement although they are selectively arranged to facilitate understanding of what happened. The approach can be characterised as thematic analysis: a method for identifying, analysing and reporting patterns across a data set that, thereon, minimally organises this information in rich detail (Braun & Clarke, 2006). This organisational structure pays heed to both the structuralist and interpretive traditions by providing spaces in which the lawyers' voices can be heard without ceding my responsibility as researcher.

In deploying this approach, the key issue for this paper will become clear: how do we reconcile the difference between what the lawyers say in interview with the situation I collated through my account of the observation? For clarity, it is important to try and explain the different accounts of the lawyer–client relationship that emerge from balancing these two methodological approaches. In particular, I offer the line that psychological insight might be of benefit. Ahead of considering the value of locating the results in a psychoanalytic context, however, it is important to first consider the data arising from the research in interviews and under observation.

Lawyers in interview

Throughout the interviews the lawyers in this study talked with much passion about the importance of access to justice. Many identified this as the chief motivation that drove them into legally aided criminal defence and pushed them to work as hard as they were able thereafter. The following quote presents one lawyer's reason for entering this branch of the profession:

> I wanted to go into legally aided work – I had idealistic views on helping people: the less advantaged, etc. So I was looking at crime, justice, human rights aspects. I had spent a year working for a charity before that. It was all about helping people for me.

In the next quote, another lawyer discusses how driven they are in their practice:

> I'm very passionate about justice. I wouldn't even consider doing anything else. I mean, I know logically, if I did another type of law, I might earn twice what I'm being paid. But that wouldn't interest me. It's access to justice I believe in.

These excerpts from interviews are entirely representative of the practitioners from the three firms studied. Two thirds of the lawyers – 24 out of 35 – identified access to justice reasoning in their rationale for entering this branch of the profession while every single lawyer presented such a worldview as underlining their continued practise. Lawyers would talk about the importance of preserving a criminal justice system "based on fair play" that provided "equal treatment for all". In particular, almost all – 32 out of 35 – explicitly identified their own role in, what was labelled as, "maintaining the rule of law". The following quotes highlight the importance such lawyers found in their role serving justice:

> I am proud to be in criminal defence. It's an ego thing, I suppose; I think it's hugely important. You have a member of the public who knows nothing and they have the might of the state against them and we are the knights in shining armour standing between the individual and the dragon of the state.

> Criminal defence work is important and I think societies are often judged on how they treat the sick, the mentally ill and their own criminal population. There is part of me that feels incredibly privileged to be a part of all of this, to have a perception of this and

> a knowledge and an understanding of our society that means, one, I am not scared of it, and, two, I'm trying in some small way to do something that contributes perhaps to improving it.

By assuming this crucial position helping to deliver justice for all, the lawyers saw themselves as noble professionals representing a public service ethos that one practitioner branded a "social agenda". This social agenda entailed the lawyers claiming to practise for, what were often referred to as, "altruistic" reasons, with lawyers stating that they "wanted to be on the side of the underdog", "standing up for the vulnerable" or "fighting for the little guy". The lawyers saw themselves as part of the welfare state, providing a vital public service; facilitating a public good. This was clear in the frequent comparisons with medical professionals that lawyers provided throughout the interviews. More than half of the lawyers – 20 out of 35 – drew such parallels with other areas of public service or identified legally aided criminal defence within the context of the welfare state, as in the following extract:

> What we are doing here is most accurately described as part of the welfare state. We're the part that goes ignored and people don't think about until they actually have to use us for whatever reason. Doctors, teachers, social security, everyone sees those parts and recognises their importance: we all rely on them and we all value them. But do we all need lawyers? Maybe we will, hopefully not. But there will always be some people who do, quite often the lower rungs of society, people who were failed by the education system and have no life chances and need someone to help them. They can't pay for lawyers, so it's us that come between them going to prison and getting into gangs, drugs, generally wasting their life or helping them to get out of it, to get help, keep their family together. We help the people that no one thinks about or certainly don't care about.

Accordingly, there was a great sense of self-importance amongst these lawyers with a clear theme running throughout the interviews that their work was "important to society" and "supporting those who are forgotten by society". The social agenda these lawyers served made them perceive themselves as a fundamental element of the welfare state.

In order to meet the social agenda, it was apparent that client-centred practice was the ideal these lawyers professed to adhere to. At some stage of the interview every lawyer highlighted that their practise was solely focused on meeting the wants and needs of those suspected or accused of crime. The following quotes give a flavour of the lawyers' explanation on how they delivered a client-centred service:

> Always put the clients first, that's the first rule of being a lawyer … you always work your hardest to give the client a result that they are happy with.

> At the end of the day, I'm happy if they're [the client] happy. When you break it down, it isn't complicated what we do: someone comes to us for help and we help them. End of story.

> It's all about the clients .... We wouldn't be here without them so it's important to remember that.

Many lawyers appeared to take pride in their serving clients in this way, with more than half – 19 out of 35 – explicitly making clear the satisfaction they derived from doing their best for clients. The lawyers talked about clients with no little sense of affection, expressing empathy and even respect for those they served, with several explaining that they were happy to "go above and beyond" for their clients. While only two addressed individual clients in their examples, most – 30 out of 35 – talked of their clients as a whole in positive terms extolling the "long-term relationships" that were built up, as in the following quote:

> We are a community practice and I am very proud to say that I represent this community. The strong relationships I am able to build with clients means that the community recognises me as one of them. I'm not from [the local area] but I feel accepted because I serve them .... This is very important to me.

With clients so exalted within the lawyers' vision of themselves as professionals fighting for justice, it followed that almost all – 33 out of 35 – lawyers in these interviews would emphasise the manner in which they fought hard for their clients at all times. The following quotes reflect the strong message that the lawyers saw themselves as practising active defence:

> You always fight for them [the client] ... stand tall for them because they need you.

> I am robust in my efforts to always push my client's case. We all are, it's what we do and why we are so popular: we stand up for them [the clients].

> Whether you are in a trial or not, it's a battle, all of it is .... The defendant asks us to fight their cause; they trust us to stick up for them. So we fight .... I still call it going into battle ... for them [the clients].

Lawyers were resolute in the idea that they always stood up for their clients; it was identified at the heart of a client-centred practice, the *raison d'être* of their public service remit and the essence of what it meant to be a professional. The lawyers were not unrealistic, and they explained how cases that went to trials were the minority and that many clients wanted to plead guilty, but all the same they presented this combative ideal of what they did for clients.

Overall, then, the interviews presented client-centred practice across all of the firms with lawyers who placed great stock in their public service role serving the vulnerable and needy. This image was in glaring contrast with that which emerged from the observation.

Lawyers under observation

While the interviews saw lawyers talking encouragingly about their clients, locating clients at the centre of their work, the observation showed quite the opposite scenario in practise. Lawyers displayed deeply negative feelings towards their clients, conceptualising clients in a most disparaging manner. First and foremost, the lawyers adopted a uniform approach of treating clients as if they were idiots, with all 35 lawyers at some point referring to an individual client by such condemnatory terms as "stupid", "moron" or "so stupid he makes me want to cry". The tone lawyers adopted when considering their clients' level of intelligence is reflected in the following quotes made to me, in turn, before, after and, in an aside, during meetings with clients:

> Look at this fool, have a read of that [his statement to police] .... It always seems to be me who gets stuck with these idiots.

> Well, he won't be joining Mensa any time soon. I doubt he could even read; he could barely talk.

> How are you keeping a straight face? This tosser is thick as shit.

Beyond simply pointing out how mentally deficient the lawyers believed their clients to be, the lawyers appeared to revel in the comedy they found mocking the supposed stupidity of those they were tasked with serving. Joking about their clients was something that every lawyer drew on as a foundation of their relationship with me and each other as in the following exchange between two lawyers:

> Lawyer 1: You want to stick around and check my guy out.
> Lawyer 2: Bit of entertainment is he?
> Lawyer 1: Thick like you wouldn't believe. I wouldn't be surprised if he gets his name wrong.

That the lawyers I observed did not think much about the understanding of their clients highlighted how the lawyers appeared to look down on their clients as inferior. The superiority displayed by these lawyers was taken a stage further in the moral judgement that was made of clients' characters.

Again and again in this research, lawyers – 35 out of 35 – would pass comment on the "type" of client, sneering about how "low" or "vile" clients were and that they were a "waste of space". While lawyers may be pleasant to a client's face – there were only a handful of occasions I saw lawyers openly rude to clients – lawyers were frequently patronising and could be extremely keen to communicate their distaste for the client as soon as they were out of earshot. Lawyers would pass judgement on the clothes clients were wearing or the way they looked. The following quotes represent some of the aversion displayed by these lawyers and the perception that clients were offensively lower class than them:

> He came in here looking all smart. It's just a pity his trainers didn't match his suit

> I did not expect someone with such a posh name to look like that. Typical inbred.

> What a dirty bastard. I want to wash myself now, I tried everything I could to avoid shaking his hand . . . . I bet he stunk.

Some clients were damned for the area they came from ("have you seen what comes from that estate?"), others for their family ("I wouldn't expect anything different, I know his mother too … she's a sight") and others for the offences they were charged with even before guilt was ascertained ("not a pleasant man at all"). Seeing clients as representatives of an "underclass", to use the term offered by at least five of the lawyers, lawyers were willing to condemn the moral culpability of those who presented themselves to them at court. Demeaning comments of the type that these lawyers would regularly offer on clients could be taken to reflect a view of these clients as somehow deserving of their status as criminals, a view that saw its realisation in a widespread presumption of guilt.

Lawyers in this study routinely believed their clients to be guilty throughout the observation, with all 35 displaying such prejudices at one point or another – sometimes before the lawyer had talked to the client, others even before they had received any of the prosecution material or their client's statement. Such practise is reflected in the following examples of comments made to me:

> I recognise this name . . . . He's going to be guilty, he comes from a family full of them.

> Look at the colour of this file. Never believe a client from there.

> I hope this idiot doesn't waste our time. I bet he wants to have a trial, pointless.

Past simply believing clients guilty, at some stage, I saw every lawyer push clients to plead guilty, in many cases despite the client asserting their innocence and wanting to plead not guilty. There are numerous reasons why a lawyer might convince their client to plead guilty, including systematic factors such as communicating the sentence discount, the expectation for plea bargaining since *R v. Turner* and the Criminal Procedure Rules that oblige the defence to cooperate with the prosecution. Another possibility is financial incentives, whereby it is more efficient for a lawyer to conclude a case early to get a fee for doing little work, with criminal legal aid increasingly a volume-based industry whereby processing lots of cases quickly is imperative to financial survival. McConville & Marsh (2014) would suggest the reasons combine so that defence lawyers work to serve the interests of the state (not necessarily the client) in ensuring a conveyor-belt of guilty defendants. The negative attitude of lawyers acts to ensure their complicity in making sure clients go guilty.

The following quote shows the approach taken by many lawyers, whereby they set out to persuade a client to change their plea:

> Our job today will just be persuading the client to plead guilty. It's an assault. So, really, our job today is to explain to him that there's no point in having a trial and he might as well plead guilty. He's usually alright, usually listens.

In a similar vein, I witnessed around two-thirds of the lawyers – 22 out of 35 – explicitly encouraging clients to plead guilty without getting the client's side of the story despite the client insisting they were not guilty. In the following extract, a lawyer begins a meeting with a client by making it clear that there should be a guilty plea:

> Lawyer: So, how are we pleading? Oh, I should warn you that the judge you'll be appearing before is very tough on public order offences. He's also very tough on breaches, and he's been sending people down all day for failures to surrender.
>
> Client: Oh, right. I wanted to go not guilty, I didn't do anything.
>
> Lawyer: I think you need to think very carefully about this before you come to a decision. There might be a deal on the table.

If clients were resistant to pleading guilty, the lawyers could get quite angry and at least half a dozen engaged in agitated rants about clients following a meeting, complaining that "he just won't follow instructions", "this idiot just doesn't listen" or "who does he think he is ignoring me like that?". Lawyers were so sure in their assessment of the moral deprivation and legal blameworthiness of the clients they encountered that client attempts to resist these stereotyped identities were met with consternation. In short, the lesser beings represented by these clients should listen to the lawyers and accept what the lawyer wants.

Overall, instead of a client-centred practice, the lawyers under observation showed a practitioner-centred practice in which the clients were, at best, a bothersome irrelevance, and, at worst, a problem to be eliminated. This image was in stark contrast to that produced from the interviews, a contradiction explored in the remainder of this paper as I bring in insight from the psychological literature.

Positive or negative attitudes

This study produced two contrasting images of the lawyer–client relationship. To read the interviews, lawyers had positive attitudes towards their clients. Under observation, there emerged negative attitudes. It seems important, therefore, to try to account for the difference between the attitudes claimed and displayed. Perhaps the immediate explanation that springs to mind is that someone is lying in this research. First and foremost, I may be claimed to be lying; perhaps this is what the lawyers would say: the positive attitudes they described in interview are true but I twisted the events depicted in the observation in order to produce a salacious story to make my written account more interesting. Maybe I had a hidden agenda all along that looked to cast lawyers in a bad light as so often happens when academics write about them. It would be hard for me to defend myself to such accusations, all I can offer is my word and to hope that readers credit me with more integrity than that.

Alternatively, maybe the lawyers were lying – and this seems a common-sense approach to take when presented with self-justifications that do not tally with the facts as witnessed. The events shown in the observation are the reality of lawyer attitudes while their interviews represent an attempt at image management to cover up any malpractice. There is an argument that lawyers would need to attend to the bad impression created by their practise because there was a real possibility it could be used to show that they fall short of the expectations outlined in the Solicitors Regulation Authority (2007) *Code of Conduct*, which posits their central responsibility to clients. The observation lasted for a long time and I built up good rapport, thus the lawyers were off-guard and acted naturally. This meant the possibility of maintaining a superficially client-centred practice could not be realistically achieved so they had to engage in damage limitation after the matter when they reflected on what might be written about them. Under observation, the lawyers had no control over what I was writing in my notebook but, in taped interviews, their views were a matter of record, which would inevitably focus the mind on presenting a constructive picture of their practise. In such circumstances, perhaps it would be hard to envisage them doing anything other than engaging in a public relations charm offensive.

While I recognise many will be convinced by the latter reasoning, I believe it is possible to take issue with such explanation. It seems a little crude to reduce understanding to a rehashing of the stereotypical 'lying lawyer' trope. Personally, I felt as though I would be making a knee-jerk reaction to just write off the fieldwork in such simplistic terms and wondered whether there was something more to the jarring juxtaposition of these two accounts. Better would be a rationale that gives more depth to the issue and can be read either in place of or, at least, side by side with the notion that the lawyers were purposively telling lies. Rather, I explore an alternative approach whereby lawyers could legitimately claim to hold positive attitudes even while displaying negative attitudes and, crucially, do so while unaware of any apparent inconsistency. As such, the explanation explored in the remainder of this paper is premised on lawyers having learnt to differentiate between the client in general and a client in particular. What we are dealing with here is a question of attitude, which is an internal psychological construct developed over time and subject to change under the influence of external factors.

An attitude can be understood as "a summary evaluation of an object" (Bohner & Wanke, 2002: 5). Attitudes are made up of two elements: an object and a response to that object. The object could encompass any of a wide array of stimuli, from the inorganic to the animate, the non-figurative to the tangible. The response to that object involves a collection of cognitive, affective and behavioural parts, best conceptualised as beliefs, emotions and responses (Rosenberg & Hovland, 1960). Classical conditioning suggests that frequent and recurrent connection between the object and, either, positive or negative stimuli shapes (and can reshape) the nature of an individual's evaluation of the object (Staats & Staats, 1958). In a famous study, researchers consistently paired the names Ed and Ben with variously positive and negative stimuli to condition participants to see people with those names in a certain way (Berkowitz & Knurek, 1969). Attitudes, then, are learnt and can alter; a person's attitude to an object depends on the associations they have with that object at any particular moment of their life. Such insight can be applied to the lawyers who might be said to have learnt to hold particular attitudes to their clients. The learning of these attitudes, however, has not been a simple process, as various challenges to the self-image of these lawyers have complicated the issue of lawyer attitudes leading to internal mental conflict and the ability to harbour conflicting positive and negative attitudes concurrently.

Lawyers' self-image

Katz' (1982) work on the lawyer–client relationship has shown that the lawyer's professional self-image is the most salient factor to consider when looking at the approach to practise, with clients dependent on state provision essentially finding themselves reliant on the perception a lawyer has of themselves and their work. Self-image refers to the representations that people have of themselves (Meffre, 2005). In psychoanalytic theory, self-image is developed by interacting with others. When considering self-image, Freud represents the most notable authority. Indeed, it was Freud's work that legitimised the seeking of the impact subconscious processes exert on personality. Freudian theory entered day-to-day life and popular culture many years ago, from references to Freudian slips to searching for the underlying meaning behind irrational acts. In contrast, Freud has been much maligned in the social sciences – especially in the UK (Bocock, 1981). Sociologists have resisted treating Freud as a social theorist, marginalising him as a therapist. While his work centred on the unconscious, it did not exclude the social and Freud himself saw sociology as applied psychology providing a testing ground for his concepts of the mind. His theories operate at the intersection between the individual and society, allowing us to fully consider the relationship between the two. It has perhaps been easier for sociologists to avoid the complexity that engaging with the individual necessarily imported into their theory (Craib, 1989). The result, however, has been at times a stunted social theory, which operated on the surface and failed to understand how individuals related to one another.[8] Freudian theory, then, offers latent potential to improve our social knowledge.

Freud's theory was far from perfect though. He was mistaken in claiming psychoanalysis as a science because it cannot satisfy the falsifiability criterion. Further, the theory has tended towards dogmatism without allowing room for criticism. These drawbacks can be overcome through using select Freudian concepts as and when they are judged to add value to an analysis under Butler's

(1999) 'bricolage' approach. A loose and reflexive appropriation of the Freudian toolbox allows for a social theory that can properly examine the concealed processes that influence social actors but may otherwise be ignored (Young, 1940). Most useful for the purposes of this paper is Freud's (1989) treatment of self-image, which centres on his understanding of the ego. The ego is one of the three components of the mind in Freudian analysis, operating together with the id and the super-ego. The id is the lowest level of the mind, which contains the basic, instinctual drives. The id is unconscious and driven by the pleasure principle that seeks constant gratification through the avoidance of pain and discomfort. In contrast, the super-ego is the highest level of the mind, the organised part of the personality structure, largely (but not completely) unconscious that internalises cultural rules. The super-ego strives for perfection as it attempts to attain social acceptance through imposing the moral judgements of the surrounding society. It is the ego that mediates between the id and super-ego as it attempts to balance between the primitive drives of the id and the critical calculations of the super-ego.

The ego is the site of human consciousness, whereby the largely conscious sense of self operates to determine the role individuals should take in wider society. While the id is driven by pleasure, the ego follows the reality principle and looks for socially acceptable ways to satisfy our base instincts, thereby arbitrating between the id and the social world. While self-image arises from the interplay of all three parts of the mental structure, the extent to which the ego constitutes the organised part of the personality attributes it the central role in shaping self-image. The ego-ideal emerges here as the inner image of the self whereby the ego attempts to realise the perfection demanded by the super-ego. The super-ego is "the vehicle of the ego ideal by which the ego measures itself, which it emulates, and whose demand for ever greater perfection it strives to fulfil" (Freud, 1995: 81). To achieve perfection, the ego establishes a series of rules to follow that enforce standards that must be achieved. The attainment of these goals leads to a sense of accomplishment with a strong feeling of pride in success in meeting the targets essential for a healthy self-image. Considering this process of striving for perfection and a positive self-image illuminates the lawyers in this research.

In interview, the lawyers in this study proudly self-identified as professionals. There was a sense of self-satisfaction in the professional position they saw themselves occupying. The ego-ideal's quest for perfection was realised by their perceived professional standing. These lawyers were imbued with an awareness of their own importance, revelling in the responsibility placed in their hands. The professional is a designation imputably linked with high social status owing to the rise of the original three learned professions (legal, medical and clerical) in Medieval times when to be a professional was to stand with aristocracy and nobility (Freidson, 1994). In particular, the legal profession was considered to confer gentlemanly status and has been shown to hold particularly high regard as a "status profession" (Elliot, 1972: 14). The legal profession has long fought to uphold social closure to individuals with the greatest levels of cultural capital (Francis & Sommerlad, 2009). It is a profession determined to maintain itself as a class apart. The lawyers' self-image as professionals in this study was thus largely centred on the high status they believed it to hold. This belief, however, was problematic because the lawyers' wages did not reflect those of a high-status professional, thus challenging their self-image.

The challenge of lesser remuneration

Legally aided criminal defence trails many other professions in terms of remuneration. Despite their high levels of qualifications and years of training often achieved at a considerable level of debt, the average wage of criminal legal aid lawyers at the time of the research was £25,000, in line with the national average and well below the other public service providers with whom such lawyers are want to compare themselves such as teachers (£34,000) or general practitioners (£56,000) (Baksi, 2013).[9] In addition, the cost of providing legal services extends beyond simply paying lawyers, it must finance the cost of running an entire office with overheads such as rent, business rates, utilities, insurance, information technology, furniture, audit costs, transport, tax and national insurance on top of support staff and management working alongside fee earners. Hourly rates received by such lawyers were generally below the rate required for such firms to break even (Parry, 2015). The break-even figure would be £35.02 per hour, while a healthy business would require an hourly rate of £105.[10] A comparison with the national average, then, is inappropriate. So it is that legal aid lawyers also compare themselves with other areas of the legal profession and those with whom they studied but now work in far more lucrative areas such as commercial practice, wherein it has been reported that lawyers can earn £850 per hour (Owen, 2013).

The stark comparison whereby criminal legal aid lawyers can earn a little over 1.5% that of their City brethren will be degrading to those in the former position. The lawyers in my study were sharply alert to this financial reality. Throughout the fieldwork, I was subjected to endless complaining about the lawyers having lower remuneration compared with their peers. During the observation, I regularly noted this as the chief topic of discussion. Indeed, lawyers lamented this situation to anyone who would listen – each other, prosecutors, court staff, clients and, particularly, me. In the interviews, every lawyer brought up remuneration of their own accord and all complained about their lot, often telling stories of lawyers they knew in other areas of practice who earned so much more than them. It was also common to complain about how little they were paid for duty work, especially in comparison with the call-out fees charged by tradespeople (who were deemed inherently inferior). For these lawyers they were not simply undervalued in financial terms, meaning they might not be able to drive the car or have the second holiday they desired, but the level of their wage meant they were not treated with the respect they felt they deserved.

Most of these lawyers understood that they were not valued as high-status professionals in financial terms. This may have challenged their self-image as professionals. Such would be logical when the basis of, what Larson (1977: xvii) labelled, the professional project was status elevation and marketability, with "professionalization … an attempt to translate one order of scarce resources – special knowledge and skills – into another – social and economic rewards". Take, for example, the image presented by the large City firms when they appeal to students at law fairs; they do not sell commercial practice on moral good but present it as the domain of the high-flyer earning lots of money and able to fund a champagne lifestyle (Collier, 2005). With big commercial training contracts held in highest regard, these lawyers could be considered failures in the professional project in juxtaposition to their high-earning City peers. This unfavourable comparison would have an emotional impact bringing pain and discomfort because, for these lawyers, their market value fell well below that of their self-image or, in Freudian terms, their ego-ideal. Their egos strived for perfection and, to realise this, the lawyers needed to play by a different set of rules and establish alternative criteria. Instead of achieving the high status that professionals were seen to get via economic reward, these lawyers gave primacy to the social agenda. In this way, they would be able to meet their ego-ideal and feel proud with a sense of self-worth and accomplishment, at the same time managing to dodge the pain and discomfort that would accompany being financial failures.

This entailed a process of rationalisation, whereby the pain and discomfort represented by an external threat is circumvented by distorting reality. A 'disavowal defence', rationalisation allows the individual's ego to avoid having to deal with circumstances that would otherwise cause it anxiety through setting up a fallacy of reasoning at a level below consciousness. In this process, previous choices made for one reason can be reframed as if they were made under quite different motivation. The result is that the truth of an individual's decision-making can be obfuscated and mistakes ignored to protect the ego from any harmful reality. In place will be substituted a false but preferable understanding allowing a positive self-image to be maintained in spite of challenge. For these lawyers, the social agenda was offered up as a rationalisation for why they entered practice in place of any desire for a financially rewarding career.

The interviews showed the prominence the lawyers attributed to these values. The majority of lawyers earnestly identified themselves as engaged in a vocation, doing something essential and making a difference. This relied on a traditional professional evocation: that they could use their specialist knowledge to fulfil a socially important role (Eraut, 1994), imbuing the assumption that public service and professional status were linked (Abbey & Boon, 1995). In this situation, it was the social agenda and not financial remuneration that provided their rewards, and it was meeting those aspirations that earned the designation 'professional', with the high status that accompanied it. However, this claim to possess a social agenda is not something that should be accepted uncritically. The observation data demonstrate such a discrepancy from these values that they must cause us to question its substance. In particular, highlighting the importance of the social agenda may be deemed an act of rationalisation, thus providing an alternative explanation for lawyers' engagement in legally aided criminal defence.

That criminal legal aid carried such low levels of remuneration highlighted its place at the bottom of the profession and the difficulty with which it could be claimed as high status. The relatively poor remuneration would be a clear signifier of the lowly position of legally aided criminal defence, which could provide a major blow to the lawyers' egos, one that would disappoint the ego-ideal and deny it in its quest for perfection. There would be no pride at the low remuneration, which would deposit the lawyers well below the standards set for themselves as long as professional status was to be associated with earnings. To overcome this failure and the associated pain and discomfort to the ego, they required an alternative means to meet their ego-ideal. Sidestepping the link between accomplishment and financial reward, the lawyers found solace in establishing a rule that tied success into their realising the social agenda. However, previous research shows that the social agenda is not a major pull-factor in terms of law student motivation compared with financial considerations.[11] Large-scale surveys have shown how "practical and selfish aspirations came far above altruistic aspirations" (Boon, 2005: 236). Legal qualifications were most likely to be sought with an eye towards employment concerns. Public service desires lag behind both individual and vocational priorities as relevant variables. By this view, lawyers enter the legal profession because it represents a sensible career choice; financial considerations are to the fore.

Perhaps lawyers were in a poorly remunerated branch of the profession because they were unable to obtain better-paid work. Demand for training contracts with the top commercial firms is notoriously intense with many losing out and having to enter further down the professional ladder. No lawyer in this study pointed to their own inadequacies leading to their practising in a relatively low-paid branch of the profession and it would not be fair to assert otherwise without evidence. However, many lawyers suggested that other lawyers around them at the courts were only in legally aided criminal defence because they were not good enough for the alternatives. While it needs to be recognised that such suggestions are unsubstantiated hearsay, this is worthy of note; it was a common complaint amongst the lawyers in this study that standards were slipping and that criminal legal aid was becoming something of a dumping ground for those who could not get anything better. Lawyers would always identify the professional disappointment in others, while shielding their own egos from pain and discomfort by never countenancing the possibility that they were similarly engaged in this supposedly lower branch of the profession.

The social agenda, then, acted to protect the egos of these lawyers from any sense of failure with regards to their lower wages relative to peers. Whatever adverse judgement could be implicit in lesser remuneration, the lawyers could still assert their professional merit due to the valuable and meaningful function they played for the social good. The rationalisation that they were still high-status professionals despite the fiscal reality, however, relied upon others accepting the value of this social agenda. That the social agenda may not have been universally held in such high regard means its place as a support to the lawyers' self-image was precarious.

Problems with professionalism

Hughes (1962) developed the sociological understanding of dirty work, job-holders undertaking the tasks others avoid and dealing with the types of people that mainstream society would rather not know about. All occupations have a dirty work component but it is more significant in some jobs than others, with the sort of work that involves engaging with criminals amongst the highest so that "contact with psychical, social or moral dirt leaves a taint" (McMurray, 2012: 128). Accordingly, the legal profession in England and Wales has been labelled:

> A core of high status practitioners, concerned chiefly with the functions of capital, surrounded by a peripheral majority who deal in personal services for private clients ... a lower form of legal practice somewhat similar to social work. (McDonald, 1982: 273)

Such a view reflects a widely held lack of respect within other branches of the legal profession whereby criminal legal aid is looked down upon and held in contempt (Goriely, 1996).[12] There exists an "element of distaste, sometimes even of disdain which is to be found amongst some solicitors of standing for those who do legal aid work" (White, 1976: 233). Indeed, criminal legal aid lawyers in previous studies recognise such a lowly designation (Thomas & Mungham, 1983). It is important to question, then, the validity of the social agenda talked about by the lawyers in this research and whether it has any validity across the wider profession. To judge from Sadefur's (2001) survey of legal prestige the answer would be no: from 42 areas of legal work, lawyers ranked criminal practice 31st. That study identified two key reasons why criminal work held such a low status amongst lawyers, a professional purity thesis and a client-type thesis. Both theses undermine the status of criminal lawyers due to the very nature of legal aid work, which invariably entails working with clients who may not be able to finance their own representation; a lower socio-economic class than will be dealt with by many other branches of the profession.

Theories of professionalisation show that clients' socio-economic class plays a key role in determining the standing of the profession (Larson, 1977), so it can be said that "the importance of the clients affects the status of the professional providing the service" (Eraut, 1994: 5). This is as true for law as any other profession, perhaps even more so considering the wide disparities that exist between clientele such as the juxtaposition between criminal lawyers and the low-value crimes often committed by addicts, and commercial lawyers who service executives and glamorous companies. Studies have shown that lawyers who deal in higher status clients are particularly likely to make judgements of their fellow professionals who work with clients that they deem inferior (Heinz & Laumann, 1982). More so, criminal work in particular involves dealing not simply with the working class but with what are sneeringly referred to as the 'criminal classes', perhaps the social group looked down upon more than any other in contemporary society. Working with those written off as criminals rubs off badly on the lawyers, who become guilty by association, in what Sommerlad (1996: 298) has described as a "clear reflection of the connection between the status of the client and the lawyer". When the lawyers' clients are demonised, so are the lawyers and, if few value the practice or the practitioner, this seems to undermine the value of the social agenda in giving these lawyers a high status. Rather, the social agenda actually adds to the lower status bestowed by the lesser financial rewards on offer. Without validation, research has shown that public service professionals can become sullen and dejected (Parker, 1999). Through their association with such a lowly clientele, the social agenda of these lawyers could not allow them to achieve the perfection required to satisfy their ego-ideals meaning that, as it was with remuneration, the lawyers were to be disappointed. At least they would be if another Freudian defence mechanism had not kicked in.

If rationalisation could be said to have protected these lawyers' egos from sensing failure at their lesser remuneration, displacement sheltered them from realisation of the failure of their social agenda to give them any standing of note. A neurotic defence, displacement involves transferring the pain and displeasure brought about by a dangerous object onto one considered safe. This displacement shields the ego from having to deal with trauma, thus lessening anxiety. There were several targets that could have been identified for the lawyers' ire if they were reeling against the undermining of their social agenda. These include the media who created a populist anti-defendant line, the public that bought into this and demanded action, the government that reflected this in their policy-making, judges who convicted innocent defendants or sentence them too harshly, prosecutors who bring unjustified charges and police who may lie. All contributed to the debasement of the practise of these lawyers by ensuring that those suspected and accused of crimes were generally looked down upon and little respect was given to those who represented them. While the lawyers might have criticised the role of these parties on an intellectual level – as they did frequently in this research – these were powerful groups and largely beyond the reach of the lawyers when they were satisfying their emotional drives. Displacement involves selecting a weak, vulnerable and readily accessible victim to cast as a scapegoat. Clients provided the perfect soft target.

Displacement, then, can be picked out as a contributory factor in the lawyers shifting between professing positive attitudes to clients but concomitantly acting in quite the opposite manner. The clients were the reason they practised under their client-centred approach yet those very clients were also the reason they were largely looked down upon and had their self-image challenged, therefore the clients could be blamed for any resultant pain and discomfort. In these circumstances, the lawyers resented the clients as evident in the sheer contempt shown throughout the observation. Displacement allowed such resentment to fester below the surface, with lawyers thus able to continue to trumpet their social agendas and resultant claims to high status as their egos were being protected from the reality by this defence mechanism. They would be unaware of this process while any pain and discomfort that might otherwise be internalised if they were to perceive themselves as failures for how little due was given to their social agenda was simply channelled outwards in their treatment of clients.

Conclusion: are lawyers neurotic?

This paper has offered an account whereby the lawyers studied learnt to take out the pain and displeasure caused by challenges to their self-image upon their clients. I have suggested that lawyers can hold both positive and negative attitudes simultaneously without necessarily being conscious of this distinction or its contradictory nature. Rationalisation and displacement combined to allow these lawyers to deceive themselves and protect a self-image as high-status professionals whatever the reality.

As a final consideration, Jung's particular understanding of psychoanalysis offers a neat way to tie together the themes described in this paper. Jung is more radical than Freud and so his usage here is made with similar, if not greater, caveats to that of Freudian theory: his ideas offer a means for exploring the issues of this disjuncture in lawyer attitudes, not offered as a perfect theory to be strictly adhered to but one sufficiently illustrative and with potential illumination for the immediate goal of stimulating this debate. For Jung (2009: 414), an attitude can be understood as "the readiness of the psyche to act or react in a certain way". Jung (2009: 415) holds that attitudes are organised in pairs: one conscious, the other unconscious, a distinction which means that "consciousness has a constellation of contents different from that of the unconscious, a duality particularly evident in neurosis". Neurosis reflects an unresolved tension between opposing attitudes of the conscious and the unconscious. They arise when the conscious attitude is unable to distinguish or integrate elements deemed important to the unconscious attitude. As a result, a duality emerges between abstractism and concretism. These represent two ways of thinking and feeling – the former more sophisticated, rational and logical, and the latter primitive, based entirely on perception through sensation. Concretism is useful for the manner in which it allows recognition of external reality; however, it is lacking in how that is subsequently interpreted.

Jung's duality offers insights that can be appropriated to conclude the psychoanalytic explanation for the conflicting accounts of lawyer attitudes. The lawyers suffered from a neurosis, a split between their consciously professing positive attitudes and unconsciously propagating negative attitudes. The lawyers were differentiating between 'the' client and 'a' client: the general and the particular. The client was that considered in abstract, regarded in theoretical terms through the lens of access to justice and, as such, reflecting the social agenda discussed in interview. On the other hand, a client was the concrete experience, that client dealt with in the here and now, connected with the pain and displeasure of their professional standing, which they subsequently appeared to resent under observation. When thinking objectively – detached and reasoning – the lawyer held positive attitudes towards the client. This is what happened in the interviews where lawyers were given time and space to reflect. It was only when lost in the moment – reacting to demanding situations, working on instinct – that the lawyers displayed these negative attitudes towards a client. It was thus that the observation showed the unfiltered image of the lawyers in action and without time for pontification.

This process necessitated a further act of rationalisation on the part of these lawyers. So as to resolve the tension that separated the negative attitudes shown as lawyers engaged in their routine practise with the higher ideals signified within the positive attitudes, they were acting out an elaborate fantasy. In this way, lawyers were able to show complete disdain for their clients, disrespecting and debasing them at will, while still able to assert to holding positive attitudes as long as they felt they were doing their best in the job. As a result, the lawyers could actually believe they held positive attitudes, thus allowing them to claim to be realising the social agenda and, therefore, meeting their ego-ideal. Realising the ego-deal meant achieving perfection as they kept to the rules set and realised the standards that they primed themselves to hold to. As a result, lawyers were able to feel proud and experience a sense of accomplishment. The rationalisation defence mechanism thus had a double value here, protecting the lawyers from the realisation that they had failed to achieve high remuneration or be valued for upholding the social agenda. The reality of their two failures was successfully rebutted, keeping their egos free from pain or discomfort. Returning to the idea that the lawyers may have been lying to me, then, this consideration makes it entirely reasonable to suppose that they were lying without realising it rather than being malicious or self-serving. By this line, they were not simply lying to me, however, they were lying to each other and, crucially, to themselves. I was treated as one of them and they talked to me as a peer, which meant presenting a professional, positive attitude in theoretical terms but showing the opposite in reality. When given the opportunity to muse at length on their attitudes to clients, the lawyers were thinking in the abstract and thus falsely convincing themselves that this abstract was something more than a self-justificatory myth. I also saw the concrete and, as a result, have been able to document the discrepancy that existed between the two.

Regardless of the lawyers being aware of the reality, they were seen to display negative attitudes to their clients so the consequences for the state of the lawyer–client relationship need to be further considered by those with an interest in ensuring access to justice. By bringing psychoanalysis into the lawyer–client relationship, this paper has sought to offer a new perspective for traditional discussions of access to justice. The issues covered here are, of course, open to other explanations and readers are not expected to necessarily agree with the analysis offered. There are a number of other possibilities for the distinction between what the criminal defence lawyers purport to think and the way they behave. For example, other areas of more rational psychology might be relevant such as the concept of cognitive dissonance, and Chemerinsky (1980) has applied this to lawyers in exploring what happens to lawyers that have to practise in ways which counter their own beliefs and values, which could be built on further. Elsewhere, the author has applied Marxist alienation to speculate that funding cuts and financial pressures may have debased the social perspectives of once altruistic lawyers and reduced the lawyers' ability to relate to clients (Newman, 2016). Perhaps the way lawyers talk to each other about their work is frequently just an exaggerated version of their real views and does not necessarily translate into their actual working practices, as has been shown in the criminal justice context through explorations of the police canteen subculture (Waddington, 1999). On the other hand, Blumberg (1967) has depicted a much more knowing and aware approach among criminal defence lawyers when he describes practice as a confidence game, with lawyers purposefully tricking their clients into thinking they are getting a better service than they are.

In light of the above, some readers will not be convinced that psychoanalysis is the most relevant framework to apply to legal practice, perhaps viewing it as out of date or too unorthodox. These may be valid observations and, indeed, could damage the argument of this paper were the paper seeking to follow the (flawed) line of Freud that psychoanalysis was a scientific theory, using it as some manner of authoritative grand narrative. This paper is not, however, claiming to offer a definitive reading of the lawyer–client relationship; it rather provides an innovative approach to the subject by drawing these two disparate literatures together in order to create a new way of looking at the problems of access to justice. In particular, the argument here is intended as a provocation that will stimulate original responses from others and take the debate in a fresh direction.

In so doing, it is important to proceed with the conviction that access to lawyers alone is not enough to achieve access to justice; those lawyers need to be client-centred and fully serve their clients. While legal aid cuts threaten advice deserts whereby those suspected or accused of crimes may find it difficult to get lawyers to represent them, it is as, if not more, important to ensure that the legal aid cuts do not intensify the defence mechanisms and resultant bad practice considered in this paper by posing even bigger threats to lawyer egos. Assessing the future impact requires properly understanding the nature of the lawyer–client relationship and fully exploring issues such as the attitudes lawyers hold towards their clients. Such studies could also bring in issues such as gender and social class, as means to engage with the relationships between lawyers and clients. Considering such additional factors of identity and self-understanding may take the research into new directions and provide yet more valuable perspectives. Further research also needs to be done with those suspected and accused of crimes in order to draw out their experience of the lawyer–client relationship. Because of the lack of empirical study in this area, it will be important to find out what clients perceive in relation to the issues raised in this paper, since they are also a material element in the process. An ethnographic research study with the defendants in the criminal process would provide a valuable follow up to broaden our understanding. The implications of all such further examination may have great significance in attempts at promoting ethical practise amongst criminal legal aid lawyers.

Notes

1. It should be noted that Shapiro's (1999) work suggests that everybody displays some neurotic states and that these are not necessarily problematic.
2. While this paper considers criminal legal aid lawyers and the criminal justice system, it is important to note that issues of access to lawyers are both pressing and present different challenges in other areas of the English legal system. For example, following the cuts to legal aid enacted by the coalition government in the Legal Aid, Sentencing and Punishment of Offenders Act 2012, funding for lawyers has been removed from large areas of the civil law system. In civil cases, what emerges are issues around access to justice in terms of literal access to lawyers, the quantity of legal advice available. In criminal legal aid, the issue is much more the quality of legal advice.
3. Also, by extension, reliant upon legal aid. Access to justice specifically requires access to lawyers funded by legal aid. See Ashworth (1996).
4. For example, in Article 6 § 3 (c) (right to legal assistance) of the European Convention on Human

   Rights: "Everyone charged with a criminal offence has the right to defend himself in person or through legal assistance of his own choosing or, if he has not sufficient means to pay for legal assistance, to be given it free when the interests of justice so require". The decision of the European Court of Human Rights in *Salduz v. Turkey* went further, stating that "as a rule, access to a lawyer should be provided as from the first interrogation of a suspect by the police".
5. A full discussion of the methods and methodology that underpin this research can be found in Newman (2013). The present paper builds on arguments around the role of defence mechanisms in the lawyer–client relationship first developed in this book.

They have benefitted from being rewritten into the more concise and accessible format of this paper as well as gaining through being updated. Rather than use previously published data, this paper utilises mostly data from the fieldwork that were not included in the book and will thus be research presented for the first time here.

6. See, for example, the exemplary studies offered by Sommerlad (2001) and Tata *et al.* (2004).
7. Reconvened here as Bridges *et al.* (1997).
8. Parsons (1964) posits social theory as lacking if it does not give due attention to such psychic mechanisms.
9. These levels have since dropped further with the 8.75% cuts to legal aid fees introduced in 2014.
10. Talking of break-even costs here is putting an optimistic sheen on incomes as received wisdom suggests that a company needs to do more than break even to stay in business and, rather, should reinvest at least a third of earnings to grow the business and take a third in profit for the owners.
11. See, for example, Sherr & Webb (1989) and Boon *et al.* (2001).
12. McIntyre (1997) shows this to be a trait of state-funded lawyers dealing in criminal matters outside the UK as well.

Disclosure statement

No potential conflict of interest was reported by the author.

References

Abbey, R. & Boon, A. (1995) The provision of free legal services by solicitors: a review of the report of the Law Society's Pro Bono Working Party, *International Journal of the Legal Profession*, 2(3), pp. 261–280.

Abel, R. (1988) *The Legal Profession in England and Wales* (Oxford, Basil Blackwell Ltd).

Ashworth, A. (1996) Legal aid, human rights and criminal justice, in: R. Young & D. Wall (Eds) *Access to Criminal Justice* (London, Blackstone Press Ltd), pp. 55–69.

Baksi, C. (2013) Juniors 'on £14 a day' after legal aid cuts, MPs hear, *Law Society Gazette* 10 June.

Berkowitz, L. & Knurek, D. (1969) Label-mediated hostility generalization, *Journal of Personality and Social Psychology*, 13(3), pp. 200–206.

Blumberg, A. (1967) The practice of law as confidence game: organizational cooptation of a profession, *Law and Society Review*, 1(2), pp. 15–40.

Bocock, R. (1981) British sociologists and freud: a sociological analysis of the absence of a Relationship, *The British Journal of Sociology*, 32(3), pp. 346–361.

Bohner, G. & Wanke, M. (2002) *Attitudes and Attitude Change* (East Sussex, Psychology Press).

Boon, A. (2005) From public service to service industry: the impact of socialisation and work on the motivation and values of lawyers, *International Journal of the Legal Profession*, 12 (2), pp. 229–260.

Boon, A., Duff, L. & Shiner, M. (2001) Career Paths and choices in a highly differentiated profession: the position of newly qualified solicitors, *Modern Law Review*, 64(4), pp. 563–594.

Braun, V. & Clarke, V. (2006) Using thematic analysis in psychology, *Qualitative Research in Psychology*, 3(2), pp. 77–101.

Bridges, L., Hodgson, J., McConville, M. & Pavlovic, A. (1997) Can critical research influence policy?: a response to max travers, *British Journal of Criminology*, 37(3), pp. 378–382.
Butler, J. (1999) *Gender Trouble* (London, Routledge).
Cain, M. (1983) The general practice layer and the client: towards a radical conception, in: R. Dingwall & P. Lewis (Eds) *The Sociology of the Professions* (London, Macmillan), pp. 106–130.
Caudill, D. (1991) Freud and critical legal studies: contours of a radical socio-legal psychoanalysis, *Indiana Law Journal*, 66(3), pp. 651–697.
Chemerinsky, E. (1980) Protecting lawyers from their profession: redefining the lawyer's role, *Journal of the Legal Profession*, 5, pp. 31–43.
Collier, R. (2005) 'Be smart, be successful, be yourself… '?: representations of the training contract and trainee solicitor in advertising by large law firms, *International Journal of the Legal Profession*, 12(1), pp. 51–92.
Cornell, D. (1997) Where love begins: sexual difference and the limit of the masculine symbolic, in: E. Feder, M. Rawlinson & E. Zakin (Eds) *Derrida and Feminism: Recasting the Question of Woman* (New York, Routledge), pp. 161–206.
Craib, I. (1989) *Psychoanalysis and Social Theory* (Brighton, Harvester Wheatsheaf).
Eraut, M. (1994) *Developing Professional Knowledge and Competence* (Abingdon, Routledge Falmer).
Ericson, R. & Baranek, P. (1982) *The Ordering of Justice* (Toronto, Toronto University Press).
Elliot, P. (1972) *The Sociology of the Professions* (London, Macmillan).
Felstiner, W. (2001) Synthesising socio-legal research: lawyer–client relations as an example, *International Journal of the Legal Profession*, 8(3), pp. 191–201.
Francis, A. & Sommerlad, H. (2009) Access to legal work experience and its role in the (re)production of legal professional identity, *International Journal of the Legal Profession*, 16(1), pp. 63–86.
Frank, J. (2009) *Law and the Modern Mind* (New Brunswick, NJ, Transaction Publishers).
Freidson, E. (1994) *Professionalism Reborn* (Cambridge, Polity Press).
Freud, S. (1989) *The Freud Reader* (New York, WW Norton and Company).
Freud, S. (1995) *New Introductory Lectures on Psychoanalysis* (New York, WW Norton and Company).
Goldstein, J. (1968) Psychoanalysis and jurisprudence, *The Yale Law Journal*, 77(6), pp. 1053–1077.
Goriely, T. (1996) The development of criminal legal aid in England and wales, in: R. Young & D. Wall (Eds) *Access to Criminal Justice* (London, Blackstone Press Ltd), pp. 26–54.
Heinz, J. & E. Laumann (1982) *Chicago Lawyers* (New York, Russell Sage Foundation and American Bar Foundation).
Hillyard, P. (2002) Invoking indignation: reflections on future directions of socio-legal studies, *Journal of Law and Society*, 29(4), pp. 645–656.
Hoyle, C. (1998) *Negotiating Domestic Violence* (Oxford, Oxford University Press).
Hughes, E. (1962) Good people and dirty work, *Social Problems*, 10(1), pp. 3–11.
Larson, M. (1977) *The Rise of Professionalism* (Berkeley, University of California Press).
Luban, D. (2014) Is there a human right to a lawyer?, *Legal Ethics*, 17(3), pp. 371–381.
Jung, C. (2009) *Psychological Types* (London, Routledge and Kegan Paul).
Katz, J. (1982) *Poor People's Lawyers in Transition* (New Brunswick, NJ, Rutgers University Press).
Mather, L., Maiman, R. & McEwan, C. (1995) 'The passenger decides on the destination and i decide on the route': are divorce lawyers 'expensive cab drivers'?, *International Journal of Law, Policy and the Family*, 9(3), pp. 286–310.
McBarnet, D. (1981) *Conviction* (London, Macmillan).

McConville, M. & Marsh, L. (2014) *Criminal Judges* (Cheltenham, Edward Elgar Publishing).
McConville, M., Hodgson, J., Bridges, L. & Pavlovic, A. (1994) *Standing Accused* (Oxford, Oxford University Press).
McDonald, P. (1982) 'The class of '81': a glance at the social class composition of recruits to the legal profession, *Journal of Law and Society*, 9(2), pp. 267–276.
McIntyre, R. (1997) The public defender: the practice of law in the shadows of repute, in: R. Abel (Ed) *Lawyers: A Critical Reader* (New York, New Press), pp. 262–272.
McMurray, R. (2012) Embracing dirt in nursing matters, in: R. Simpson, N. Slutskaya, P. Lewis & H. Hopfl (Eds) *Dirty Work: Concepts and Identities* (Hampshire, Palgrave Macmillan), pp. 126–142.
Meffre, P. (2005) Self-Image, in A. de Mijolla (Ed) *International Dictionary of Psychoanalysis* (Michigan, Thomson Gale), pp. 133–151.
Newman, D. (2013) *Legal Aid Lawyers and the Quest for Justice* (Oxford, Hart Publishing).
Newman, D. (2016) Are lawyers alienated workers?, *European Journal of Current Legal Issues*, 22(3). Available at: http://webjcli.org/article/view/463.
Owen, I. (2013) Justice costs: Fury as lawyers' fees top £850 an hour, *The Lawyer*, 26th November.
Parker, C. (1999) Compliance professionalism and regulatory community: the Australian trade practices regime, *Journal of Law and Society*, 26(2), pp. 215–239.
Parker, C. & Evans, A. (2007) *Inside Lawyers' Ethics* (Cambridge, Cambridge University Press).
Parry, J. (2015) *What are Criminal Legal Aid Lawyers Paid?*, Parry Welch Lacey. Available at: https://parrywelchlacey.wordpress.com/what-are-criminal-legal-aid-lawyers-paid/.
Parsons, T. (1964) *Social Structure and Personality* (New York, The Free Press).
Rosenberg, M. & Hovland, C. (1960) Cognitive, affective and behavioural components of attitudes, in: M. Rosenberg, C. Hovland, W. McGuire, R. Abelson & J. Brehm (Eds) *Attitude Organization and Change: An Analysis of Consistency Among Attitude Components* (Connecticut, Yale University Press), pp. 1–14.
Sandefur, R. (2001) Work and honor in the law: prestige and the division of lawyers' labor, *American Sociological Review*, 66(3), pp. 382.
Sarat, A. & Felstiner, W. (1988) Law and social relations: vocabularies of motive in lawyer/client interaction, *Law and Society Review*, 22(4), pp. 737–770.
Sarat, A. & Felstiner, W. (1995) *Divorce Lawyers and their Clients* (Oxford, Oxford University Press).
Schoenfeld, C. (1973) *Psychoanalysis and the Law* (Illinois, Charles C Thomas).
Shapiro, D. (1999) *Neurotic Styles* (New York, Basic Books).
Sherr, A. & Webb, L. (1989) Law students, the external market, and socialization: do we make them turn to the city?, *Journal of Law and Society*, 16(2), pp. 225–249.
Shiner, M. (2010) Post-lawrence policing in england and wales: guilt, innocence and the defence of organizational ego, *British Journal of Criminology*, 50(5), pp. 935–953.
Smith, T. (2013) The 'quiet revolution' in criminal defence: how the zealous advocate slipped into the shadow, *International Journal of the Legal Profession*, 20(1), pp. 111–137.
Solicitors Regulation Authority. (2007) *Solicitors' Code of Conduct* (Redditch, Solicitors Regulation Authority).
Sommerlad, H. (1996) Criminal legal aid reforms and the restructuring of legal professionalism, in: R. Young & D. Wall (Eds) *Access to Criminal Justice* (London, Blackstone Press Ltd), pp. 292–312.
Sommerlad, H. (2001) 'I've lost the plot': an everyday story of legal aid lawyers, *Journal of Law and Society*, 28(3), pp. 335–360.

INTERNATIONAL JOURNAL OF THE LEGAL PROFESSION  29

Staats, A. & Staats, C. (1958) Attitudes established by classical conditioning, *The Journal of Abnormal and Social Psychology*, 57(1), pp. 37–40.

Suseno, Y., Pinnington, A., Gardner, J. & Schulman, A. (2006) Social capital and knowledge acquisition in professional–client relationships, *International Journal of the Legal Profession*, 13(3), pp. 273–295.

Tata, C., Goriely, T., McCrone, P., Duff, P., Knapp, M., Henry, A., Lancaster, B. & Sherr, A. (2004) Does mode of delivery make a difference to criminal case outcomes and clients' satisfaction? The public defence solicitor experiment, *Criminal Law Review*, pp. 120–136.

Thomas, P. & Mungham, G. (1983) Solicitors and clients: altruism or self-interest, in: R. Dingwall & P. Lewis (Eds) *The Sociology of the Professions* (London, Macmillan), pp. 131–151.

Travers, M. (1997a) Preaching to the converted? Improving the persuasiveness of criminal justice research, *British Journal of Criminology*, 37(3), pp. 359–377.

Travers, M. (1997b) *The Reality of Law* (Aldershot, Ashgate).

Tyler, T. (1988) What is procedural justice?: criteria used by citizens to assess the fairness of legal procedures, *Law and Society Review*, 22(1), pp. 103–136.

Waddington, P. (1999) Police (canteen) sub-culture. An appreciation, *British Journal of Criminology*, 39(2), pp. 287–309.

White, R. (1976) The distasteful character of litigation for poor persons, in: N. MacCormick (Ed) *Lawyers in their Social Setting* (Edinburgh, W Green and Son), pp. 1571–1572.

Young, K. (1940) The impact of freudian psychology on sociology, *American Journal of Orthopsychiatry*, 10(4), pp. 869–876.

Young, R. & Wall, D. (1996) Criminal justice, legal aid and the defence of liberty, in: R. Young & D. Wall (Eds) *Access to Criminal Justice* (London, Blackstone Press Ltd), pp. 1–25.

Section A

1. What debate about the nature of client-lawyer relationships is the author of the article addressing?
2. Why does the author think that understanding the nature of lawyer-client relationships is important?
3. What two kinds of new data does the author put forward from his own research? Which does he think is better?
4. Why does the author think that the amount that criminal legal aid lawyers are paid might be relevant to how they thought about the nature of their job?

Section B

1. The author says that lawyers he observed regarded some of their clients as being of low education or intelligence (p.11). Does he show that the lawyers were incorrect in thinking this? If a lawyer's client is either of low intelligence or education what are the arguments for and against them treating the client differently because of this?
2. If the answer to the author's question in his title, are lawyers neurotic, is yes with regard to criminal legal aid practitioners, what are the advantages to this being the case and what might be the possible problems?

3. If criminal legal aid lawyers are neurotic what arguments are there for saying that some lawyers will not be in the same position?
4. What arguments can you suggest which might show why it is not useful to use Freud's work to analyse the lives of lawyers?

9
Studying at University

9.1

University isn't all about studying. Most students want to make friends and have a good social life, as well as getting a degree. Many have lots of other goals, such as participating in sporting activities, travelling or earning some money. However, getting a good degree, and thereby opening up a really wide range of employment possibilities, often features quite highly on many students' wish-lists. In order to achieve your full academic potential, and graduate with a degree that you really think reflects your true abilities, it helps to think about the study skills you might need to acquire, or develop, to help you. The purpose of this chapter of *How to Study Law* is to help you achieve your goals. It suggests some strategies to help you study law more effectively, so that you can improve your academic performance. It also aims to make studying law a more enjoyable and satisfying experience for you, and one which leaves time for all the other things you want to do while you are at university.

Successful study does not simply involve spending a lot of time working. Students who spend a lot of time on their work do not necessarily receive high marks (although clearly there is some correlation between the effort you put in to your academic work and the results you can expect to achieve). You need to make sure that you are using your study time effectively, so that you can succeed academically, but also have time for a social life and leisure activities. The purpose of this chapter is to suggest some techniques which you can apply to the tasks which law students are asked to carry out, such as writing essays or participating in seminars, which will enable you to get the most out of the degree you have chosen to study in the most effective way.

LEARNING INDEPENDENTLY

9.2

As a student in a college or university, you will be expected to take responsibility for your own learning. Your tutors will assume that you can work on your own without supervision, develop your research skills, complete assessment tasks and hand them in on time. You are likely to spend a much smaller proportion of your time on timetabled activities than you did at school. Your tutors will generally be helpful, but they are not school teachers, and they will not expect to guide your day-to-day learning in the same way as your teachers may have done. You will be responsible for ensuring that you know what lectures and small group sessions you need to attend, where they are held (online or in person) and at what time. You will be expected to know whether you have to prepare work in advance of a seminar or tutorial, and to do it in time. You will also be responsible for meeting any deadlines set for coursework or assessment tasks. The freedom to learn in your own way is very rewarding, but some people find this approach very challenging, because it is extremely different to the one they were used to before they came to university.

It is up to you to organise your time and plan it so that you can get everything done which you need to do, both in terms of your academic work and your social life, as well as any paid employment you might be engaged in. The next section of this chapter is devoted to time management, because it is one of the most useful skills you can learn. It will not just be useful whilst you are a student; it is one of the skills that are commonly called "transferable", because it can be used not just while you are a student, but also throughout the rest of your life.

MANAGING YOUR TIME

9.3 As a law student, you will be expected to do a number of different things: attend classes or lectures, prepare work for discussion in tutorials, seminars or classes, write essays and sit exams. Coursework will have to be submitted by a set deadline, in the form required by your university. At the same time as fulfilling all those obligations, there will be other things you want to do, such as going out with your friends, going shopping or playing sports. There will also be things that you pretty much *have* to do (unless you can get someone else to do them for you) like buying food and doing the washing. In order to fit everything in, it's best to work out a plan, so that you don't forget to do something or start getting behind with your work.

- **Buy a diary or use the calendar on your mobile device**
  You can use your diary or electronic calendar to plan your time. To be effective, it needs to contain a complete record of what you have to do. You need to carry it with you and add new appointments as you make them. You could start by putting in all your academic commitments—lectures, tutorials/seminars, deadlines for coursework and so on. Often your university will make this easy for you by giving you access to a virtual learning environment (BlackBoard or Moodle, for instance) which includes an online timetable. Then you can add in social engagements and other things you want or need to do. Get into the habit of writing commitments into your diary or calendar as soon as you know about them.

- **How much time should I spend on my law degree?**
  No-one would suggest that you spend all your time studying. The whole point of managing your time is to have enough time *both* to study effectively *and* to do all the other things you want to do. It is impossible to tell anyone precisely how much time they need to spend studying. Everyone is a unique individual and has different requirements. But, if you are a full-time student, then think of working for your degree as being similar, in terms of time, to a full-time job—around 40 hours a week. At certain times, if you have an assessment to prepare, or exams to revise for, you will find you need to spend considerably more time. The important thing is to work out how much time you personally need to spend in order to fulfil the requirements of your course of study.

- **Become good at prioritising**
  Much of the time you will have multiple things you need to be making progress with—seminar preparation, buying lunch, meeting friends, listening to music, attending lectures and so on. You clearly can't do everything at once. Many people find it helpful to make lists, covering what they want to get done on a particular day or in a certain week. Consider installing a list app on your mobile device. Get used to prioritising items on your list—highlight those that you absolutely MUST get done, and fit the others in around them.

- **Find out if there are hidden institutional time constraints**
  Even if you are good at time management, your plans can be upset by the arrangements made by your institution. It is all very well planning to do lots of research for an essay during the vacation, but not if the library is going to be closed for building alterations for three weeks. Equally, you may come across the problem of "bunched deadlines", where several of the courses you are doing require assessed work to be handed in on the same day. You can alleviate these problems by finding out about the library, computers, and other support services well in advance and by asking tutors to give you assignments in good time, but you may not be able to overcome such difficulties completely. If you are planning your time well in advance, however, that should give you sufficient flexibility to deal with the resulting pressure on your time, and you will be in a much better position than someone who has given no thought to such problems.

- **Be realistic when planning your time**
  Although you will often be working to deadlines imposed by your tutors, it will be up to you to organise your time around those deadlines. Be realistic about how much time you need to set aside in order to complete your essays or tutorial preparation. It is counterproductive to set yourself a deadline that you cannot possibly hope to meet. Many activities will take longer than you think; for instance, most law students are surprised how long it takes them to do the research for an essay!

  When you are planning your time, you need to be realistic about your own strengths and weaknesses, too. If you are the sort of person who can stay in and write your essay on a Saturday afternoon when all your friends are going out together, that's fine. On the other hand, if you are the sort of person who cannot wake up before midday, it is unrealistic to plan to write your essay at 8.30 in the morning. If you do not allow yourself sufficient time to do something, you may start to feel depressed and frustrated. If your schedule is realistic, you will gain satisfaction from knowing that you have achieved what you set out to do. Of course, everyone underestimates the time they need sometimes, but you should try to avoid this happening to you too often.

- **Don't leave things until the last minute**
  This especially applies to preparation for tutorials and seminars, and the research you will need to do for assignments. If you leave things to the last minute, you may well find that most of the hard-copy books and articles you need to use have already been borrowed by other students (and remember that even e-books may have restrictions on their use). You can sometimes rescue the situation by finding the information you need elsewhere, but it takes a lot of thought, time and energy to discover alternative sources of information. Your tutors are unlikely to be sympathetic if you miss deadlines simply because you left everything to the last minute.

MAKING LECTURES WORK FOR YOU

9.4

Lectures usually last one to two hours, and are delivered to large groups of students at once. They allow the lecturer to explain the main ideas in an area. Often, lecturers will also take the opportunity to tell students about the latest developments in an area, and to explain any particularly complex parts of a subject. Lectures are often regarded as forming the backbone of a course and it is usually assumed that most students will attend them. The content of lectures, and the handouts or powerpoint slides that often accompany them, also form the basis for further independent study.

Lecturing style is closely related to the personality of an individual lecturer, so you are likely to come across a wide variety of lectures delivered in many different styles. Some will be excellent, some less so. As a student, you will need to develop a good technique for dealing with lectures, which you can then adapt to cope with the different lecturing styles you come across.

- **Prepare in advance for flipped lectures**

  You may find that your tutors have decided to use what are called "flipped" lectures. This means that you will be given work which has to be prepared in advance, before the lecture takes place. Often this will take the form of reading, but it may involve written exercises or some kind of legal research task. When the lecture takes place (in person or online) the lecture time is then used for activities and discussions based on the work you have already prepared.

  Don't forget that while most lecturers want to be good at what they do, and deliver lectures of a very high standard, you are ultimately responsible for your own education. You must make lectures work for you. Here are a number of suggestions which will help you to do that.

  The idea behind flipped lectures is that in advance of the scheduled lecture slot you will engage in learning activities (which may be reading, watching a video, doing some guided research or another activity designed by your lecturer). Then the lecture time will be devoted to activities, exercises, small group discussions and similar learning activities, all of which are strongly connected to the pre-lecture preparation you have already completed. Making sure that you have done the pre-lecture preparation is an important part of ensuring that you get the most out of a flipped lecture.

- **Arrive/Log On in reasonably good time**

  Important announcements are often given out at the beginning of lectures, you may be very confused if you miss them. Equally, the first few minutes of the lecture itself are important, as the lecturer will often summarise the main points they are going to cover in the lecture, or remind you where they have got up to in their coverage of a topic.

- **Listen actively**

  Listening to a lecture can be a very passive experience. Students are not generally expected to interrupt a lecture by asking questions or making comments (although some lecturers will include interactive elements in their lectures). In a standard lecture, it is very easy to "switch off" and lose the thread of the lecture. To avoid this, take notes to help you to concentrate. Do this even if you are permitted to record the lecture: you may never get round to listening to it again, but your notes will be very important for revision when you come to do your exams. When you are listening to the lecture, try to relate what you are hearing to your existing knowledge of the subject and think how the new information fits into it. A lecture can be very boring if the lecturer has a monotonous delivery, but as an effective listener, you need to train yourself to ignore poor delivery, and concentrate on the content of what is being said, which you can briefly record in your notes.

- **Eliminate distractions**

  In order to help you concentrate in lectures, you need to eliminate as many distractions as possible. Switch your mobile phone off; texting your friends might appear more fun than taking notes in the short term, but it won't help you when you are revising for exams. The same goes for Facebook! Make sure you are comfortable; use a clipboard if there is no desk. Use a convenient size of paper, which gives you enough space to set out your notes clearly. If you have a series of consecutive lectures you may become uncomfortable because you are sitting for long periods; try to move your limbs slightly during the lecture and use any brief gaps between the lectures to get out of your seat and move around a bit.

- **Take notes for future use and to aid concentration**
  Since one of the main purposes of taking notes is to use them in the future to help you write assignments and to use as a revision aid, it is important to devise a system of note-taking which produces a clear set of notes which you will understand when you come to look at them again, weeks or months after the original lecture. Handouts or powerpoint slides that support the lecture can make the task of note-taking easier, if they are well used; they should show you the broad structure of the lecturer and the main topics which will be covered. The lecturer may help you by summarising their main points; they may also try to aid your understanding by including examples or illustrations; these are good to include in your notes, as they will help to remind you of the workings of the arguments. Note the names of cases, statutes and academic writers who are mentioned; if there is a lecture handout, this should help you as it will contain names of cases and statutes and other technical legal terms, so you don't need to get all these perfectly during the lecture; you can insert them when you review your lecture notes.

- **Take notes which you will be able to use**
  There is no single "best" way of taking notes. Some people will take quite detailed notes; others will take down the key points in a diagrammatic form. Many people find it helpful to use headings and sub-headings to emphasise the main points made, and to indicate changes in topics. Numbered points can provide a quick way of noting a large quantity of information. Underlining and the use of different coloured pens can direct your attention to particular points.

  The most important factor here is to establish a style of note-taking which results in a useful set of notes for you to refer to after the lecture has finished. Since law degrees generally rely on lectures as the main source of information, you may feel you need to write down quite a lot in order to be sure that you have everything you need. However, don't attempt to write down everything the lecturer says, as you won't be able to do this, and you will lose the sense of what they are saying. When you have taken some notes in some lectures, it is worth reviewing them and asking yourself whether they will be useful to you in the future. If they are too messy, too short or too confusing, you can take steps to improve your note-taking technique. If you are unsure about the best way in which to take notes, you should consult one of the study guides that are listed in the "Further Reading" section at the end of this chapter. You may also wish to consult a member of the academic support team in your institution.

- **Review your notes as soon as possible**
  It is important to review your notes while the lecture is still fresh in your mind. You may need to expand what you have written, or add headings, or do a little research on a point which you have not understood. Some people like to summarise their notes in diagrammatic form at this stage.

TUTORIALS AND SEMINARS

9.5 Tutorials involve small groups of students who meet regularly with an academic tutor to discuss questions that have generally been set in advance by the tutor. Seminars are similar, but usually involve larger groups of students; sometimes seminars may be led by one or more of the students. These names for small group work are often interchangeable, so you may find something labelled "tutorial" which is attended by 30 students. The title is not important; it merely indicates a "teaching event" which is usually smaller scale and more interactive than a lecture. In both tutorials and seminars, all the students are generally expected to have prepared the topic under discussion in advance and tutors usually expect that all the students involved in the group will participate, by joining in the discussion. The following points will help you get the most benefit from these sessions:

- **Ensure you know what is expected of you**
  Many tutors set specific work for tutorials and seminars. Ensure that you obtain this in good time, so that you can prepare the topic properly. If you are unprepared, and unfamiliar with the subject matter, you won't get much out of the session, because you won't be able to participate in the discussion and you will find it hard to understand what is going on. Different tutors will run these groups in very different ways. You will need to be adaptable, to fit in with different teaching styles. Some tutors will make this easy for you, by having explicit "ground rules"; with others you will have to work it out for yourself.

- **Try to participate**
  Often, you will attend tutorials and seminars with the same group of people for a whole module. Clearly, the experience will be more pleasant if the members of the group get on with each other, but this is essentially a learning experience, so you have to balance your desire to be friendly with your learning needs. No one wants to make a fool of themselves in front of a group of other people, but if you do not try out ideas in discussion, you are not going to develop your thinking, so a little bravery is called for. Try not to be so worried about what the others will think that you do not participate at all. Everyone is in the same situation, so people are generally sympathetic to contributions made by others. If your tutorial is online, then ideally you should turn your camera on, although many people do not like doing this. Remember you can select a background before you join the session – you do not have to show everyone your private space if you don't want to; this might make it easier for you to turn the camera on. Even if you don't turn it on, you can generally participate in online tutorials via the "chat" function.

- **Consider making a contribution early in the discussion**
  If you make a contribution to the discussion at a fairly early stage, it is likely to be easier than if you delay participating, for a number of reasons. In the early stages of discussion, it is less likely that other people will have made the point you have thought of. Tutors who are keen to involve the whole group may single out people who have not said anything and ask them direct questions; this is much less likely to happen to you if you have already made a contribution. If you are less confident about talking in front of other people, the longer you wait to say something, the more difficult you may find it to join in.

- **Think about the art of polite disagreement**
  The aim of academic discussion is to try to develop the ideas you are considering. Often, this involves members of the group disagreeing with one another's ideas. Remember that you are challenging the argument which is put forward, not the person who is advancing it. It is also important to remember this when your ideas are challenged. Saying something like "Perhaps there's a different way of looking at this" is less confrontational than saying "I think you've got that wrong"!

- **Expect to be challenged**
  During group discussions, tutors will try to teach you not to make assumptions. Their aim is to help you to think critically and precisely. They will therefore challenge many of the things you say. Most people are not used to being challenged in this way, and the ability of tutors to question almost everything you say can seem unduly negative. However, if you are going to succeed in thinking rigorously, you need to be able to question your own ideas and those of other people, and tutors whose sessions are the most challenging may turn out to be the best ones you have.

- **Do not expect to take notes all the time**
  If you take notes of everything that goes on in a tutorial or seminar, you will be so busy writing that you will not be able to participate in the discussion. Not only will you not be able to say anything, but note-taking also detracts from your ability to think about the points that are being made. Try to limit your note-taking to jotting down the main issues raised and the outline of any answer given. You can then read over your notes later and follow up any points of particular interest.

- **Learn to take advantage of small group learning situations**
  It is much easier to learn in small groups than in large lectures, because small groups should give you the opportunity to ask questions about aspects of the subject under discussion that you do not understand so well. Clearly, you do not want to dominate the discussion, or interrupt with too many questions, but small group situations do give you an opportunity to raise issues that are of particular concern to you.

RESEARCHING A TOPIC FOR AN ESSAY/PROBLEM, TUTORIAL OR SEMINAR

When you are preparing for a tutorial or seminar, or preparing to write an essay or problem answer, you will need to carry out some research in order to find the information you need. In the case of tutorials and seminars, you will often be given specific reading lists, so some of the research has been done for you, but you will still need to use the information to the best advantage. Here are some suggestions to help you research effectively.

▶ 9.6

In this section we will use the following question as an example:

"How successful is the operation of s.1 of the Police and Criminal Evidence Act 1984 (PACE)? Discuss"

- **Read the question carefully**
  Before you start gathering materials, you need to be clear about what you are being asked to do. Titles that invite you to "discuss" or "critically analyse" mean that you are expected to

engage in reasoned argument about the topic; you are not being invited merely to describe something. Here, you are being asked "how successful" is s.1 of PACE when it "operates". So you need to know:

- That s.1 of PACE is about stop and search powers given to the police.
- "Operates" suggests you are being asked to think about how these powers actually operate in practice, on the street, not just what the statute says should happen.
- "How successful" and "Discuss" invites you to make a judgment about whether you think the powers work well or not when the police put them into practice.

One of the easiest traps to fall into is to fail to answer the question which is set because you are concentrating on conveying as much information as possible about the general area of law, rather than focusing on the specific aspect which is the subject of the question you are answering. Keep the question in mind the whole time; write it out and keep it in front of you while you are researching.

- **Identify your key words**

  First, define the general area you are interested in. In our example, this might be "criminal justice" or "police powers of stop and search". At first, you may find it difficult to identify the terms lawyers would use to classify an area of law, so you might need to ask your tutor or law librarian to help you with this.

  Now you know the areas you are looking for information on, you can look for materials in those areas. If you are unfamiliar with the topic, you might want to look for a textbook first, so that you can read it and gain some broad understanding of the topic; while you are reading, keep the question in mind and see how it relates to what you are discovering through your reading.

  You may need to re-define your phrases or words if, for instance, you find that the first few words you think of bring up too many references. In that case, try to think of much more specific terms which you can search.

- **Use the references in the text**

  In any good textbook, you will find references to other materials on the topic which is being discussed. If the textbook you choose does not have any such references, it is not going to be helpful for your assignment, so choose another one. Academic writing, found in journal articles and books, contains a lot of references and footnotes. At first, this can be confusing, and you may tend to ignore them. However, when you are researching a topic, footnotes and references are an important source of further information.

  A good way to start your research on a topic is to look in the footnotes or references of any textbooks, journal articles or specialist books that you have found; they often contain references to more books or journal articles, and you can make a note of these. Then you can consult your library catalogue and find out whether your library keeps copies of that material. Footnotes and references can direct you to other relevant material in a number of different ways:

  (a) They can give full references to articles or books that are just mentioned or summarised in the text. This is useful if the material referred to is relevant to your work, because you can then read the full text.

(b) They can give references to other books or articles on the same topic, which put forward a similar argument (or the opposite one often indicated by the word "contra" in front of the reference). Again, you can extend your knowledge by following up the references.

(c) They can give further explanation about points made in the text.

All these types of reference can provide you with further information about the topic which you are researching. That is why footnotes and references are so useful.

- **Organise your research notes carefully**
  When you are identifying the materials for your assignment, it is easy to lose track of what you have found. You get so involved in tracking down a potentially interesting article that you forget where you read the footnote which mentioned it, so you can't go back and find other useful references from the same place. This is very frustrating, so make sure you write down a note of where you found a reference, as well as the reference itself, so that you can easily get back to it. We talk more about recording your research in the next section of this chapter.

- **Use a variety of sources**
  Searching the library catalogue will generally direct you to books with titles that include your key words. Most modern catalogues will also direct you to journal articles. Once you get an idea of the journals which are the most important in a particular area of law which you are interested in, you can locate them in the library or online and look through the contents pages of the latest issues to find the most up-to-date articles.

  You can also locate books and articles by using any relevant electronic databases that your library subscribes to. Your library should have instructions about how these work; if it doesn't, you can ask one of the librarians to explain them.

  You can use specialist law databases, such as Westlaw, to locate both cases and statutes on a particular topic; they also contain references to some journal articles.

  There are a number of specialist databases, such as HeinOnline, which concentrate on providing access to journals, and these are the best place for you to locate journal articles.

  If you are researching a statute, you may also find it helpful to consult the website of the Government department which is responsible for the area of law covered by the statute, since Government websites often contain copies of consultation papers and other official documents which can provide useful background information and help you to understand the statute more easily.

  There are a number of hard copy publications that give details of all British books in print, arranged by subject, as well as by author and title. The Index to Legal Periodicals will help you to find articles in legal journals and there are similar publications relating to social science literature, often called "Abstracts". Using these sources will help you find a wider range of materials than those referred to on your reading lists. You may then be able to use these as alternatives to the ones that everyone else is using or which are unavailable when you wish to consult them.

- **Be time-sensitive**
  Start with the most recent literature on your chosen topic, i.e. the latest books and the most recent issues of relevant journals. These items may not appear on reading lists, so may have been missed by others.

  If you are using a legal textbook (usually at the beginning of the research process), remem- ber that new editions are produced quite frequently, so you need to be sure that you are using the latest edition. You can usually check this by looking on the publisher's website. Even if you have the latest edition, do not rely on it as your sole source of information; there may have been a lot of recent developments in that particular area of law, which are not referred to in the textbook, because they have occurred since it was written. Similarly with articles in journals: remember that the law changes frequently; check that any legal points made by the author are still valid.

- **Make the best use of your library**
  You need to ensure that you are using your library as effectively as possible. There may be leaflets designed to help readers find their way around the different catalogues, or there may be a resource page for law on the internet homepage of your law department or the home-page of the library; see if any of these can help your research. You will probably find that your university library has a helpdesk, so that you can ask for assistance from one of the librarians. You will find that they are immensely knowledgeable and helpful. There will always be someone to help with your enquiries. Try to help yourself first, but do not ignore the experts whose job it is to help you.

- **Use the internet appropriately**
  Many students find the internet a very convenient source of information. However, it is unlikely that you can rely on the internet as your only research tool. And when you do use it, you need to use it appropriately. Many students just rely on Googling a topic, and think that this is sufficient. Google is often a useful place to begin your research, but it is unlikely that you will find sufficient material if you just rely on Google, and do not use any other sources of information. You need to be aware that much of what you find using Google will not be appropriate for use in an essay or assignment which you submit at university. A lot of material on the internet is journalism, which is interesting, but not authoritative enough to be used in an academic essay. You should only rely on journalism or opinion pieces if that is the only information you can find on a topic (which will rarely be the case). Thus it will only be very occasionally that you can directly use a newspaper article, or the opinion of a pressure group, which you have found on Google, to back up your arguments in a piece of academic writing. You will need to use the specialist electronic resources provided by your university, or look at a government website, or that of the Law Commission, to follow up the leads you have found on Google and build on those leads by retrieving academic articles and books on the topic you are researching.

  However, if you go beyond just using Google, the internet can be a useful research tool. In addition to following up leads you find on Google itself, you can use Google Scholar to locate academic materials, and you can also use the internet to find a range of official publications, published by government departments, or by official bodies such as the Law Commission, and such documents can be very useful for research purposes.

- **Researching for different approaches to law**
  Bear in mind the perspective you need to adopt in order to answer the essay or problem question you are working on. Problem questions focus on a "black-letter" or "doctrinal" approach to law; they demand that you use decided cases and statutory materials to justify the points you make. In general, it is not appropriate to include references to other materials, such as academic articles, when writing a problem answer.

When you are answering an essay question, you may have the opportunity to introduce a wider range of materials; in addition to any relevant cases and statutes, you may be expected to discuss Law Commission materials, consultation papers and reports from relevant government departments, academic articles and books, and materials from other disciplines, such as criminology, sociology, economics or politics. You need to find out from your lecturers and tutors which approach you will be expected to adopt when you are writing your essay.

Our example essay title is clearly asking you not only to briefly discuss the relevant area of law (s.1 of PACE), it is also asking you to evaluate how well this section of the statute works in practice, and to do that you will need to find out whether there is any empirical evidence (produced by researchers who have, for example, gone and observed the police, or interviewed people who have been stopped and searched). Since this is a matter of criminal justice, you will find that criminologists have researched it a lot, and therefore you will need to use books and articles from the criminology section of your library to answer this part of the question.

- **Be prepared to search other nearby libraries**
  Sometimes you may find that your library does not have sufficient information on a topic that you are researching. Perhaps everyone else in your year has been set the same essay, and there just aren't enough books and journals to go round. Think of other libraries in the area that you could use and have a look in their catalogues to see if it would be worthwhile visiting them. Perhaps their students are not all doing the essay on offences against the person that your year has been set. Often, universities have schemes which allow students of other universities to have limited borrowing rights; it is often worth finding out if one of these schemes applies to a nearby university library other than your own which you might wish to use.

- **Find things out for yourself**
  When you are gathering and using written materials, remember that you must always find out things for yourself. The insertion of a footnote in a piece of academic writing that has been published in a journal or book does not necessarily mean that the footnote is accurate. Sometimes, when you find the article or case report that is referred to, you discover that it cannot possibly be used as justification for the proposition which you have just read. In order to find out whether a footnote is accurate, you will need to look up the reference for yourself. You should never merely replicate a reference without looking it up for yourself.

- **Enjoy Research!**
  Although researching is hard work, it can also be very enjoyable. It is immensely satisfying when you find some material which backs up a point you want to make, or you discover lots of information about a topic that you are going to write about. Researching is like many other things in life—the more you put into it, the more you get out. Give yourself a chance to enjoy your research by allowing sufficient time to do it and developing your research skills as much as you can—ask your librarian for help if you need it, so that you can learn how to find materials as quickly as possible.

RECORDING YOUR RESEARCH

Research can be very enjoyable and interesting, and it helps you discover the subject of law for yourself, but if you don't write down accurately the sources you find when you are researching, you can waste a lot of time. You will need to give full references to anything you want to rely on when

9.7

you write an essay or answer to a problem question. If you do not write down the details of the material you find, it's very tedious to have to go back and try to find them again.

- **Always write down a full reference**

  Whenever you read something which you think might be useful, you should write down its full reference; this not only means you will be able to find it again quickly, it also means you have all the information you will need if you want to refer to it in a footnote and/or bibliography.

  For a book, you will need the author, title, edition (if it is not the first edition), publisher, place of publication and date of publication. You may also like to make a note of the catalogue reference so that you can retrieve the item from the library easily; this will usually be a Dewey decimal reference number. Your reference should look something like this:

  Bradney et al. *How to Study Law* (3rd edition) Sweet & Maxwell, London, 1995. (340.07 HOW)
  If you are recording a journal article, your reference will be something like this:
  Addison & Cownie "Overseas Law Students: Language Support and Responsible Recruitment" (1992) 19 JLS p.467 (PER340 J6088).

  It is important to write down references in such a way that you can easily distinguish between references to books, and references to articles. The system that has been used here is to italicise the titles of books, but put titles of articles inside inverted commas. You may be told by your tutor what system of "citation" or referencing to use; it is important to follow any instructions you are given.

- **Make concise notes**

  Always begin by asking yourself why you are taking notes. Refresh your memory as to the question you are trying to answer. Remember that you can take different types of notes on different parts of a text—detailed notes on the directly relevant parts, outline notes on other parts, while some parts you will be able to read through without taking any notes at all.

- **Make clear notes**

  Your notes will be more use to you if they are reasonably neat. Try to develop a standard way of recording the source you are taking the notes from, perhaps always putting it at the top right-hand corner of the page, or in the margin. You can use this reference for your bibliography, or for footnotes, or for your own use if you need to clarify a point at some later stage. In order to make it even easier to find your way around the original text, you might like to make a note of the actual page you have read, either in the margin, or in brackets as you go along. Here is an example of some notes on the first few pages of a chapter of a book:

  H. Genn (1987)
Hard Bargaining
Oxford Uni. Press, Oxford.
(344.6 GEN)

  Chapter 3 "Starting Positions"
  Structural imbalance between the parties (p.34).
  One-shotter pl. v Repeat-player def. See Galanter 1974 (p.34).
  Repeat players—advance intelligence, expertise, access to specialists, economies of scale. See Ross 1980 (p.35).
  Distribution of personal injury work (p.35) Pls huge variety of firms.
  Defsinsurance co/specialist firm.

Defs solicitors allowed few mistakes (p.36 top) Defs solicitors nurture relationship with insurance companies Contrast position of general practitioner.

The student who wrote these notes has not only noted the full reference to the book they are working on, and the main points made in Chapter 3 of the book. He/she has included a couple of references to work by other researchers (Galanter and Ross) which can be followed up later to see if those experts have anything to say which is relevant to the essay the student is writing. The student has also been careful to note down the page number in Genn's book that contains the points which are important.

- **Do you need to photocopy the bibliography?**
  When you are taking notes, you will often note down references to other articles or books referred to in the text you are reading. You will have to decide later whether you need to look these up, but many people find that it disturbs their train of thought to look up the full reference for each of these as they occur in the text. If that is the case, it is important to have access to a copy of the bibliography of your source (on-line or in hard copy), so that you have a copy of the full reference in case you need to refer to it later. In the example above, the student would need to have access to the bibliography of "Hard Bargaining", otherwise they wouldn't know what they meant by references to "Galanter 1974" or "Ross 1980".

- **Keep notes and comments separate**
  It is a good idea to think critically about the content of what you are reading. However, if you want to make comments, keep these separate from your actual notes in some way, such as by highlighting. Otherwise, when you come back to the notes, you might find it impossible to distinguish your great thoughts from those of the original author.

- **Good presentation is important**
  Remember that clear presentation of your notes is just as important when you are taking notes for an essay or seminar as it is when you are taking lecture notes. Use headings and sub-headings, and remember that underlining and highlighting can direct your attention to particular points.

READING FOR RESEARCH

It is important to develop a strategy for dealing with the large amount of reading you will have to do. All students have to face this problem, but if you are studying law, you have a particular problem, because studying law requires you to read a great deal of material quickly. In addition, although by this stage you are an expert reader, you are unlikely to have had much experience, if any, of reading legal materials, such as case reports and statutes, so in this respect you are a novice again. When you are researching, you need to be able to read quickly through the material you locate, so you can decide whether it is sufficiently relevant to look at in more detail, and perhaps make some notes from it. 9.8

The chapters in this book which deal with reading cases and statutes will help you develop an effective method of reading these new types of text, and once you have practiced, you will find that you can process them as quickly as other types of text, such as articles or textbooks, with which you are already familiar. There are many different ways of reading; for example, you can skim quickly through something, or you can read it slowly and carefully. In order to decide what kind of reading you should be doing at any particular time, you need to think about the purpose of your reading. You also need to be aware of the different techniques of reading and be able to use each type as it becomes relevant.

- **Scan the text first**
  To check the relevance of a text, skim through it, looking for the key words and phrases that will give you the general sense of the material and enable you to decide whether it is relevant for your purposes. When looking at a book, the title and contents pages will give you a broad outline of the information you will find. Sub-headings within an article perform the same function. You can use these headings to decide whether or not to read a piece of text in more detail.

- **Approach the text gradually**
  Even when you have decided that a particular chapter of a book or an article is relevant, check it out before you begin to take notes; you may not need to take notes on the whole chapter, but only a part of it; similarly, with an article. It is often suggested that you should read the first sentence of each paragraph to find out more precisely what the text is about.

- **Reading statutes**
  As you have discovered in Chapter 5 of this book, statutes must be read carefully and precisely. At first, they can seem very complicated to read, because they are so detailed. When you read a section of a statute, try to establish the main idea first, then you can re-read it and fill in the details on the second reading. You might find it helpful to copy the parts of the statute that you have to read, so that you can use a pen or highlighting to mark the main idea. There is an example below:

  Sale of Goods Act 1979 s.11(3)

  Whether a stipulation in a contract is a condition, the breach of which may give rise to a right to treat the contract as repudiated, **or a warranty**, the breach of which may give rise to a claim for damages but not to a right to reject the goods and treat the contract as repudiated, **depends in each case on the construction of the contract**; and a stipulation may be a condition, though called a warranty in the contract.

  The main point that is being made is quite simple, and can be identified by reading the phrases in bold type "Whether a stipulation in a contract is a condition or a warranty depends in each case on the construction of the contract". Having established what the section is basically about, you can now go back and find out what the section says about the effect of a stipulation in a contract being classified as either a condition or a warranty.

- **Reading cases**
  Although reading a reported case might seem more straightforward than reading a statute, it is important to remember that reading the judgments in a case and extracting from them both the facts and the decision requires practice.

  Sometimes you will be able to get an indication of the important aspects of a decision from a textbook or from a lecture. However, if you are faced with a decision about which you know very little, you can read the headnote first, which will summarise both facts and judgments for you. Many students are tempted to regard reading the headnote as sufficient, but this is not a good strategy; you need to read the whole of the leading judgment to understand the ratio of the case properly. (You will be able to tell which is the leading judgment by noticing from which judgment most of the points in the headnote are taken.)

Reading dissenting judgments is also helpful. It is a good way to understand the complexities of a legal argument. Often, your tutors will ask you to think critically about decisions; reading dissenting judgments are a good source of ideas about the strengths and weaknesses of a decision.

WRITING ASSIGNMENTS (ESSAYS AND PROBLEM ANSWERS)

During your law course, you will be set various types of assignment to submit to your tutor. The most common of these are essays and problem questions. Writing an assignment is a challenge, but it is also one of the most rewarding aspects of studying law. When you focus on a particular area of law for the purposes of writing an assignment, you bring together a lot of the skills you are developing; you need to research, organise the material, reflect on the question and engage in some critical thinking.

9.9

- **Clarify the task**
  Before you do anything else, read the question carefully. Identify which area of law it is asking you about. This may not be immediately apparent, particularly in a problem question. Read the whole question through carefully to help you understand which area(s) of law are involved. Then make sure you understand exactly what the question is asking you about the area of law involved. It is highly unlikely that it will just ask you to write down all you know about, for example, the tort of negligence. It is much more likely to ask you to criticise a particular part of the law of negligence, or explain the strengths and weaknesses of an aspect of the law of negligence.

- **Make a plan**
  The next stage of the writing process is to make a plan. A plan provides a structure for your argument and allows you to organise your arguments into a coherent whole. It is a vital stage of the research process and you need to produce one as soon as possible. You may want to do a bit of basic reading first, but generally, the plan should be one of your first tasks. Plans for problem answers are easier to produce than those for essays, because the events that make up the problem give you a structure for your plan. In all cases, jot down the main points of your answer; later, you can refine your plan and fit in subsidiary points in the most logical places.

Example

"Discrimination in the legal profession is a thing of the past" Discuss.

Introduction — *much discrimination on grounds of both race and sex in the past- refer to numbers of women / members of ethnic minorities qualifying as solicitors and barristers, also women not able to qualify as solicitors till well into the twentieth century — see Bebb v The Law Society.*

First section *Currently, still a lot of discrimination on grounds of sex — refer to small numbers of women partners in solicitors' firms, small numbers of female QCs and small numbers of female judges. Also refer to research reports on women in the legal profession.*

Second section *Equally, still a lot of discrimination on grounds of race — refer to small numbers of solicitors, barristers and judges drawn from ethnic minority communities, also research reports on racial discrimination at the Bar and in the solicitors' profession.*

Conclusion *Although it appears there is still a lot of discrimination on grounds of race and sex in the legal profession, it is arguable that the situation is improving — use statistics to show increased participation in the legal profession by women and by members of ethnic minority groups.*

Your plan is there to help you; you do not have to stick with your original structure too rigidly. If you can see a better way of organising your argument once you have done a bit of reading, then adjust the plan. The plan in the example above is just a first draft. It provides a basic framework, but it does not contain enough ideas at this stage. In order to add more ideas, the student needs to go and do some more research and reading before amending the plan in the light of the additional information. However, this is a good start.

- **Reflect and evaluate**
  When you have gathered the basic information, it is time to review your plan in the light of what you have discovered. Read through your notes, bearing in mind all the time the question you have been asked. Have you changed your mind about any of the points you want to make? Have you discovered additional information that you want to include in your answer? Where does it fit in to your argument? Now you will be able to make a new plan, indicating not only the main points you are going to make, but also any arguments or pieces of information drawn from your research that you wish to include.

- **Write a first draft**
  Once you are satisfied with your revised plan, you can embark on the first draft of your essay. Before you start, read through the plan and make sure that all your points are relevant. To do this, look at the question again, and then look at your plan. Every argument you make should relate to the question you have been asked. This is what makes it relevant.

  Here is an example of a first plan for an essay whose title is "Settlement of major litigation is a necessary evil." Discuss.

  - Settlement definition.
  - Settlement is necessary because a) saves court time b) saves expense c) saves litigants' time.

- But settlement is an "evil" because a) litigants are not equally experienced and do not have equal resources b) inexperienced litigants often go to lawyers who are not specialists in the relevant field & are not well advised c) inexperienced litigants can easily be put under pressure, e.g. by payment into court, delays (often manufactured by the other side), worries about cost, risk-aversion.
- Conclusion settlement is a necessary evil, but currently is so evil it is immoral and unacceptable.

Every point that is made relates directly to the quotation that is under discussion. This is an initial plan. After some research, you would be able to expand some points, and to insert the names of books or articles that you could use to justify the points being made. But you would still ensure that everything related to the quotation that you had been asked to discuss.

- **Remember the audience you are writing for**

  When you write an academic essay in law, you can assume that you are writing for a reasonably intelligent reader who knows almost nothing about your subject. That means you have to explain clearly every step of your argument. At first, many students are ignorant of this convention. They know their essay is going to be marked by an expert, so they do not bother to include all the information about a topic, only to be told by their tutor "I cannot give you credit for anything, unless it is written down in your essay. It's no use keeping things in your head".

- **Acknowledge your sources / avoid plagiarism**

  During the course of your writing, you will often put forward arguments and ideas that you have discovered in books or articles. If you do this, you must acknowledge that the idea is not an original one. You can do this expressly in the text by saying something like "As Bradney argues in 'How to Study Law'". Or you can use a footnote to indicate the source of the idea. What you must not do is pass off someone else's idea as if it were something you had thought of for yourself. That is stealing their idea, and it is a practice known as plagiarism. In academic life, where people's ideas are of the utmost importance, plagiarism is regarded as a form of cheating, and you will find there are severe penalties if your work is found to be plagiarised. In order to avoid this, you must always acknowledge the source of your argument. Students often worry about doing this, thinking that their work will not be "original". But originality lies in the way you put together your argument, not just in what you have discovered. So do not worry too much about originality. The thing to worry about is making sure you have acknowledged your sources. In time, you will use other people's ideas as a base from which to develop thoughts of your own, acknowledging their idea, and then going on to say something original about them. But it takes time to learn enough about your subject to do this. It is the sort of thing you can expect to be doing in the final year of your study, but not really at the beginning! This is the kind of critical thinking which you are trying to develop over time.

- **Do not make assertions**

  In academic writing, you must always be able to justify what you say. You cannot make assertions (an assertion is when someone says "X is the case", but provides no justification that proves that X is the case). You must always be able to provide reasons for your statements; in an essay, this is done by providing a reference or footnote. In a problem question, all the points of law you make need to be substantiated by a reference to some legal authority—usually the ration of a case, or a section of a statute.

Example

If someone writes "Small claims are proceedings involving £5,000 or less" that is an assertion. There is no evidence that the statement is true, the author is just expecting us to take their word for it. After a little research, it is possible to rewrite the sentence so as to include the evidence which proves the statement: "Under Part 26.6 of the Civil Procedure Rules, small claims are proceedings involving £5,000 or less." Alternatively, you could include the justification in a footnote. Then the statement would look like this:
Small claims are proceedings involving £5,000 or less.[1]

- **Consider the style of your writing**
  An academic essay is a formal piece of writing, so the style in which you write should not be too colloquial. Shortened forms of phrases, such as isn't and mustn't, are inappropriate. However, pomposity is equally inappropriate. Phrases such as "I submit that. . ." are out of place. Advocates make submissions in court, but you do not make submissions in an academic essay, even in a law school!
  Aim for a clear, direct style, which conveys your arguments in a way which can be readily understood. Use paragraphs to indicate a change of subject, and keep sentences reasonably short. In general, academic writing is written in an impersonal style, so writers do not use phrases such as "I think that. . .". They use alternative, less personal, phrases, such as "This indicates that. . ."
- **Be prepared to write several drafts**
  Before you arrive at the final version of your essay, you should have produced several drafts. You should read each draft carefully, making additions and alterations that you then incorporate into the next draft. Although it is important to correct the spelling and the grammar in each draft, the primary reason for having several drafts is to give yourself the opportunity to examine your argument and make sure that it is as clear and convincing as possible. Think about what you are saying. Have you justified all the points you have made? Does the argument flow logically from one point to another? Is the material relevant?
- **Do not describe too much**
  In general, the object of writing academic essays is to engage in critical analysis, i.e. thought and argument. Your tutors are not looking for detailed descriptions of subjects that they could, after all, read in any competent textbook. A certain amount of description is necessary, to explain what you are talking about, but the main emphasis in any academic piece of work will be on analysing. You are interpreting for the reader the significance of what you have described, and it is this process that is most important.

- **A few points about problem answers**

  It is often said that it is easier to answer a problem than to write an essay, but this is largely a matter of personal preference. Problem answers are certainly easier in one sense because they provide a framework for your answer by posing certain issues that you must cover. The research and planning process described above will help you when you are answering a problem question, just as much as an essay.

  Problem answers do not need lengthy introductions. The convention is that you need to introduce a problem answer by identifying the main issue in the problem. Whenever you make a statement about the law, you must give the relevant legal authority; for example, "When X wrote to Y saying that if he did not hear from Y, he would assume that Y agreed to the contract, this has no legal effect, because silence does not imply consent (Felthouse v Bindley (1862) 11 C.B. 869)."

  Remember that socio-legal information is not usually relevant in a problem answer. Strictly speaking, problem questions are just asking you to identify the relevant legal rules relating to the issues raised. There may be very interesting research studies on a topic, but these are not relevant to a problem answer.

EXAMS AND ASSESSMENT

It is likely that you will experience a number of different forms of assessment, including continuous assessment, based on written work submitted during the course of the academic year, and the traditional three-hour unseen examination. The strategies discussed above will help you to cope with the various forms of continuous assessment which you are likely to meet. This section will therefore concentrate on strategies designed to help you cope with the traditional unseen examination.

9.10

- **Make a revision timetable in good time**

  It is important to make a realistic revision timetable well in advance of the examinations, allocating a certain amount of time for each subject you have to prepare. Most people find it best to study all their subjects concurrently, doing a bit of each one in turn, rather than finishing one before going on to the next one, which brings the danger that you might never get round to the last subject.

- **Reduce your notes to a manageable size**

  At the beginning of the revision period, you are likely to find that you have a large amount of notes. It is a good idea to reduce the size of these, by taking even briefer notes from your original notes, so that you end up with a manageable quantity of material to work with. As the examinations approach, most people reduce their notes again, perhaps several times, so that a whole topic can be covered comprehensively, but speedily.

- **Question-spotting is a risky strategy**

  It is sensible to consider what sort of subjects might come up in the examination. Consulting old examination papers is a useful way of finding out what is expected of you in the exam. However, it is unwise to "question spot" too precisely. It is unlikely that you will be able to revise the whole course; indeed, this would often be a waste of effort, but you need to cover several subjects in addition to the three or four which you hope will come up, so that you have plenty of choice when it comes to deciding which questions you will answer in the examination. Being familiar with a range of subjects is a sensible strategy because:

(a) Your favourite topics might not come up at all.
(b) Some topics might come up, but in a way which is unfamiliar to you.
(c) Your favourite topic might be mixed up with another topic which you have not revised.

- **Consider practising timed answers**
  If you find it difficult to write answers quickly, it is a good idea to practice writing some answers in the same time that you will have in the examination. Use questions from old examination papers.

- **Make sure you get enough rest**
  Studying hard for examinations is a very tiring experience. Try to ensure that you get sufficient sleep and exercise, so that you remain as fresh as possible. Burning the midnight oil is not necessarily a sensible strategy.

- **Feel as comfortable as possible during the exam**
  Before you enter the examination room, make sure you have all the pens, pencils and so on that you need. Wear something comfortable, preferably several layers of clothing so you can discard some if the room is hot, or add additional layers if you are cold. Check whether you are allowed to take drinks or food into the examination room. If you are allowed to do so, it is a matter of personal choice whether you take advantage of this facility or not; some people find it helps to have a can of drink, others find it a distraction. Check that you know where you have to sit, and whether there are any attendance slips or other forms that you have to fill in. Ensure that you know whether or not you will be told when you can start the examination; you do not want to sit there, waiting for an instruction that never comes.

- **Read the instructions on the exam paper very carefully**
  Make sure that you read the instructions at the top of the examination paper very carefully. The paper may be divided into different sections and frequently candidates must answer a certain number of questions from each section. Sometimes you will be asked to write certain questions in certain answer books. Always make sure that you comply with any instructions of this kind; the examiner may not give you any marks for material you have written in contravention of such instructions.

- **Develop good examination technique**
  In the examination, plan your time carefully. Provided that all the questions carry an equal number of marks, you should allow an equal amount of time for answering each question. Sub-divide your time into reading the question, planning the answer, writing the answer and checking it. Planning is a very important part of good examination technique. If you spend a few minutes setting out a good plan, it will allow you to write a much fuller answer than if you are thinking out your answer as you go along, because all the basic thinking will be done at the planning stage, and you will be able to concentrate on writing a relevant answer. Do not spend more than the time that you have allocated for each question. If you run out of time, leave that question and go on to the next one, returning to the unfinished question if you have some spare time later.

- **Answer the question**
  Read the question carefully. To gain the maximum number of marks, your answer must be relevant to the question you have been asked. If you are familiar with a topic on which a question is set, it is tempting to write down a version of your notes, which includes all you know about that topic, in the hope that you will get a reasonable number of marks. However, if you merely write all you happen to know about a topic, it is unlikely that you will be answering the question. You need to slant your information to the question, showing how the things you know relate to the precise question that you have been asked.

- **Answer the correct number of questions**
  Under pressure of time, some people fail to answer the whole examination paper by missing out a question. Examiners can only award marks for what is written on the examination paper. By not answering a question, you have forfeited all the marks allocated to that question. However, it is often said that the easiest marks to gain are the ones awarded for the beginning of an answer, so if you do run out of time, it is much better to use those final minutes to start the final question, rather than perfecting answers you have already finished.

- **Remember that examiners are human, too**
  When you are writing an examination paper, you often feel as if the examiner is the enemy "out there", determined to catch you out. In fact, examiners do not want candidates to fail. They generally expect students who have done a reasonable amount of work to pass examinations.

INTERNATIONAL STUDENTS

The study skills discussed in this chapter are required by all law students. However, if English is not your first language you may feel that you would like some extra assistance with studying in the UK. Most institutions which welcome students from around the world have a support service which offers different classes covering a range of English Language and study skills, and you should try and find out about these at an early stage in your course. Even if your English is very good, you might be able to pick up some useful tips about studying in the UK from such classes. The support service will also be able to help you familiarise yourself with the particular types of teaching and learning situations which you will find in British educational institutions, what might be termed the "hidden culture" of learning, such as particular ways of writing essays or behaving in seminars, which might be different to those with which you are familiar at home. This sort of information can be very useful, as it is impossible to discover beforehand, however good your English is. Many institutions also offer self-access materials, which you can go and use at a time that is convenient for you.

9.11

FURTHER READING

If you would like to find out more about any of the topics covered in this chapter, you will find that there are many books on study skills available. The following book covers a wide range of study skills.

9.12

S. Cottrell, *The Study Skills Handbook*, 54th edn, Palgrave Macmillan, (2019).

You will find that this author, Stella Cottrell, has also written a large number of other books on specific aspects of studying at university, which you might also find helpful.

There is also a series of books called "Pocket Study Skills", published by Palgrave Macmillan. You might find some of the titles in that series useful in giving you hints and tips about particular aspects of study skills. Titles in this series which you might find helpful include:

- *Brilliant Writing Tips for Students*
- *Getting Critical*
- *Planning Your Essay*
- *Reading and Making Notes*
- *Referencing and Understanding Plagiarism*
- *Writing for University*
- *Time Management*

Exercise 6

STUDY SKILLS

The exercises below concentrate on some of the most important study skills which you will need at college or university. They may help you decide if these are areas you need to improve in order to get the most out of your course. 9.13

Note-Taking

You will find that you have to take a lot of notes, in lectures, and when you are researching for essays and other assignments. Being able to take very good notes as quickly as possible is a very useful skill.

1. For this exercise, you are going to take notes on the first three pages of the article entitled "Are Lawyers Neurotic?" by Daniel Newman which you will find in Exercise 5 of this book. Before you start, re-read the suggestions about taking notes in Chapter 9 of the book, in the sections headed "Take Notes to Aid Concentration" and "Take Notes Which Will Be Useful in the Future".

   Once you have finished taking notes, compare them with the three pages of the article you were working on, and assess your notes according to the following criteria:

   - *Presentation* Can you read what you have written? Have you used underlining or highlighting effectively? Could you have used diagrams or lists?
   - *Clarity* Can you remember what your abbreviations mean? Are there words or phrases which occur frequently that you definitely need to invent an abbreviation for? Have you remembered to write down the full reference of the article you are working on?
   - *Content* Have you included all the main points? Do you have a full reference to any useful articles or other documents which were mentioned in the footnotes? Have you written down too much, so that your notes are not really notes, but involve copying out nearly the whole extract?

2. Find some notes that you took in one of your lectures. Now use the criteria above to assess how useful your notes will be to you if you need to refer to them in the future. Do they make sense to you now? Will you be able to refer to them when you are writing assessments or revising for exams? Have you noted down the references to any cases or statutes that were mentioned? Do you need to make any changes to the way you take notes in order to make them more useful to you when you want to use them?

Essay Writing Skills 1—using footnotes and references

One of the new skills you will have to master at this level is the ability to use footnotes or references in essays to justify what you are saying. Everything you write in an essay must be justified, and in order to do this, you need to include a reference to an appropriate document in your essay. You can do this by including footnotes or Harvard-style references. These two styles of reference are explained below. The explanation is followed by an exercise to help you practice the skill of referencing. You should find out from your tutor which style of referencing they want you to use, and then learn to use it as early on as possible in your course, so that when you have to submit an assignment, you know how to reference appropriately.

Using Footnotes

It is likely that your tutors will require you to use footnotes when you submit an essay for assessment. If you use footnotes, your essay will look like this:

Historically, women were debarred from entering university law schools.[1] Today, women are to be found in larger numbers than men in university law schools.[2]

Note that the footnote number is inserted *after* the punctuation. The footnotes themselves are located at the foot of the page; look at them now. They contain the full reference to the work referred to, *including the page number*; it is very important to include a page number, so that the reader of your work can look up your reference and check that the material upon which you are relying really does back up what you have written.

You must adopt a consistent order for the information included in your footnotes: author; here is an example for a journal article:

> Author: date: title: volume number of journal: name of journal: page number.
> F. Cownie & A. Bradney (2003) *"Divided Justice, Different Voices: Inheritance and Family Provision"* p.23 *Legal Studies* p.56.

Computers make it very easy to insert footnotes; in Microsoft Word, you will find a drop-down menu called "References"; you can then click on "insert footnote" and a footnote number will appear in the text. Practice inserting footnotes in a piece of text, so that you know how to do it *before* you have to submit your first essay.

Harvard-Style References

References can be included in the text (these are known as "Harvard-style" references), so that your essay would look like this:

> Historically, women were debarred from entering university law schools (Sachs & Hoff Wilson, 1978, 27–28). Today, women are to be found in larger numbers than men in university law schools (Law Society, 2006, 34).

Note that the reference in the text includes the page number at which you can find the material which is being relied upon.

If you use Harvard-style references, you <u>must</u> include a list of the *full* references to all the materials you have included in your essay. So at the end of this essay, the references would look like this:

> Law Society (2006) *Annual Statistical Report 2005* London, The Law Society. Sachs, A. & Hoff Wilson, J. (1978) *Sexism and the Law* Oxford, Martin Robertson.

1 A. Sachs & J. Hoff Wilson (1978) *Sexism and the Law* London, Martin Robertson, pp.27–28, 31–33 & 170–174.
2 Law Society (2006) *Annual Statistical Report 2005* London, The Law Society, p.34.

Note that the order of the information provided is: author(s); date of publication; title; place of publication; publisher. This order remains the same every time you write a reference.

Cownie et al., *English Legal System in Context*, 4th edn, (Oxford, OUP) p.209.

Reference Exercise 1

Here is a piece of writing about private security firms. Read it through. Imagine this is part of your essay. The footnote numbers have been inserted for you, but there is no content in the footnotes. On a piece of paper, write down the TYPE of material you would use to justify what you have said. The first footnote is completed for you as an example, to show you what to do.

Private Security

(adapted from Cownie et al., *English Legal System in Context*, 4th edn, p.209)

An increasingly important form of social control which has hitherto been largely ignored by those writing about the English legal system is the world of private security. Private security personnel are those persons engaged in the protection of information, persons or property. They are privately employed, have different legal powers to the public police, and are accountable for the exercise of those powers to a private individual or institution, rather than to the public.[1]

The term 'private security' is used, rather than 'private policing', partly to avoid confusion with the public police, but also because that term conveys more accurately the wide range of activities carried out by private security personnel in contemporary society, activities which go far beyond the policing activities carried out by the public police. The range of activities undertaken by the private security sector is very wide. It involves the provision of manned services – guarding, patrolling, transporting cash etc, as well as providing bodyguards, private investigators and involvement in the management of prisons and escort services.[2] Private security entities are also involved in the provision of physical or mechanical devices, such as locks, safes and cash bags, supplying electrical and electronic devices, such as alarms, video motion detection devices etc. and 'security hardware' i.e the manufacture, distribution and servicing of a wide variety of security equipment.[3]

It is impossible to obtain accurate figures relating to the number of persons involved in private security in Britain today. Estimates vary greatly, partly depending on the definition of private security which is used. Figures reported by the Home Affairs Select Committee in its 1995 report on the industry ranged between 126,900 and 300,000.[4] The 1999 White Paper *The Government's Proposals for the Regulation of the Private Security Industry in England and Wales* estimated that there were then a total of 240,000 individuals employed in some 8,000 companies.[5] All commentators are unanimous, however, in agreeing that the number of persons employed in the sector is growing rapidly and many have noted that it is probable that the number of persons employed in the private security industry is larger than the number of persons working in the police service.[6] Thus in terms of quantity alone, we are dealing with a significant factor in the criminal justice system.

The answers to this exercise can be found at the back of the book.

1 Reference to book or article about private security, which discusses what private security personnel do, and how their employment status, powers etc. differ from the public police.

Essay Writing Skills 2—Avoiding Assertions

A common mistake made by law students is that in answering essay questions, they fail to *justify* what they have written. Writing a statement without providing justification for it is called making an "assertion". Assertions are completely unacceptable in academic law essays.

Virtually every statement you write in an essay should be justified by reference to something which proves that it is a true statement. This might be, among other things, a reference to a case report, section of a statute, a particular page of an academic book (monograph), or a page of an academic journal article. In the exercise above the footnotes were inserted at appropriate places for you. In this exercise, you have to decide where to put the footnotes, as well as indicating what should go in them.

Reference Exercise 2

Read the following extract and identify the assertions that it makes. Do this by deciding where footnotes need to be inserted to support the author's arguments. Then, for each footnote, indicate the *type* of material which could provide the evidence which is needed (e.g. a section of a statute, a journal article, a Government document etc.). The first footnote is completed for you as an example.

Uncovering Crime

(adapted from Cownie et al., *English Legal System in Context*, 4th edn, pp.224–225.

It is generally accepted that the number of crimes dealt with by the criminal justice system is less than the actual number of crimes taking place. This is because a large number of offences are not reported to the police, so they do not feature in statistics which record the number of crimes taking place. It is surprising to find that the police play a relatively small role in uncovering crime. Research for the Royal Commission on Criminal Procedure (the Phillips Commission) showed that most offences were reported to the police, either by the victim, or someone acting on the victim's behalf; many crimes were also reported by witnesses. When all these instances were taken into account, the researchers concluded that 75–80% of crimes are reported to the police, rather than the police discovering the crimes for themselves. This data is confirmed by other research studies, including research carried put for the Royal Commission on criminal Justice (the Runciman Commission) which found that the initial source of information linking the suspect to the offence came from the police in only 37% of cases.

Write down your answers like this:

Footnotes needed as follows:

Location	**Content**
After "place" in line 3.	Reference to precise page of book or article discussing the fact that there is a large amount of unreported crime.

APPENDIX I

MOVING ON: FURTHER STUDY AND CAREERS

This short appendix to *How to Study Law* helps you consider what you might do after your course of study has ended.

From School to University

▶ A1.1

You might be reading this book because you are studying Law with the idea of going to university to study for a law degree. Sources of information about degree courses can be obtained by looking at the websites of individual universities, by consulting official websites such as: *https://discoveruni.gov.uk/* or by looking at some of the readily available commercially-produced university guides.

Whenever you are looking at such information, one important consideration to take into account is that if you wish to go on and join the legal profession as a solicitor or barrister, you would generally be advised to ensure that your law degree will enable you to study what are often called "the foundation subjects". More information about this can be found at: *https://www.barstandardsboard.org.uk/training-qualification/becoming-a-barrister.html*.

From Undergraduate to Postgraduate

One of the things you might consider doing after you have got your law degree is to do a postgraduate degree. Most universities offer a range of Master's courses in Law (often designated LL.M., which means Master of Laws). These are generally one-year taught programmes, during which you usually take three or four different taught modules in a specialist area, such as Human Rights or International Trade Law, and then from approximately Easter to September you write a dissertation on a topic of your choice which is related to your Master's degree.

The idea of taking a taught Master's degree is to allow you to specialise in an area of law that interests you, so that you can gain more expertise than you were able to do in your undergraduate studies. Obtaining a Master's degree can also contribute to your ability to differentiate yourself from other candidates when you are applying for a job.

If you really enjoy researching the law and academic work in general, you may decide that you want to do a PhD. In Law, a PhD is generally undertaken by people who have an interest in pursuing a career as an academic. It allows you to pursue a research project over three years, under the supervision of an established academic who is an expert in your chosen area. If you are interested in doing a PhD, you should talk about it with your tutors, especially the lecturers who teach you the subject in which you are hoping to pursue your research. They should be able to discuss all the options with you, and to signpost those individuals who could be potential supervisors for your chosen project.

Using your law degree

Having a law degree gives you many options in terms of career. Many employers regard law graduates favourably, and the employment rates among law graduates are high, compared with other subjects. There are a number of websites which carry a large amount of information about careers for those who wish to consider all their options, and you may find it helpful to look at them at an early stage. Two of the main websites for students looking for law related careers information are *http://www.prospects.ac.uk* and http://www.targetjobs.co.uk/.

Legal Careers

Traditionally, law graduates wishing to pursue a legal career made a choice between being a solicitor or a barrister. Nowadays, the legal services market contains a wide variety of legal occupations; the most commonly found are legal executives. You might want to investigate all of these before reaching a decision about which career path is right for you. Here are some ideas about how you might go about finding out about legal careers.

Becoming a Solicitor

The Law Society represents solicitors in England and Wales. Helping members of the profession by providing a range of advice for solicitors, and helping the general public by providing information to help people find the legal support they need. The Law Society's website has an area dedicated to providing information and assistance for people who want to become a solicitor at: *https://www.lawsociety.org.uk/career-advice/becoming-a-solicitor/*. The website encourages you to find out as much as you can about what a career as a solicitor is really like, and it contains a number of useful documents, including a comprehensive toolkit with guidance, tools and resources to help you find out about a career as a solicitor.

Becoming a Barrister

The Bar Council is the body that represents barristers in England and Wales. It promotes the role of barristers as being at the heart of the justice system. It has a section on its website especially designed to provide information for people interested in becoming a barrister: *https://www.barstandardsboard.org.uk/training-qualification/becoming-a-barrister.html*. The website includes profiles of practising barristers to give an insight into the lifestyle and culture of the profession, as well as taking you through the steps generally taken by those wishing to become a barrister.

Becoming a Legal Executive

Under the Legal Services Act 2007 Chartered Legal Executives are "authorised persons" undertaking "reserved legal activities" alongside, for example, solicitors and barristers. The Chartered Institute of Legal Executives is the professional association which represents trainee and practising Chartered Legal Executives. Its careers website: *https://www.cilex.org.uk/membership/getting_qualified* provides a range of information for those wishing to find out about a career as a legal executive, stressing its attractions for those who want to pursue a cost-effective flexible path to a legal career. Fully qualified and experienced Chartered Legal Executives are able to undertake many of the legal activities that solicitors do. For example, they will have their own clients (with full conduct of cases) and they can undertake representation in court where appropriate.

Becoming a Paralegal

The term "paralegal" covers a wide range of roles found within the legal sphere of employment. The Institute of Paralegals is the oldest representative body of paralegals in the UK and has a useful area on its website: *https://theiop.org/joining-paralegal-profession/*, which includes information about who hires paralegals, what skills, personal qualities, qualifications and experience is needed, and how to go about getting a job as a paralegal. It also discusses how you can progress from being a paralegal to a solicitor and explains how paralegals can apply to become judges of First-Tier Tribunals.

Finding Out More About Legal Careers

LawCareers.Net is a website developed in association with the Trainee Solicitors Group. It provides information about how to begin your career in Law, whether you are looking for a training contract to become a solicitor or a pupillage to become a barrister or if you want to find out more about the paralegal or legal executive route: *https://www.lawcareers.net/*.

APPENDIX II

ABBREVIATIONS

A2.1 The short list below contains some of the standard abbreviations that you are most likely to be referred to early in your course. It is not exhaustive. It will help you whilst you are beginning your study of law. The most complete and up-to-date list of abbreviations is to be found at *http://www.legalabbrevs.cardiff.ac.uk/*. This can be searched both by abbreviation, to find out what journal or law report is being referred to, and by journal or law report, to find out what the accepted abbreviation or the journal or law report is.

A.C.	Appeal Cases (Law Reports).
All E.R.	All England Law Reports.
C.L.J.	Cambridge Law Journal.
Ch. D.	Chancery Division (Law Reports).
C.M.L.R.	Common Market Law Reports.
Conv.(n.s.)	Conveyancer and Property Lawyer (New Series).
Crim.L.R.	Criminal Law Review.
E.L.R.	European Law Reports.
E.L.Rev.	European Law Review.
E.R.	English Reports.
Fam.	Family Division (Law Reports).
Fam. Law	Family Law.
H. of C. or H.C.	House of Commons.
H. of L. or H.L.	House of Lords.
I.L.J.	Industrial Law Journal.
K.B.	King's Bench (Law Reports).
L.Q.R.	Law Quarterly Review.
L.S.Gaz.	Law Society Gazette.
M.L.R.	Modern Law Review.
N.I.L.Q.	Northern Ireland Legal Quarterly.
N.L.J.	New Law Journal.
P.L.	Public Law.
O.J.	Official Journal of the European Communities.
Q.B.D.	Queen's Bench Division.
S.I.	Statutory Instrument.
S.J. or Sol.Jo.	Solicitors' Journal.
W.L.R.	Weekly Law Reports.

APPENDIX III

EXERCISE ANSWERS

Statutes I

1. The Act applies to England and Wales, Scotland and Northern Ireland (s.4(1)).
2. The Act is part of the criminal law. It creates a specific criminal Offence (s.1(1)) for which there are specified punishments (s.1(4)).
3. The long title, which is found above the at the top of the Act under the short title and before the enacting formula, is "An act to make provision creating new offences of shining or directing a laser beam towards a vehicle or air traffic facility; and for connected purposes". The long title is not legally part of the Act. There is therefore no statutory authority for this answer. It is simply true as a matter of fact. Conversely the long title does not provide an authority for your answer to question two. The long title does talk about creating offences. However sometimes long titles can be wrong.
4. Yes (s.1(6)).
5. Yes (s.3).

Statues II

1. The short title is the Stalking Protection Act 2019 (s.15(4)). In the first statute exercise we saw that what the long title of an act is not matter of law. However short titles are now specified in acts. What the short title is then becomes a matter of law. If you said that the short title was the Stalking Protection Act 2019 because that is what you find at the top of the statute you have failed to give a legal authority for your answer. It is not enough to be correct. You need to also say why legally you are right.
2. Section 1(1) tells you that a chief officer of police can apply for a stalking protection order. Section 14(1) defines the phrase chief officer of police in such a way as to include all of the various different state police forces that there are in England and Wales.
3. Section 7(1)(a) gives defendants who have had a stalking protection order made against them a right of appeal to the Crown Court. However note that the question for the Crown Court is not was the making of the "fair" but more precisely first did the magistrates' court properly apply their power to make orders under s.2(1) of the Act. Secondly the Crown Court will need to decide whether or not the contents of the order that was made met the requirements under s.2(2) and s.2(3) of the Act.
4. Section 8(1) of the Act says that breaching a stalking protection order is an offence unless there was a "reasonable excuse" for that breach. Therefore the fact that Anne has breached the order does not tell us whether she can be punished. The first question will be did she have a reasonable excuse for the breach. If she did not have a reasonable excuse on summary conviction a 12-month term of imprisonment or a fine or both can

be imposed (s.8(2)(a))) or on conviction on indictment a five-year term of imprisonment or a fine or both can be imposed (s.8(2)(b)).

5. Under s.2(3) of the act prohibition or requirements in an order, "so far as is practicable", must not conflict with the defendant's religious beliefs (s.2(3)(a) or interfere with any times during which the defendant normally works or attends an educational establishment (s.2(3)(b)).

Cases I

1. The case was heard in the Family Division of the High Court. You are told this in the law report on the left hand side at the top of the first page. The court where a case is heard determines the authority of the precedent that the judgment sets. A judgment made in the High Court binds all courts below the High Court but is not binding on the High Court itself when hearing future cases nor is it binding on those courts above it.
2. The case was an appeal against and order for maintenance made against the respondent following a divorce between the respondent and the applicant. You will find this at para.8.
3. The judge in the original hearing decided that income streams from the franchises owned were "matrimonial property" (para.17). The judge also asked why after the divorce should the husband "live well" on the income stream from the franchises which were a "marital endeavour" if the wife was not able to do the same (para.17).
4. The court held that there were a number of authorities, most particularly *Waggott v Waggott*, that held that whilst in principle matrimonial property ought to be shared after divorce earning capacity after a divorce ought not, in general, to be shared (paras 18 to 21). The exceptions to this general rule were where there was a need to compensate party or where a party's need justified the making of maintenance payments. The judge in the original hearing had used the wrong test to decide what maintenance payments ought to be made. The authorities that are cited in this part of the judgment are all Court of Appeal precedents or higher and are thus binding on both the court in this judgment and the court from which the appeal had been made.
5. Although the judge in the original hearing had used the wrong test to calculate the maintenance payments the wife could show that she had a claim based on need. In the circumstances of the case the wife should not have to sell her capital to meet her living costs and therefore maintenance payments, albeit at a much lower rate than originally ordered, should be made (para.46).

Cases II

1. Lord Kerr in his judgment says that Ronald Stocker took issued proceedings for defamation against his former wife (paragraph 5). Defamation is part of the law of torts. The fact that people are or were married does not determine the nature of legal proceedings they might take against each other. Those who are married may, for example, sue each other for breach of contract. In this case the parties had divorced; that is a family law action. However the judgment in the case is about tort law.
2. Lord Kerr's judgment describes the judge's approach as "legal error" or "an error of law" (paras 47 and 48, para.51, para.60). The court's duty is to decide what an "ordinary reasonable reader" would think that the word meant (para.38). The meaning is not

determined by "technical, linguistically precise definitions" (para.25). Deciding that the first instance judge's approach is legally wrong is important. If deciding what the word meant was a question of fact then an appellate court, such as the Supreme Court, would be reluctant to interfere with a first instance finding even if it disagreed with it. In the case of errors of law, however, the court will have much less hesitation with substituting its own judgment.

3. If dictionaries are not used what objective criteria are there to be for deciding what a word means? How does a judge, or anyone else, know what an ordinary reasonable reader would think a word means?
4. First which dictionary is to be used? The Oxford English Dictionary, which is now available online as well as a print copy, is usually taken to be the most authoritative available. It has 20 volumes. Have you ever consulted that version of the dictionary? How often have you consulted the shorter versions of the Oxford English Dictionary which have been published? How often have you consulted any dictionary when you are writing something? You think that what you write means something. Does a dictionary determine what it means? But how am I to decide what your words mean?
5. "Justification" in this context means that in response to a suggestion that something is defamatory the argument is made that the statement is true or substantially true (para.29).

Reading Research Materials

1. The author suggests that two views about the nature of lawyer-client relationships have been put forward. One argues that lawyers have "little but contempt" for their clients whilst the other view argues that lawyers admire their clients and are dedicated to supporting them (p.6).
2. The author argues that within the criminal justice system access to justice means that there must be access to lawyers since clients are not in a position to understand and deal with the complexities of the legal system. Further to this the lawyer must be willing to act as a zealous advocate on behalf of their client, putting their clients' interest first (pp 3–4). Later in the article the author contrasts a "client-centred" view of legal practice with a "practitioner-centred" view "in which the clients were, at best, a bothersome irrelevance, and, at worst, a problem to be eliminated" (p.13).
3. The author conducted interviews with 35 lawyers from three firms (pp 8–10). He also observed the everyday behaviour of the same lawyers in a variety of different settings (pp 10–13). In the interviews the lawyers took a broadly positive view of clients and their needs. In his report of his observations the author noted many examples of lawyers taking a negative view of their clients. However in his analysis the author does not suggest that one set of information is better or more accurate than the other, instead seeking an explanation of how lawyers could legitimately take a positive view of their relationship with their clients whilst being disparaging about clients as individuals (p.14).
4. Criminal legal aid lawyers are paid much less than many other types of lawyer (p.17). It is commonly thought that being a professional involves having marketable knowledge and skills (p.18). If you are not well-paid this might suggest that you do not have marketable knowledge and skills and are therefore not a professional. Suggesting that one's job is a vocation which involves the pursuit of a particular social agenda is another way of characterising the nature of a profession. Criminal legal aid lawyers are therefore

able to justify thinking of themselves as professionals even though their pay is relatively low (pages 18–19).

Reference Exercise 1

A3.1

1. Reference to the precise page of a book or article that discusses the wide range of activities carried out by private security personnel.
2. Reference to the precise page of a book or article that discusses the role of private security in relation to the supply of physical/mechanical/electronic devices and "security hardware".
3. Full reference to the 1995 Home Affairs Select Committee Report mentioned in the text.
4. Full reference to the 1999 White Paper mentioned in the text.
5. Reference to the precise page of a book or article which discusses the growth in private security personnel and concludes that the number of persons employed in private security is larger than the number employed in the police service.

Reference Exercise 2

A3.2 It is generally accepted that the number of crimes dealt with by the criminal justice system is less than the actual number of crimes taking place. This is because a large number of offences are not reported to the police, so they do not feature in statistics which record the number of crimes taking place. It is surprising to find that the police play a relatively small role in uncovering crime. Research for the Royal Commission on Criminal Procedure (the Phillips Commission) showed that most offences were reported to the police, either by the victim, or someone acting on the victim's behalf; many crimes were also reported by witnesses. When all these instances were taken into account, the researchers concluded that 75–80 per cent of crimes are reported to the police, rather than the police discovering the crimes for themselves. This data is confirmed by other research studies, including research carried put for the Royal Commission on Criminal Justice (the Runciman Commission) which found that the initial source of information linking the suspect to the offence came from the police in only 37 per cent of cases. Footnotes needed as follows:

Location	**Content**
After "place" in line 3.	Reference to precise page of book or article discussing the fact that there is a large amount of unreported crime.
After "witnesses" in line 7.	Reference to the precise place in the report of the research carried out for the Royal Commission on Criminal Procedure which discusses the fact that offences are generally reported to the police.
After "themselves" in line 9.	Another reference to the report of the research carried out for the Royal Commission on Criminal Procedure, to the precise page where the researchers' conclusions are set out.
After "cases" in the final line.	Reference to the report of the research carried out for the Royal Commission on Criminal Justice setting out the statistics referred to in the text.

APPENDIX IV

FURTHER READING

The number of books about law and legal rules increases each day. They range from simple guides, written for the GCSE student, to thousand-page, closely argued texts, written for the academic market. Some are encyclopaedias; others are exhaustive surveys of a very small area of law. This short list of further reading is intended to be of use to those readers who want to take further specific themes raised in this book. The list is not a guide to legal literature as a whole. Readers who have specific interests should consult their library catalogues for books in their area.

A4.1

Introductory books

J. Adams and R. Brownsword, *Understanding Law*, 4th edn (London: Sweet & Maxwell, 2006).
J. Waldron, *The Law*, (London: Routledge, 1990).
G. Rivlin, *First Steps in the Law* 7th edn (Oxford: Oxford University Press, 2015).

Books on the English legal system

F. Cownie, A. Bradney and M. Burton, *English Legal System in Context,* 6th edn (Oxford: Oxford University Press, 2013).
S. Bailey, M. Gunn, N. Taylor and D. Ormerod, *Smith, Bailey and Gunn on the Modern English Legal System,* 5th edn (London: Sweet & Maxwell, 2007).
L. Mulcahy and C. Stychin, *Legal Methods and Systems: Text and Materials,* 4th edn (London: Sweet & Maxwell, 2010).
R. Ward and A. Akhtar, *Walker and Walker's English Legal System*, 11th edn (Oxford: Oxford University Press, 2011).

Index

This index has been prepared using Sweet & Maxwell's Legal Taxonomy. Main index entries conform to keywords provided by the Legal Taxonomy except where references to specific documents or non-standard terms (denoted by quotation marks) have been included. These keywords provide a means of identifying similar concepts in other Sweet & Maxwell publications and on-line services to which keywords from the Legal Taxonomy have been applied. Readers may find some minor differences between terms used in the text and those which appear in the index. Suggestions to *sweetandmaxwell.taxonomy@tr.com*.

(All references are to paragraph number)

Also available

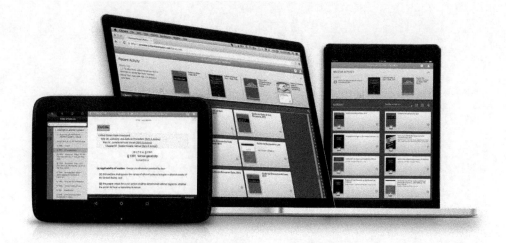